FamilyCircle

Hints, Tips & Smart Advice

EDITORIAL STAFF

Editor, Book Development—Carol A. Guasti
Editorial/Production Coordinator—Kim E. Gayton

PROJECT STAFF

Project Editor—Kendall Bradley Wood
Book Design—Bessen & Tully, Inc.
Illustrations—Roy McKie
Typesetting—R.M. Borden, Alison Chandler
Special Assistant—Kristen J. Keller

MARKETING STAFF

Manager, Marketing & Development—Margaret Chan-Yip
Promotion/Fulfillment Manager—Pauline MacLean Treitler

MALLARD
PRESS

An imprint of BDD Promotional Company, Inc.
666 Fifth Avenue
New York. N.Y. 10103

"Mallard Press and it accompanying designs are trademarks of BDD Promotional Book Company, Inc."

First published in 1988 by The Family Circle, Inc.

This bookstore edition first published in the United States of America in 1992 by The Mallard Press

ISBN 0-792-45441-3

Printed and bound in the United States by R.R. Donnelley & Sons.

Other Books by Family Circle:

The Best of Family Circle Cookbook
1986 Family Circle Cookbook
1987 Family Circle Cookbook
1988 Family Circle Cookbook

Family Circle Christmas Treasury
1987 Family Circle Christmas Treasury

Family Circle Favorite Needlecrafts

To order **FamilyCircle** books, write to Family Circle Books,
110 Fifth Avenue, 4th Floor, New York, NY 10011

To subscribe to **FamilyCircle** magazine, write to
Family Circle Subscriptions,
110 Fifth Avenue, New York, NY 10011

Table Of Contents

Introduction

In today's world of busy parents, two-career couples and fast-track singles, who wouldn't look for any way to make life a little easier? Why leave for work with a knot in your stomach when you can stop the morning madness with a few simple solutions? Why spend all of Saturday cleaning when you can get the job done in half the time?

That's what Family Circle's HINTS, TIPS & SMART ADVICE is all about: making your life a little easier. We've been doing that for years with our best-selling magazine. Now we've collected five years' worth of our finest tips and most valuable information in this special book. For instance: Turn to page 12 to discover strategies for surviving the breakfast time-crunch. You can save hundreds on heating and electric bills: just see page 66. Which medicines should you never mix? Page 258 has the answer. You'll find those solutions plus tips on child care, decorating, pet care, health and diet, beauty and much, much more. (Don't forget to take a look at our special holiday section!)

Best of all, each one of these tips works. They have been tested by our editors and our readers, so you know you're getting advice you can count on. Keep this book handy: you'll find yourself reaching for it every day!

1.
Get Organized! Get Time Smart!

Put Time On Your Side
Easy Organizers
Keeping Track
Meal-Planning Time-Savers
Surviving the Breakfast
Time Crunch
Moving Along

Put Time On Your Side

Discover the hidden time-wasters in your day!

Keep a master list

Make a list of everything you want to do, including day-to-day matters and long-term goals. Use a small notebook; keep it handy for reference and for writing additional entries.

Plan each day

Keep a daily "to do" list. Make up a new one each morning and include tasks you specifically hope to accomplish—deadlines, appointments—as well as items from your master list. Give each task a priority number—1, 2, 3. Do all the 1's first.

Learn to delegate

Assign jobs and responsibilities within the family. Kids ages 2 to 4 can put dirty clothes in the hamper or match socks, ages 4 to 7 can dress themselves and clear the table, while those over 8 years of age can put away toys and do many chores reasonably well.

A place of your own

Set up an area for yourself where you keep all your lists, calendars, menus, etc. This is *your* place to work and make schedules.

Use your best time for your most important tasks

If you're a "day person," make use of the mornings to get your hardest tasks completed, and if you're a "night person" struggling to function at 7:30 A.M., leave as little as possible to do in the early hours. For example, before you go to bed each night, set the table for breakfast and supervise the children while they get clothes and schoolbooks ready. When you get to work, ease into the day. Answer phone calls, catch up with filing and do other jobs you can accomplish with little effort. Then, as your energy level rises, take care of the more important work.

Use time- and labor-saving devices

▶ Shop by phone whenever you can and be sure to inquire about delivery. Drugstores and dry cleaners will often deliver for little or no charge.

▶ Appliances that save time include food processors, slow cookers and microwave ovens.

▶ A home computer really can help you organize your household chores. Put your Christmas card list on computer and you can update the file each year with just a few keystrokes. To make entertaining less work, keep a collection of two or three sure-fire party plans on file. For each, include a menu section with recipes, a shopping page noting the amounts to purchase and miscellaneous notes on decorating, seating arrangements, flowers and music.

Consolidate and plan ahead

▶ Group errands together. If you're going to the cleaner's, check your master list to see what else you can do in that part of town.

▶ Whenever you buy a staple, pick up two instead of one. When you start to use the second box of noodles or tube of toothpaste, enter that item on your shopping list and buy two again. You'll save yourself needless trips to the store.

▶ Buy an assortment of birthday and other greeting cards and stock up on all-purpose wrapping paper, note cards, ribbons and bows.

▶ Keep a list of your family's clothing sizes in your wallet. When you stumble upon a particularly good buy, you can take advantage of it to save both time and money.

Learn to use bits of time

No one has several free hours to clean out a closet. The key is to use the 10-minute segments you do have to accomplish a small task or make a dent in a larger one. For example, file your nails, make an appointment to see the dentist or clean just one shelf of that closet. You'll double your efforts if you do small tasks, such as writing a thank-you note, while engaged in some other activity like running a bath or waiting for a casserole to heat. Try talking into a small tape recorder to give yourself reminders while putting on your makeup or taking the bus.

Avoid peak-hour delays

Schedule appointments and shopping for times when other people are less likely to do so:

▶ Unless it's an emergency, schedule doctors' appointments early in the morning or just after lunch.

▶ See your dentist during the lunch hour, if he or she is available.

▶ Make appointments with home repair people for a time when you can be first on the list.

▶ If you must drive your car during rush hour, consult a map for a couple of alternate routes that take you away from the most crowded streets.

▶ Avoid banks on Fridays, the first, fifteenth and thirtieth of each month and any day at lunch hour. Better yet, bank by mail.

▶ Ask your doctor to have your prescription phoned in to the pharmacy. This will save you a 15- to 60-minute wait while it's being filled.

▶ Carry around a couple of postcards, a good book or some knitting for those times when you can't avoid waiting.

Beat-the-clock dressing

▶ The way to save time dressing in the morning is at the beginning of the season when you shop. Buy separates in simple shapes with a minimum of detail and stick to a single color scheme. A good year-round one is tan/gray/cream. Make sure each item you buy goes with three things you already own.

▶ Don't switch handbags. A roomy envelope clutch goes with almost anything and can be slipped into a larger tote.

▶ Have a couple of dresses that need few or no accessories.

▶ Hang clothes by category and remove the dry cleaner's plastic bags.

▶ Choose fabrics that keep their shape and don't require last-minute pressing—lightweight wools, jerseys, synthetic blends.

Budget time for yourself

Set aside whatever time you need to relax, unwind and do the things that are important to you. Here are some get-away-from-it-all suggestions:

▶ Hire a baby-sitter once a week so you and your spouse can have a regular evening out.

▶ Schedule an adult education class for one evening a week.

▶ Check out low-cost exercise or other fitness programs and sign up.

▶ Set aside an hour each evening called "private time." The kids can use it to do their homework, watch TV or play quietly, but make it clear that *no one* is to disturb you unless it's an emergency.

Easy Organizers

Sometimes all it takes to eliminate mess, clutter and confusion are a few hooks here, a basket or two there and a bit of reshuffling of items on a shelf.

Baskets do the trick

Buy one small basket for each person and hang the baskets near the coat closet door. Use them for gloves, mittens, winter hats, scarves and other small but important items such as housekeys.

Emergency shelf

Set up an emergency shelf out of reach of small children. Equip it with flashlights, candles (use votive candles in glass holders for safety), matches, a first-aid kit and an index card with all emergency telephone numbers. Make sure baby-sitters know where the shelf is.

On file

Keep household documents, such as warranties, owner's manuals and immunization records, in a handy accordion-folded envelope.

In the bag

To organize the various booklets and pamphlets that come with cooking and home-care appliances, punch holes into self-sealing plastic bags so that they will fit into a three-ring notebook. Use one bag for each appliance and seal.

Toy storage

Put books and games on lower shelves in the play room, paint, clay, scissors, crayons or anything you don't want the kids to play with unsupervised on the upper, out-of-reach shelves.

Borrower's shelf

Select one shelf in the den or playroom for storing borrowed library books. You'll know where they are when it's time to return them.

Soft storage

Use drawstring pouches made from fabric as containers for baby's blocks, puzzle pieces and other toys with dozens of parts.

Bath time

Use a zippered mesh lingerie bag for storing bath toys. Tie with string and hang it over the showerhead so toys can drip dry.

Versatile labels

When moving to a new home, order extra new address labels and send one of your personalized labels along with each change of address card to notify friends of your move. Then they can stick the labels right in their address books.

Time checks

If you conduct a lot of business by mail—like paying bills, sending for free offers or ordering merchandise—enter each transaction on a large wall calendar in the kitchen and check it periodically. This is especially helpful to verify a payment that may have gotten lost or if too much time has elapsed since placing an order.

Handy reference file

Keep a file of the instruction booklets that come with your appliances, from major ones like your refrigerator to minor ones such as your hand mixer. A few extra moments spent when you make the purchase may save you hours when service is necessary. Keep the following information:

Date of purchase, store name, service data, check number and amount paid. If a problem arises, it takes only a minute to determine whether or not the item is still under warranty and where to call for service.

Health book

Keep a health book for each member of your family (a photo album with self-sticking pages works very well) listing each illness, accident and doctor's visit, and the date, treatment, medication and doctor's instructions. Highlight important information, such as allergies to medication and the date of the last tetanus shot. A quick glance at your book will help you to be well prepared when you pay a visit to the doctor or emergencies occur.

Box it

Store envelopes of sauce and gravy mixes in a child's shoe box.

Address book

Use a pencil to write phone numbers and addresses in your address book. If someone moves, you can easily make the necessary change without messing up your book.

Assigned parking

In the garage, assign labeled "parking spaces" for bicycles, lawnmowers, gardening tools, etc. If someone fails to "park" an item in its proper place, issue a "ticket" and charge a small fine.

Keeping Track

No need for strings on your finger! Here's how to stay on top of all the little things you forget.

Closet list

The problem with storage closets and kitchen cabinets is remembering everything that is in them. Taping an overall list to the inside of the door saves the time and trouble of searching for something that may be in the back or at the bottom of the closet—or may not be there at all!

A place for everything

When you get a new reference book, such as a cookbook or gardening manual, attach a pocket to the inside flap to store clippings, notes or pictures about that subject.

Gifts by the month

To help keep track of gift giving, use an inexpensive monthly planner (purse- or pocket-size). On each special date, note the name of the person, the occasion and the gift given. Add sizes, color preferences and any tips for future giving.

Thoughtful reminder

If you can't remember when you last wrote to a distant friend or relative, solve the problem by keeping a small spiral notebook with your stationery box in which you note the names of those you have written to. After writing each letter, record the date next to the receiver's name. You will know for certain when you wrote last—and avoid the possibility of repeating old news.

Mobile address file

To keep up with the changing addresses and phone numbers of friends and acquaintances, use a 3 x 5-inch index card file box. On colored cards write names, addresses, phone numbers and other information, such as names of children, birthdays and anniversaries. When someone moves, just fill out a new card and discard the old one.

Meal-Planning Time-Savers

With these tips, you'll never have to say "I don't have anything for dinner" again.

Two-cook kitchen

With two cooks in the kitchen, it's easy to run out of ingredients and not know it. To avoid emergency trips to the supermarket, keep a pad of paper with an attached pencil in the kitchen. Whoever opens the last can, bag or box notes the item on the pad. This method also saves time making a shopping list at the end of the week.

The right match

Stop hunting through the clutter of mismatched plastic containers and lids. Use a dab of nail polish to color-code the right lid to the right container. The polish is washable and durable—and a little dab will do ya!

At your fingertips

Keep a card file in the kitchen with all the business cards and "foods to go" menus of your favorite restaurants for those evenings when you don't feel like cooking or eating out.

Joint meal planning

If you and your spouse work, you need a system for getting weekday meals on the table. Each week sit down and write out menus. For each menu jot down things that can be done in advance or by whomever arrives home first, such as peeling potatoes or defrosting meat. Writing things out each week—which takes only half an hour—pays off in faster and more efficient meal preparation.

Little helpers

Busy parents with children age 9 and older can portion responsibility for preparing the evening meal. The younger kids can do part of the preparation—scrape vegetables, set the table, pour beverages. As the children get older, their responsibilities can be increased. This creates good sharing and teaching time, and is invaluable experience for the kids as they grow.

The basics

▶ Plan weekly menus and shop only once a week.

▶ Shop in bulk once a month for nonperishables and buy the most economical sizes—as much as you can afford and can store.

▶ Arrange your shopping list to coincide with the order of the aisles in your favorite supermarket.

▶ Exchange shopping trips with a friend: Have him or her go to the butcher while you go to the fruit market.

▶ Patronize stores that deliver.

▶ Cook in quantity and use your freezer. Wrap individual-size portions for days when family members are involved in various activities. They can help themselves when they get home.

▶ Think in terms of make-ahead dishes for parties. You'll eliminate last-minute cooking and be able to spend more time with your guests.

Color coordinated

A maze of electric cords can be confusing, especially in the early morning when you're not your most alert! To the ones you unplug regularly (toaster, coffeepot, etc.), attach twist-ties of different colors. They quickly identify the appliances you want to disconnect.

Place settings

When you empty the dishwasher after dinner, wrap a flatware place setting in a napkin for each family member. This way the children are able to set the table and the job gets done faster.

A week of tasty, no-fuss dinners

▶ **Monday:** Coarsely chop cooked "sea legs" (imitation crab) or crab legs and stir into store-bought potato salad; add chopped parsley, chives and/or green onion and a dash of mustard.

▶ **Tuesday:** Heat store-bought, ready-to-use taco shells and a can of chili; spoon the chili into the taco shells. Serve with grated cheese, shredded lettuce and chopped onions.

▶ **Wednesday:** Buy canned lentil soup, grated Swiss cheese and garlic bread. Heat the soup and pour it over a tablespoon of the cheese into a soup bowl. Top with more cheese and serve with the garlic bread.

▶ **Thursday:** Heat fully cooked chicken pieces with bottled barbecue sauce; serve over sesame rolls.

▶ **Friday:** Cook a package of frozen fish sticks according to label directions. Serve in hot dog rolls and top with Russian dressing. Store-bought coleslaw makes a zesty topping or side dish.

▶ **Saturday:** Treat your family to pizza—it's delicious and nutritious. If you're eating pizza at home, serve it with salad and fixings from your supermarket salad bar.

▶ **Sunday:** Combine canned chicken gravy, precooked chicken pieces or canned chicken pieces with canned mushrooms (drained); heat and serve on toast points or prepared biscuits.

Surviving The Breakfast Time-Crunch

Say good-bye to weekday morning chaos in your house with these time-saving strategies and tips.

Spot the time-wasters in your morning routine

It's a good idea to determine exactly how time evaporates in the morning. Clock yourself performing various tasks. Decide which morning activities are essential and which can be rescheduled, delegated to other members of the family or eliminated altogether. For instance, if you love a long shower, consider taking it at night instead of in the morning. Encourage your kids to bathe before bed, too.

Begin a "pick-up-your-own-mess" policy

Get the kids—and the adults— into the habit of cleaning up after themselves, especially before bedtime. Stress the importance of waking up to an orderly house.

Avoid the "what-will-I-wear-today?" panic

Before bedtime, encourage family members to pick out what they'll wear the next day.

Stop the "where's-my-lunch-money?" confusion

Fill a glass container with lunch and bus money and keep it in a convenient location. This way you won't have to search for change at the last minute.

Get yourself up an hour before the rest of the family

Getting a headstart on your family— drinking a cup of coffee, reading the paper, planning your day's schedule—is the most effective way to avoid the A.M. frenzies.

Start a new "house rule"

Starting tomorrow, everyone is to come downstairs dressed and ready to go. School-age kids should also have their homework and books packed and placed by the door the night before.

Wake slowpokes up earlier

If your kids like to dilly-dally at breakfast, give them an extra 15 or 20 minutes so they—and you—won't feel rushed.

Dress babies and toddlers as soon as they wake

Try dressing them even before they are out of the crib and not fully awake. They won't fuss as much.

Keep all the house and car keys in one place

Hang a key holder in a convenient spot and place your keys there as soon as you enter the house.

Strategies for working moms

▶ Assemble your briefcase or tote bag the night before. Put it near the door so you can grab it on your way out in the morning. Put the money you'll need for the day in your wallet.

▶ If you take a young child to a baby sitter or day-care center, completely pack up the diaper bag the night before except for perishables. Make your child's lunch; fill juice and milk bottles in advance as well. All you have left to do is add them to the bag on your way out the door.

▶ Stop wasting precious time rummaging for lipstick and eye shadow in a cluttered makeup drawer. Throw out what you never wear; stash evening makeup in a separate place.

▶ Spend half an hour on the weekend pressing skirts and blouses and washing a week's worth of pantyhose. If a button needs replacing or a hem needs mending, try to do it as soon as you take off the garment.

Healthy rush-hour breakfasts

▶ Toast with peanut butter or plain yogurt topped with fresh fruit or raisins and wheat germ are two nutritious quickies.

▶ Here's a high-protein breakfast that is also low in calories: Top a scoop of cottage cheese with unsweetened applesauce; sprinkle with bran cereal for a little crunch.

▶ Top toasted English muffin halves with sliced Muenster or Swiss cheese and run them under the broiler for a few minutes. Add leftover diced ham, cooked vegetables or a spoonful of tomato sauce, if you like.

▶ Oatmeal is a healthy, stick-to-the-ribs breakfast. Boost its fiber and protein content by stirring in wheat germ and bran. Regular oatmeal cooks in five minutes; quick-cooking oatmeal takes just two minutes.

▶ Most youngsters adore pancakes and French toast. Make them on the weekend and freeze them in foil. Just pop them into the toaster on hectic weekday mornings.

▶ Spend an hour on the weekend frying a couple of pounds of bacon until all the grease is rendered but the bacon is not quite done. Wrap the bacon in individual serving sizes in foil and warm in a 350° oven for five minutes in the morning. Precooked bacon lasts a week in the refrigerator and can also be frozen.

► When summer fruits are in season, fill half a cantaloupe with cottage cheese, or make an all-American cottage cheese "sundae" with blueberries, sliced strawberries and a dollop of plain yogurt on top.

► If your children hate eating breakfast as soon as they get up, send it with them to school. Hard-cooked eggs, cheese cubes, oranges, small boxes of raisins, peanut butter sandwiches and whole-grain muffins are all good candidates for the brown-bag breakfast.

Divide and conquer

For today's busy two-career couple with little ones, division of labor is a must. For an efficient breakfast-time routine, one can be making breakfast while the other prepares lunch for the toddlers. Or one spouse can dress the youngsters while the other tidies the kitchen. At home as in business, teamwork can save the day!

"I made it myself!"

Youngsters age 8 and older can make their own lunch with a little parental guidance. Take time on the weekend to explain what makes a healthful lunch and give them guidelines to follow. Let them practice once or twice beforehand in the evening or on a weekend. Then do occasional spot-checks to make sure your guidelines are being followed. Because they've made it themselves, the kids are more likely to eat their lunch without complaint. It's also a good way to learn nutrition at an early age.

Moving Along

Going from one home to another can be trauma-free with this step-by-step guide.

Checking it out

If you're moving to another city, try to get acquainted beforehand with your new surroundings. Subscribe to one of the local newspapers and read up on various events. You will get a pretty good idea of your new town by the time you actually start packing.

A new house to announce

For a unique "just moved" announcement, type your new address and phone number onto a sheet of paper and, using double-stick tape, add a snapshot of your new home. Photocopy the announcement and send it to relatives and friends. Everyone will love it!

Get acquainted

Visit your new neighborhood with your children before you move, if possible. Show them their new schools, as well as the playgrounds, parks and shops in the area.

Easy going

▶ Before moving to a new house, tape easy-to-remove labels on every box and piece of furniture, designating the rooms they'll go into. It keeps the moving men from constantly asking where to put things.

▶ Pack one box or suitcase with enough sheets, pillowcases and towels to take care of your needs on the first night at your destination. Mark the container distinctly so that it's easy to find among the other luggage when you arrive.

▶ Slip a paper plate between each dish. When unpacking, don't throw away the paper plates; use them for meals while you're getting settled in your new home.

▶ Wrap dishes and glasses in damp newspaper. As the paper dries, it forms a protective wrapping in the shape of the article.

► Cardboard cartons with sectional dividers come in handy to pack just about anything. Bottles remain upright with no spillage, glasses have less chance of being broken and small, breakable objects are more secure in the smaller space.

The thirty-day plan for a hassle-free move

Fifteen to thirty days before:
► Eliminate everything you don't need.
► Prepare an inventory of goods.
► Call a variety of moving companies for estimates.
► Arrange for a method of payment.
► Purchase full coverage insurance on movables.
► Arrange for packing cartons.
► Notify your post office of your new address.
► Fill out change-of-address cards.
► Gather all medical and dental records.
► Check and clear tax assessments.
► Notify schools and request that transcripts be forwarded.
► Close local charge accounts.
► Arrange for pet shipment and immunization records.
► Make all travel plans.
► Make hotel reservations if needed; confirm them later.
► Begin to use up the food in your freezer.
► Decide what you are going to donate to charity. Get a signed receipt for what you give away to use with your taxes.

Two weeks before:
► Pack a little at a time. Don't wear yourself out.
► Use your kitchen cart or server as a mobile packing table.
► Collect clothing and items to clean or repair.
► Return borrowed items; collect those you've loaned out to friends.
► Have your bank transfer your accounts and release your safe deposit box.
► Arrange to disconnect your utilities.
► Arrange to connect the utilities at your new home.
► Have farewell parties and visits.
► Make arrangements to have your heavy appliances serviced for the move.
► Have a garage sale to get rid of things you don't want to move.
► If you're driving, have your car tuned-up for the trip. Check the oil, water, battery and tires.

One week before:
► Dispose of all flammables.
► Pack your suitcases.
► Plan for travel games and activities.
► Set things aside to pack in the car.
► If the mover has not been asked to do so, take down curtains, rods, shelves and the TV antenna.
► Get a sitter for moving day.
► Check with the phone company about returning your rented phones for a credit.
► Withdraw the contents of your safe deposit box.
► If you're traveling with pets, get pet tranquilizers for the trip. Make sure vaccinations and papers are in order.

▶ Assemble a "survival kit" containing any items needed for the last day or so in the old house and the first ones you'll need in your new house.

▶ Make up "do not move" cartons for articles to be taken with you in the car.

Day before moving:

▶ Empty and defrost the refrigerator and freezer; let them air for 24 hours. Place charcoal, coffee or baking soda in a sock in the freezer and refrigerator to deodorize.

▶ Clean and air your range.

▶ Finish packing your personal items.

▶ In urban areas, call the police to request that "No Parking" signs be placed in front of your home so you'll be assured of a parking and unloading spot.

▶ Make sure that you get a good night's sleep.

Moving day:

▶ When the moving company comes, be there or have someone there to answer any questions.

▶ Accompany the van operator during an inventory of things to be moved.

▶ Make a final check of appliances to be sure they've been serviced.

▶ Sign and save a copy of bills of loading. Be sure that a delivery address and place that you can be reached en route are included in the mover's information.

▶ Tell the driver exactly how to get to your new address, if you can.

▶ Confirm the delivery date and time.

▶ Ask to be advised of the final cost (which often is determined after the van is weighed). Make sure you'll have cash, a money order or a certified check on hand before the van is unloaded at your destination.

▶ Strip the beds but leave fitted bottom sheets on the mattresses.

▶ Have your vacuum ready to clean the bed rails, piano backs and other hard-to-move items.

▶ Load the vacuum cleaner last so you can have it in your new home first. Fast cleanups in both places really help.

▶ Before leaving the house, check each room and closet; make sure the windows are closed and the lights out.

Keep in touch

To write to friends in the old neighborhood after you've moved, buy postcards picturing a local scene. Write a short note and your new address on the postcard. Your friends will receive the news of how the move went, your new address and an idea of what your new town is like.

2.
Household
Helps

How To Clean Anything
In the House—Fast And Easy

Ways To Cut Housework In Half

Getting Rid Of Mildew

Household Miscellany

Paint Pointers

Sticky Situations:
A Quick-Fix Guide To Glues

How To Clean Anything In The House— Fast And Easy

For everything in your house that gets dirty, there's an easy way to clean it up.

Interior walls

The paint job you thought necessary may not be after all! To clean painted walls, vacuum them to remove dust and wash them with a sponge dipped in a mild detergent solution. Squeeze out excess water and rinse the sponge as soon as it gets dirty. Always wash walls from the bottom up to keep detergent from running down onto a dirty surface, making streaks that may be difficult to remove.

Wallcoverings

Many of today's wallcoverings can be washed the same way as painted walls. However, if your wallpaper is not washable, it can be cleaned with a wad of fresh bread or a dough-type wallpaper cleaner sold in many wallcovering stores. Roll the material over the surface of the paper to pick up soil and keep folding it to expose a clean surface.

Upholstered furniture

▶ Use a vacuum to remove dust and dirt from upholstery and clean with a commercial upholstery shampoo. Or combine 1 part mild dishwashing liquid with 4 parts water and whip to make lots of foam. Apply the foam with a brush. Scrub one cushion or section at a time, trying not to wet the fabric any more than necessary. Wipe off the foam with damp cloths; blot dry with towels.

▶ A rug-cleaning machine with a hand nozzle will do an even better job of cleaning upholstery. Shampoo each item by hand as described above, then go over it again with the machine to extract deeply embedded dirt.

Carpet

▶ To really get out embedded dirt, use a vacuum with a power-driven rotary brush (vacuums that depend only on suction do not do as good a job). Spots left by food or beverages usually can be removed by rubbing lightly with a cloth dipped in a solution of 1 teaspoon white vinegar and 1 teaspoon dishwashing liquid in 1 quart water. Do not wet the carpet any more than necessary. Blot dry with paper toweling. Greasy stains that are not water-soluble can be wiped clean with a cloth dampened with dry-cleaning solvent.

▶ A small plant mister or spray bottle kept filled with liquid rug shampoo and stored in a closet close to your carpeted rooms makes it easy to spray and wipe up spills and soiled areas immediately.

▶ Rather than shuffle furniture from one room to another in order to shampoo the carpet, you can save time and effort by putting a small plastic bag over each furniture leg and attaching it with a rubber band. Then move the furniture aside to shampoo the area and return the furniture to its original spot immediately; the bags can be removed after the rug has dried.

Kitchens and bathrooms

▶ Wash plastic-laminated counter and vanity tops with detergent and wipe dry. Remove stubborn stains by rubbing them with a damp cloth dipped in baking soda. If this doesn't do it, wipe with a cloth dipped in laundry bleach (test first to make sure this won't harm the top's color). Rinse thoroughly.

▶ Clean dirty ceramic tile with a commercial bathroom cleaner. To remove soap scum, wipe with a solution of 1 part vinegar to 4 parts water. Rinse and wipe dry.

▶ Grout stains caused by mildew can't be removed by detergent. Instead, scrub grout with an old toothbrush dipped in a solution of 1 part laundry bleach to 4 parts water. Rinse thoroughly and wipe dry.

Windows

Don't wash windows in direct sunlight; it tends to make them streak. Most commercial glass cleaners work well, but it is cheaper to use 1 tablespoon ammonia in 1 quart water. Squeeze the sponge almost dry before washing and avoid dripping water onto painted wood around the window. Stubborn streaks on glass can often be removed with a solution of 1 part vinegar to 5 parts water. Rinse and wipe dry.

Wipe and rinse

Keep a plastic bottle filled with diluted dishwashing liquid near your fiberglass bathtub enclosure. To get rid of the soapy film after you shower, sponge on the diluted liquid and rinse. It leaves a beautiful shine!

Soft scrubber

Use small squares of leftover carpeting to wash heavily textured plaster walls. The thick pile cleans the deep uneven surfaces without shredding and is soft enough to scrub without scratching.

Squeaky clean

When using a sinkful of hot water to rinse the dishes, add a capful of vinegar to cut excess grease or soap. It will give your dishes a clean, sparkling look.

Versatile netting

There are many uses for nylon netting: as a pot scrubber, a dishrag, a lint-remover. Another use for the stiff but not too scratchy material is to speed up the removal of ice when you're defrosting the refrigerator. Just dip the netting in hot water first.

Brush-off

When you grate orange or lemon rind, use a new toothbrush to get the grater clean and eliminate waste.

Quick dusting

For the most manageable dust cloth you can find, use an old potholder shaped like an oven mitt. Turn it inside out, spray the furniture with your favorite dusting product and wipe. For particularly tough spots, spray both sides of the mitt and rub your hand around corners or in little crevices. Cotton work gloves also do the trick.

Clear vision

The glass doors on fireplace screens collect a lot of soot. To clean the glass, try using an oven cleaner. Spray it on the glass, let it sit for about 20 minutes and wipe it clean.

Sparkle and shine

China or glassware with depressions in the design can often collect coffee and tea stains or even invisible germs. To clean the cutwork design, use an old toothbrush dipped in a water and ammonia mixture. Follow with a soap and water cleaning and rinse well.

Clean cycle

If you have hard water in your home, it is a good idea to clean the dishwasher each week by running it through a cycle with vinegar. Instead of wasting the cycle, collect all your glass knickknacks and seldom-used bar glasses and run them through as well.

Rub and shine

Don't discard squeezed lemon slices. Rub them on faucet fixtures, rinse and dry. They make chrome glisten!

Crystal clear

Wash crystal prisms from chandeliers safely and quickly in a French fry basket. Just dunk them several times in a solution of hot water and detergent until they're clean. Rinse them in clear water and drain in the basket.

Rx for vases

If a favorite vase has become dingy inside and it's impossible to get your hand in to clean it, try this: Fill the vase with warm water, drop in a denture tablet and let it sit. The vase will be clean in no time.

Worry-free rinsing

After cleaning jewelry with your favorite product, put the jewelry in a fine tea strainer and rinse each item thoroughly under the faucet without fear of losing tiny pieces down the drain.

20/20 vision

Keep a small spray bottle of glass cleaner with your cosmetics and each morning clean your glasses after putting on your makeup. Works beautifully!

Garage cleanup

▶ Cat litter is terrific for absorbing oil drips on the garage floor or the driveway. It is also a lot cheaper than commercial oil absorbents.

▶ Try pouring dry laundry detergent on oil spots. Add a small amount of water to make a paste and let it sit. The next day you'll be able to wash the stains away easily. For more stubborn stains, use a wire brush to help get oil and dirt out of the crevices.

Practical recycling

Don't throw out sample shampoos or ones you tried and didn't like. Instead, use them to wash your combs and brushes. Shampoos are specially formulated to clean the oils in your hair and work well on those same oils on your combs and brushes.

No dirty pool

When you vacuum and sweep a pool, there are always little corners by the steps that do not come clean. Try putting on a pair of old athletic socks, donning your bathing suit and running your feet and toes along these corners and cracks. Amazing results and fun, too!

Grill polish

Turn an old barbecue grill into a shiny new one. Use a cloth soaked in vegetable oil to remove ashes and polish the outside. The grill must be hot for the oil to work as a "polish," so use very heavy oven mitts to protect your hands.

Clean sweep

To clean the garage floor when the car drips puddles of winter grime, simply drop shovelfuls of snow on the puddles. The snow will absorb the puddles. If you sweep the snow out the door immediately, you will have a clean and soon-to-be-dry garage.

Petroleum protection

After cleaning the gaskets on your refrigerator, apply a thin coat of petroleum jelly. It will protect them from mildew and also prevent hardening and splitting.

Cleaners from your kitchen

▶ Lemon juice, a mild acidic solution, will gently remove hard water deposits from glassware, as well as newly formed rust stains on sinks and tubs without harming the porcelain enamel.

▶ Vinegar also removes hard water spots from glassware and rust stains from sinks and tubs. A vinegar and water solution is an effective rinse to remove soapy film from countertops, woodwork and kitchen ranges.

▶ Cream of tartar is a powdered substance commonly used in baking. When dissolved in water, it can be used to brighten aluminum ware. It also removes filmy residue from the inside of coffeepots, enhancing the coffee's natural flavor.

▶ Baking soda (sodium bicarbonate) is an all-purpose product that can be used to deodorize and clean refrigerators, remove coffee and tea stains from china and plastic dishes or remove hard water spots from glass, wall tile and porcelain. It can also be used as a gentle scouring powder on laminated countertops and stainless steel sinks. *Note:* Because it is an alkali, baking soda tends to darken aluminum. Rinse aluminum pots and utensils thoroughly after cleaning with baking soda.

Lint remover

Are lint and dust being drawn to your velvet paintings or other fabric wall hangings? No need to drag out the vacuum cleaner and the upholstery tool, which may be a bit rough on these items. A rolling lint pickup wand—designed for clothing—will do the job quickly and gently.

Sweet-smelling refrigerator

As an alternative to baking soda, place two or three charcoal briquettes in the refrigerator to keep it sweet-smelling. They last about six months and can be used in the barbecue after that.

No more rings

For all of you who have ever tried to cope with white rings on furniture from water or alcohol, here's a foolproof tip. Buff the spot with a damp cotton cloth dabbed with toothpaste. If it's a really stubborn spot, mix some baking soda with the toothpaste. This will work (unless the stain has gone all the way through the finish to the wood) no matter how long the ring has been there, and it won't hurt the furniture.

Oven clean-up

To clean up oven spills, pour salt on the area, dampen it slightly and allow it to sit for up to half an hour. Spills should wipe up easily.

The white glove treatment

The old saying about a "white glove inspection" is actually a helpful cleaning idea. If you wear cotton gloves while dusting, you'll never leave fingerprints on just-dusted furniture.

Ways To Cut Housework In Half

Wouldn't it be fantastic if you could wave a magic wand and—presto!—a spic and span house? We've got the next best thing: loads of sensible ways to minimize your cleaning chores.

Living room

▶ Apply spray-on protectors to untreated fabric to guard against spills.

▶ Wipe spills off furniture, particularly wooden furniture, as soon as possible to prevent staining.

▶ Have an emergency carpet kit on hand with rug cleaner, spot and stain removers, rags and a brush, and attack spills immediately.

▶ Place plants in saucers to avoid water spills.

▶ Install smooth plastic or metal chair glides to avoid scratching wood, tile and vinyl floors.

▶ Cut down on fireplace soot by keeping the fireplace clean (you can line the bottom with aluminum foil to make clean-ups easier), keeping your tools in a container and using a screen or glass doors.

Hall and stairway

▶ Keep your coat rack by the front door on a waterproof mat for wet boots, with a container next to it for wet umbrellas.

▶ Use a sliding door cabinet to hold outdoor shoes, hats, mufflers, etc. for quick get-aways.

▶ Keep a low chest on the stair landing for extra storage.

▶ Buy a 30-foot heavy-duty extension cord for the vacuum cleaner. It enables you to clean the entire hallway and staircase without unplugging the cord. Vacuum your way downstairs and wait until you have to go up for another reason to disconnect the cord.

Kids' room

▶ Keep a small vacuum handy for mini-pickups.

▶ Put up a blackboard or vinyl board to discourage drawing on walls.

▶ Use extra-large wastebaskets with plastic garbage liners.

▶ Organize toys in plastic boxes, milk crates, decorated cartons.

▶ Install low closet rods so kids can hang up their own clothes.

▶ Give kids only washable art supplies: water-based markers, watercolors, washable crayons.

▶ Limit snacking in bedrooms.

Kitchen

▶ Put down nonskid, washable mats at the sink and work areas.

▶ Clean up spillovers in the oven and on burners immediately.

▶ Spray the inside of the garbage can with disinfectant before putting in a plastic bag.

▶ Save the styrofoam trays from meat and, after rinsing, place in the bottom of a brown paper bag for drier garbage.

▶ Install a clear plastic sheet over the painted/papered area behind the stove for quick wipe-ups.

Bathroom

▶ Use weighted shower curtains. They don't billow out to let water leak onto the floor.

▶ Prevent mold by not letting moisture accumulate. Set this after-bath/shower routine for the family: Wipe off the shower curtain/door with a sponge, open a window or turn on the ventilator for half an hour and be sure the floor is dry before putting back the rug.

▶ Spray the shower door/curtain with disinfectant twice weekly.

▶ Avoid film and crust build-up in the soap dish by cutting an ordinary sponge to fit the dish (try to match or contrast the color). Now the film runs into the sponge and clean-up is simply a matter of wringing it out.

Attic

▶ Hold a garage sale.

▶ Use labeled boxes and industrial shelving for neater storage.

▶ Put up wall hooks for sports equipment, instruments, etc.

▶ Assign each family member a carton for his or her mementos.

Getting Rid Of Mildew

Answers to all your questions—from the cause to the cure.

What causes mildew?

Mildew is a growth caused by molds, which are simple organisms in the fungus family. The spores are almost everywhere in the air around us and thrive in damp places where there is little or no ventilation. That's why mildew is typically found in basements, crawl spaces, bathrooms and closets, as well as exterior parts of the house that are constantly damp and shaded from the sun. As the mildew spreads, it can cause deterioration and eventual rotting of the material it feeds on and often leaves behind a musty odor that is hard to get rid of.

Musty odors caused by mildew

When practical, take the item outside to air. Scatter baking soda in closets. Household disinfectant/deodorant sprays may help, but must be used repeatedly to have any lasting effect.

Preventing mildew

The best defense against mildew is to eliminate the conditions in which it can thrive.

▶ Provide plenty of ventilation in bathrooms, basements, crawl spaces and similar areas. To ventilate closets, install vents in the doors or replace solid doors with louvered ones, which let air circulate freely.

▶ Dry out damp places with exhaust fans. Install air conditioners in living areas where high humidity is a problem. Vent clothes dryers directly to the outside. Use dehumidifiers in damp basements that are kept closed. Hang bags of dehumidifying chemicals in closets and storage chests. When the bags are damp, dry them out in a low-heat oven and reuse.

▶ Use mild heat in closed-off spaces. For example, leaving a 25-watt bulb burning in a closet where mildew is a problem will help dry out the air inside. An even better solution is to tape an electric heating cable to the back wall of the closet with duct tape, weaving it back and forth. Most heating cables are flat and come in lengths that cannot be cut, but one round type (Frostex) can be cut to any length needed.

▶ Outside the house, prune away branches or large shrubs that grow close to the house and keep some of it always in shade. Don't allow sprinklers to keep siding and trim constantly wet.

Is it dirt—or mildew?

Fight mildew as soon as you discover it. Since it is a growth, it's not enough merely to wash it off; you have to actually kill the molds that cause mildew or they will grow back. Dirt stains are often mistaken for mildew stains on paint, bathroom tile and plastic surfaces. If in doubt, try this simple test: Wet a cloth with liquid laundry bleach and hold it against the stain for about one minute. If the stain disappears or gets considerably lighter without rubbing, it's mildew. If the stain is hardly affected, it's dirt.

To clean mildew off painted surfaces, inside or outside

Mix 1 cup liquid laundry bleach with 2 quarts water. Add about 2 tablespoons of a powdered cleanser containing trisodium phosphate (Soilax and Spic 'n' Span are widely sold brands). Scrub on the mixture, allow it to dry on the surface and rinse it off thoroughly with lots of plain water. When dry, repaint as soon as practical.

To remove mildew in bathrooms

On ceramic tile and shower curtains, use a mildewcide spray (X-14 or Tilex). Spray on, wait a couple of minutes, rub in with a soft brush, rinse off and wipe dry. To clean tile grout mildew stains, scrub with an old toothbrush dipped in a solution of 1 part laundry bleach to 4 parts water. Rinse thoroughly and wipe dry.

Removing mildew from fabric

▶ When mildew is found on clothing or fabric, more care is required. Take the article outside and brush off all visible growth. Spread the material out to air in direct sunlight if possible. Launder washable articles. If the material is colorfast, use a bleach solution to take out mildew stains that remain: Mix 2 tablespoons bleach with 1 quart warm water and sponge this on. Allow the solution to remain on the fabric for about 10 minutes and rinse thoroughly.

▶ Items that cannot be washed should be dry-cleaned. Upholstered items that cannot be taken outside should be vacuumed, but the vacuum bag should be emptied outside to keep the mold spores from being scattered inside the house. Clean furniture with an upholstery shampoo and dry with fans.

Household Miscellany

A quick read through this section can solve many household mysteries!

Quick action

When cooking oil or grease spills on the kitchen floor, throw cold water on it immediately to keep it from spreading and (if the spill is on a wooden floor) from soaking in.

A crumby idea

To keep toast crumbs that fall through the toaster from continuously scattering across your kitchen counter, buy an inexpensive, shallow baking pan, spray-paint it to match the kitchen decor, glue on a felt bottom and place the toaster in it. No more crumbs on the counter!

Paste-up

Almost anything can be attached to walls by using a hot-glue gun. If you later decide to remove the item, you can do so easily by reheating the glue for a few seconds with your hair dryer. This method avoids surface marks and nail holes on walls.

Rags for the kitchen

Try soft, inexpensive cotton washrags for kitchen sink use. They are more absorbent than commercial sponges, do not deteriorate with bleaching and smell fresh from the dryer.

Longer "shelf-life"

To eliminate the twice-a-year hassle of replacing shelving paper in cupboards and drawers, line each with lightweight, no-wax, self-stick floor tiles. These are attractive, inexpensive, very easy to install and make the task of cleaning almost effortless.

Warning sign for dehumidifiers

Float a small, brightly painted block of wood in the collection tray of your dehumidifier. When the water rises near the brim, the block will catch your eye and you'll know it's time to empty the tray.

Change of seasons

To remember when to change the baking soda you use to absorb odors in your fridge, put in a new box on the first day of a new season.

Effective air freshener

A wonderful way to freshen the air in your home and rid it of cooking or stale odors is to place a pan of water with spices simmering on the stove. Try cinnamon and nutmeg or spices for mulling wine. It smells delightful, especially during the winter holidays.

Handmade garbage disposal

Throw away a gallon-size plastic milk jug? Never! Rinse the jug well, cut a big hole in the top with a sharp paring knife and use it as a temporary garbage pail. You can place it on the counter and toss in eggshells, coffee grounds, hot grease, peelings or anything wet. It doesn't leak or tip over and can be carried out later to the big trash bin.

Sparkling silver

▶ Frequent use is the best way to keep silver from tarnishing. After using your silver, always wash it promptly in hot, soapy water (never in the dishwasher) and dry thoroughly. If you'd rather use your silver on special occasions only, the best way to keep it clean between times is to wrap it in the tarnish-preventive cloth sold by the yard in the household/notions department of big stores.

▶ Rotate your place settings. All the pieces will remain tarnish-free and will acquire the soft patina of wear at the same rate.

▶ Right after polishing, store seldom-used silver or silver-plated serving pieces in separate self-closing plastic bags. Since the bags are sealed, the silver isn't exposed to air and will not tarnish.

▶ To protect your hands when polishing silver, slip plastic bags over them and secure with rubber bands.

Caring for heirlooms

Beautiful table linens from Grandmother's day are well worth preserving. Since folding textiles weakens the fibers, loosely roll linens, lace and other delicate fabrics onto cardboard tubes. The tubes, used for mailing posters, are available in most office supply stores. An added advantage: Rolled items require little or no ironing when you're ready to set a pretty table.

Protecting your good china

To protect fragile china and crystal while washing it, place a towel in the bottom of the sink.

Take out the sag

An excellent way to tighten a sagging cane chair seat is to shrink it, using a damp cloth. Turn the chair upside down and apply the moistened cloth. Let it stay in place at least half an hour. The cane will shrink and the sag will disappear.

Toothpick tool

To get rid of the dirt that collects where metal and Formica edges meet, push a toothpick along the groove. It's amazing how much dirt comes out . . . fast!

Bottom of the barrel

For a time-saver, store extra kitchen garbage bags and ties at the bottom of the garbage can. When one bag fills up, take it out and there's another one at hand, ready for use.

Decal remover

Have you tried everything to remove the adhesive left by the decals that slip-proof the tub? Pour liquid drain cleaner into the tub. After the solution drains, wipe out the tub and the glue will come right off.

Protective coat

Coat a metal bathroom scale with paste wax to ward off rust from water splashes. The wax will add years— and shine—to the scale.

A perfect fit for candles

Slip the small fluted paper cups that come in a box of chocolates over the ends of candles that are too small for their holders. The cups will help the candles fit snugly. Or try putting a strip of self-stick foam weatherstrip tape around the base of each candle. It will instantly adjust to the candlestick opening and remain securely in place. The narrow foam will not show above the holder.

Flower holders

A plastic mesh vegetable bag or fruit bag rolled up and placed in the bottom of a vase will help hold flowers in place.

Protecting your furniture

Slice rubber discs from a pencil eraser with a razor blade and glue them to the bottoms of alarm clocks, ashtrays and similar articles. The rubber "pads" protect furniture from accidental scratches. They will also cut down on the noise created by vibrations.

Beautiful brass

Protect brass trim on fireplace tools, andirons and fire screens with a thin coating of clear shellac.

Keeping in shape

While your satin-bound blankets are still new, sew the binding together ¼ inch from the edge. This helps the decorative border hold its shape and prevents ragged edges when the binding eventually starts to fray and split.

Rug renewer

When the rubber backing on your throw rugs has worn off and the rugs are no longer skid-proof, replace the backing with silicone-rubber tub and tile sealant (which comes in a tube). Place dabs of the sealant on the backs of the rugs and they will be skid-free for many more months.

Keeping out winged visitors

If the buzzing of unwelcome insects alerts you to the fact that your window screens need repair, here's a great remedy: plastic needlepoint canvas. It can be cut to any size (make the patch a bit larger than the hole) and easily laced in place with fishing line.

Your cleaning closet

Tools:

▶ A vacuum cleaner with a set of attachments for carpets and rugs.

▶ Floor polisher/scrubber, dust mop and steel wool for wood floors.

▶ Brushes, sponges, a mop with a detachable head and a bucket that's divided for washing and rinsing.

▶ Clean rags for dusting and polishing.

Cleansers:

▶ Baking soda to clean glass, wall tile and porcelain enamel.

▶ Ammonia to wash windows and mirrors, loosen wax and clean ovens.

▶ Bleach to remove stains, whiten laundry and clean toilet bowls.

▶ Liquid and powder detergents for dishes, clothes and household cleaning, all-purpose cleaners to remove grease and grimy dirt, cleaners and scouring powders to remove tarnish and stains.

▶ Polishes, waxes and oils for wood, leather and metal surfaces.

▶ Spot removal products for carpets and upholstery.

Cold contact

Contact paper is easier to handle if you pop it in the freezer for about an hour before you are ready to use it. A rigid section of sticky paper is much easier to maneuver than a limp one.

No strings attached

The straightening out and tying of newspapers for recycling can be a tedious job. Instead, put the papers in supermarket bags! Two weeks of newspapers to a bag works perfectly.

Hanging made easy

When taking down your draperies, store the hooks by sticking them into a bar of soap. This will make them slide more easily into the fabric when hanging up the drapes again.

Paint Pointers

Sometimes it takes more than enthusiasm to do a good job!

Cover-up

Wear a garbage bag as a coverall when you're painting up high. Cut a hole in the top for your head and two in the sides for your arms. You can keep your head covered with an old shower cap.

"Coat" to protect

When painting woodwork, cover the doorknobs, locks and other hardware with a generous coat of petroleum jelly. If paint splashes where it shouldn't, it can be wiped off easily.

Soot-free windows

Apply transparent adhesive vinyl to your freshly painted window sills after the paint has dried. Particles of soot and grit are easily brushed away and leave no dirt to be imbedded in the fresh paint. When it is time to repaint, simply lift off the old covering, leaving a clean surface for painting.

A smooth trick

Sanding furniture before staining or painting? To be sure the surface is smooth, cover your hand with an old nylon stocking and glide it over the wood. The stocking will snag on any rough spots and pinpoint where more sanding needs to be done.

Newspaper trick

Instead of using masking tape to protect the glass when painting window frames, try dampening straightedged strips of newspaper and sticking them on the glass along the frames. When the paint job is finished, the strips of paper can be peeled off easily while still damp.

Reaching hard-to-get gaps

When staining or painting window frames, use an eye shadow sponge applicator to reach all the cracks and crevices. You'll get great coverage.

Easy paint remover

Round typewriter erasers—the kind with a brush on the end—are excellent for removing dried paint splatters from window panes. The abrasive eraser takes off the spots quickly and easily and is a lot safer to use than a razor blade.

All in a row

To simplify spraying screws for cabinet hinges, stick them into a piece of plastic foam packing material. The screw heads all will be facing the same direction, ready to be sprayed neatly and easily with just one pass of the can.

Just in case

When painting at home, stopping to take phone calls or attend to small emergencies often results in dried-out paint and stiff brushes. A good solution: A kitchen-size plastic trash bag slipped over the paint tray and closed with a twist-tie keeps the paint and brushes soft.

One wall at a time

If you find that you will run out of paint before completing a project, try to *finish* one section (ie., one wall). Paint often varies from can to can and the new can may yield a slightly different shade. By completing one section, the difference will be less noticeable.

Paint clean-up

Use vegetable oil to clean hands after working with oil-based paints. This is an especially good idea if children have gotten into the paint, because the oil is safer than paint thinner, is mild on delicate skin and has no fumes. After using it, wash hands thoroughly with soap.

Quick repairs

When you have finished painting a room in your house, fill a small jar with some of the leftover paint and store it with a container of spackle. When you want to rehang pictures or shelves, you'll be able to quickly fill and touch up nail holes.

Catch that drip!

Glue a heavy-duty paper plate (plastic coated is best) under a gallon-size paint can to catch any spills. For smaller cans, a plastic lid from large-size containers (ie., vegetable shortening) will also do the trick.

Spring Cleaning Made Easy

Save yourself time and muscle this spring by following these helpful hints to cleaning the whole house in one all-out attack.

Safety First!

Before tackling your major cleaning, follow these guidelines to use your cleaning products and equipment more safely.

▶ Read each label carefully and follow the directions. Some cleaning products may not be suitable for households with small children.

▶ Make sure that there are no broken, loose, worn or dirty parts on a cleaning product or appliance because it could prevent the product from performing correctly.

▶ Know what you are mixing. Some chemicals can be extremely hazardous if mixed together. Bleach combined with ammonia releases a highly toxic gas that can be fatal.

▶ Don't be too generous when applying a product—a little usually goes a long way.

▶ Store *all* cleaning products safely—flammable products should be kept away from a heat source, and oily rags, poisons and other potentially hazardous products should be locked up away from children and pets.

▶ *Never* transfer cleaning products into another container—particularly one that previously contained food.

▶ Make sure there is proper ventilation when using any cleaning product, but particularly those products with fumes or gases.

▶ Keep all aerosol cleaners away from heat sources—they are extremely flammable.

Walls and ceilings

A thorough cleaning of your walls and ceilings should be done twice a year. Of course this depends on the area and how it's used, for instance; kitchen walls and ceilings attract grease and should be cleaned often while you may only need to spot clean around light switches, doorways and door handles to keep an entire wall looking fresh. Here are some general cleaning rules to get you on your way:

▶ Remove all surface dirt and soil with a vacuum cleaner attachment, wall mop or soft cloth tied to the end of a broom.

▶ Dust the ceiling first, then work downward, gently brushing the walls as you go. Change the cloth whenever it gets dirty to avoid leaving streaks on the walls.

▶ If necessary, before washing the walls, move the furniture and/or cover it with dropcloths or old sheets to protect your floors or carpets.

▶ If you are washing both the walls and ceiling, start with the ceiling; then wash the walls from the bottom upwards, cleaning overlapping areas with a circular motion.

▶ Prevent streaking by washing an entire ceiling or wall in one operation.

▶ Concentrate on one small area of the wall or ceiling at a time. Change the wash water and rinse water frequently to keep the sponge clean.

▶ If a wall covering has to be washed more than once, let it dry completely between washings.

Surface savvy

Before attempting to wash any surface, determine the type of surface you are cleaning—washable, non-washable or scrubbable. If you aren't sure, do a spot test on an inconspicuous area; if there is no change of color or appearance, it can probably be cleaned as a washable surface.

▶ **Washable:** Refers to most flat painted walls and to wall coverings with a plastic or vinyl coating, with a lightweight backing. To wash most flat painted walls, use an all-purpose cleaner in a bucket of hot water following the label directions. Use a new sponge and rinse often. In particularly soiled areas, use full strength cleaner on the sponge, then rinse the area well. Water should be used sparingly on paper wall coverings; use a sponge or cloth that has been slightly dampened in sudsy water. When using a foam cleaner, spray a four-foot square area, and wipe off soil and foam with a clean, damp sponge. Then wipe the wall with a rinsing cloth or sponge, and dry it with a clean bath towel. After washing flocked paper, lift the nap with a soft brush.

▶ **Non-washable:** Most walls covered with silk, burlap or grass paper should be considered non-washable, but make a patch test first to be sure. Felt wall coverings cannot be washed because they change color and shrink; use a granular rug cleaner as a spot remover. Greasy stains often can be cleaned with paste spot removers; after the paste dries to a powder, just brush it off; second application may be necessary for imbedded spots. Again, be sure to spot test any wall covering before reusing a product or technique.

▶ **Scrubbable:** When choosing wall coverings for high traffic areas in your home, keep in mind that if they are scrubbable, they are the easiest to maintain. Most woodwork and walls covered with high-gloss paint *are* scrubbable. To clean, just spray a cleanser right onto the heavily soiled area. Rub with a sponge to remove the soil, and then rinse completely for a real shine. For areas on the wall that are less soiled, use an all-purpose cleanser that has been dissolved in hot water following the label directions. Wipe the solution onto the walls with a damp sponge. *Never* use steel wool or abrasive cleansers on your walls.

Window coverings

When laundering or dry-cleaning your draperies, you might want to clean your curtain rods, pulls or carriers. You can wash them in a bathtub or sink using a detergent and water solution or a foam cleaner; dry thoroughly. If the cords become wet, leave the rods in a closed position until the cords are dry.

▶ **Shades, washable:** Unroll the shade and place it on flat surface. Clean the shade with detergent and warm water or a foam cleaner. Apply with a circular motion in small overlapping areas and rinse with a damp, clean cloth. You can rehang the shade after cleaning, but do not re-roll it until it is dry.

▶ **Shades, non-washable:** If vacuuming has removed surface soil and dust but stains and spots remain, use a dough-type wall cleaner (available in hardware or paint supply stores) or an artgum eraser (available

in art supply stores). Roll the shade out on a flat surface, and use light strokes over a small area, giving special attention to stained or streaked portions.

▶ **Venetian blinds:** Light cleaning and dusting can be done with a damp cloth or vacuum cleaner brush attachment. Place the blinds in the extreme up or down position before cleaning. If you wish to wash your blinds, and they can fit in a tub or sink, place them in a solution of warm water and mild detergent for five minutes. Rinse and drain out the head rail and bottom rail. Dry the blinds with a soft towel to avoid water marks, or hang the blinds upside down to air dry (the gear mechanism is heavier at the top of the blind than the metal bar at the bottom so you can anchor the blind more firmly this way). You also can hose-wash your blinds, making sure you rinse and dry them thoroughly. To clean larger blinds which cannot be taken down, wash them with a solution of mild detergent and warm water. Place a towel on the floor or window-sill, and wash the blind in sections using a soft cloth, sponge or medium-soft brush. Blinds that have tapes that are dirty or stained can be cleaned in mild detergent, like regular blinds, if the tapes are washable. If the tape on the blinds is non-washable, clean it with non-flammable dry-cleaning fluid.

▶ **Stick blinds or roll-ups:** Blinds made of plastic can be washed with a sponge dampened in a mild detergent or with a foam cleaner. *Never* wash bamboo roll-up blinds.

Spot & Stain Removal for Upholstered Furniture

Oil Borne: To remove an oil-borne stain, blot or scrape off the excess spill carefully. Apply a spot remover or solvent directly to the fabric itself using a clean cloth or sponge. Be sure to dampen the cloth or sponge with the solvent frequently so you don't redeposit the stain on the furniture. Start from the outer edge of stain and work inwards, drying off the dampened area with a second clean cloth or towel as you go. If spot remover dries to a powder, clean off residue by vacuuming.

Water Borne: To remove a water-borne stain, lightly blot the stain with cool water and scrape off the excess spill. (Always use cold water to remove blood stains as hot water will set the stain into the upholstery). If the stain persists, apply a water-based detergent cleaner (following the label directions) and work in a circular motion from the outer edge of the stain inwards. Dampen a clean cloth and gently wipe off any excess cleaner from the fabric. Blot the area with a clean, dry cloth or towel to dry it as quickly as possible.

Combination: Try the Water-Borne method of stain removal first; if the stain persists, use the Oil-Borne method.

Type of Stain	Oil Borne Oily Materials & Grease	Water Borne Food Stuff & Sugars	Combination Air & Oil
Alcohol, beer, mixed beverages		☐	
Blood		☐	
Butter, margarine	☐		
Candy, chocolate, cocoa			☐
Carbonated beverage		☐	
Catsup, tomato juice		☐	
Cheese		☐	
Coffee		☐	
Cold cream	☐		
Cosmetics	☐		
Cough syrup		☐	
Crayon	☐		
Deodorant	☐		
Egg		☐	
Fruit, berry stain		☐	

Type of Stain (continued)	Oil Borne Oily Materials & Grease	Water Borne Food Stuff & Sugars	Combination Air & Oil
Furniture stain	☐		
Glue, household		☐	
Grass		☐	
Gravy			☐
Grease	☐		
Hair oil	☐		
Ice cream		☐	
Ink, fluid		☐	
Jam & jelly		☐	
Lipstick	☐		
Mayonnaise	☐		
Milk drinks		☐	
Mustard			☐
Oil, cooking & salad	☐		
Oil, machine, mineral	☐		
Paint, waterbase wet		☐	
Peanut butter			☐
Rubber cement	☐		
Shoe Polish			☐
Soot	☐		
Soup			☐
Syrup			☐
Tar, asphalt	☐		
Tea		☐	
Toothpaste		☐	
Vegetables & juice		☐	
Vomit		☐	
Wine		☐	

Rug & Carpet Cleaning

Method	Application	Advantages	Disadvantages
Dry Powder	Spread powder evenly on carpet & work in well. Use applicator designed to spread powder and massage into carpet. Let stand specified time (1-3 hours), then vacuum to remove.	Controlled amount of moisture; good on delicate and non-colorfast carpets. Good for lightly soiled carpets or between shampooings in high traffic areas, such as doorways, stairs.	Less effective on heavily soiled carpets and water-based stains. Old cleaners tend to lose strength. Complete removal of powder is difficult and it shows on darker rugs.
Aerosol Foam 1-Step	Spray on carpet (or spot); let dry completely; vacuum to remove the loosened soil and the cleaning compound.	Convenient, quick-drying, no applicator needed. Good for lightly soiled carpet, surface cleaning, emergency spot removal, corners and lightly soiled stairs.	Cleans surface of rugs and carpets only; doesn't penetrate; not appropriate for thoroughly or heavily soiled areas; more expensive than the liquid method.
Aerosol Foam 2-Step	Spray on carpet; sponge mop into carpet; let dry thoroughly; vacuum.	Convenient; sponging into carpet gives better cleaning results than aerosol foam 1-step.	Same as above in 1-step method.
Liquid	Dilute concentrated rug shampoo according to manufacturer's directions; apply with shampooer (manual or electric); let dry completely; vacuum to remove loosened soil.	Good for thorough cleaning of medium to heavy soil; brightens color; fluffs pile; most economical for large rug and carpet areas.	Drying time is slightly longer than powder or 1-step method. Possible over-wetting can cause shrinkage and discoloration.
Hot Water Extraction (Steam Clean)	Hot water and detergent are sprayed on under pressure to flush out dirt; solution is immediately extracted by vacuum action of special extraction machine.	Satisfactory soil removal from rugs and carpets; little or no distortion of carpet pile; 1-step operation.	Heavily soiled areas and spots should be pretreated; great risk of over-wetting; longer drying time than other methods; promotes resoiling unless carpet is treated after cleaning; most expensive method.

Stain Removal From Carpets

Use this alphabetical listing of stains to get rid of blemishes on your carpet. The methods of stain removal follow the listing of stains. Follow each step given in the order that it appears.

Acids: ADTL	Food Stains: PCDAVTS	Ointment: CDAVTS
Alcohol: DVTS	Fruit Juices: CDAVTS	Paint: P
Bleach: DVTL	Glue: DAVT	Rust: P
Blood: DAVTP	Grease: CDVT	Shoe polish: CDAVTR
Butter: CDVAVTR	Household cement: CDAVTP	Soft drinks: DAVTR
Candy: DAVCTR	Ice cream: DAVCTR	Tea: DVTR
Chewing Gum: CDAVT	Inks: PCDAVTR	Unknown stains:
Chocolate: DAVCT	Lipstick: PCDAVTR	PCDAVAVTS
Cocktails: DCTS	Medicine: PCDAVTS	Urine: DVTL
Coffee: DVTR	Metal polish: CDVTP	Vomit: DAVTS
Cologne & perfume: CDVT	Mildew: P	Water colors: PCDAVTR
Cooking oil: CDAVT	Milk: DAVCT	Water stains: PDVTR
Cosmetics: CDAVTS	Nail polish: PCR	Wax: C
Dye: PCDAVTR	Oil: CDAVT	Wine: DVTS

A - Ammonia Add ¾ cup water to tablespoon ammonia. Place a small amount directly onto the stain and blot with paper toweling. Continue until no stain remains.

C - Dry Cleaner Place a small amount of dry cleaning solvent (a spot remover for clothing) directly onto the stain and blot with paper toweling. Continue until no stain remains. Only small amounts of the dry cleaning solvent should be used to prevent damage to the latex on the carpet's backing and do NOT use carbon tetrachloride, gasoline or lighter fluid.

D - Detergent Mix one teaspoon mild dishwater detergent (a carpet detergent is ideal but if not available use a non - alkaline detergent that doesn't contain bleach) with one cup lukewarm water. Use a small amount of the solution on the stain then blot with paper toweling. Continue until stain is removed.

L - Loss of Color Change in color of the carpet normally signifies dye loss in the fiber of the carpet. A professional rug cleaner can help by redyeing the stained area.

P - Professional Use a professional rug cleaner.

R - Redyed Fiber If discoloration remains, it is probably due to a stain which is affecting the fibers. Have the carpet redyed professionally.

S - Similar Staining Materials Such types of stains are not all composed of the same chemical formulas. Some may act as a dye (**R**) while others may look like a loss of dye (**L**).

T - Tissues and Weight Place ½-inch layer of tissues or other white absorbent material over damp area. Stack books, or any heavy material, over the tissues to weigh them down. Allow the area to dry for six hours, or overnight if needed.

V - Vinegar Mix ⅓ cup white vinegar with ⅔ cup lukewarm water. Apply a small amount of the solution onto the stain and blot with paper toweling. Continue until no stain remains.

3.
Caring
For
Clothes

Laundry
Handle With Care
So-Easy Sewing
How To Do Your Own Alterations
Needleworks: Knitting,
Crocheting and Embroidery

Laundry

*Do you dread laundry day? Don't
hide those dirty clothes in the
closet any longer. Armed with a
little know-how, you can send
dirt and stains down the drain.*

Easy sorting

Tired of a laundry hamper that
continually overflows? Buy four
plastic milk crates and label them
"whites," "towels," "colors" and
"work clothes." The result: presorted
laundry and no more overflowing
hamper.

Laundry I.D.

If you do laundry in a laundromat, tie
a colorful ribbon around your soap
container before leaving home and tie
a bow on the handle of the machine
you use. You then can quickly
identify *your* machine.

Slip-proof

If the drawstring of your sweat pants
keeps slipping through the casing, try
this easy solution: Sew a medium-size
button on each end of the drawstring
and it won't slip through again.

No tangled ties

To machine-wash a wrap-around skirt
without having the ties tangle around
the agitator, tie them together in a
large single bow. The skirt comes out
of the washer without a problem.

Wrinkle remover

If clothes get wrinkled from sitting in
the dryer, throw in a damp towel and
run the load for four minutes at the
end of the low cycle.

Less fading

When hanging clothes on the line to
dry (especially in strong sun), hang
them inside-out. They are much less
likely to fade on the "good side."

Pin it!

Use large safety pins to fasten
jumpsuit buckles to the insides of the
pockets. Now the buckles won't hit
the sides of the washer and dryer.

The scoop

Can't find your laundry measuring cup? Don't play the guessing game and add too little or too much detergent to your wash. Try using the scoops included in large-size powdered fruit drinks cans. Each scoop measures one-fourth of a cup. Use them not only to portion out detergent but also to measure powdered bleach.

The lint trap

Can't get the lint out of your dryer's lint trap? Try wiping it clean with a used fabric-softener sheet then toss them both away. When you need to clean beyond the removable lint trap, use your vacuum cleaner to suck the dirt out. A small hand-held model works well to clear the air vent opening. If all else fails, use a damp cloth and clean by hand.

Set and match

After removing laundry from your dryer, fold the contoured bottom sheets and pillow cases and insert them in the last fold of the top sheets. Not only will the matching sheet sets be easier to find, they'll fit more compactly on the closet shelf. Your towels can be folded into a set as well by placing the wash cloth and hand towel into the last fold of the bath towel.

No more sags

There's nothing more frustrating than hanging your clothes on a clothesline that sags and puts your clean clothes in the dirt. The next time that happens, try this simple solution: Tie one end of your clothesline to the last link in a small length of chain. Then, if the line sags, place the next link of the chain over the hook. It's easier than trying to pull the clothesline tighter.

Laundry cart

An old baby bassinet makes a great laundry cart for your laundry room. It will cut down on your need to reach and bend for your dirty clothes, and you can wheel it easily between the washer and dryer.

Button repair

A machine-sewn button can often unravel and fall off in the wash. To prevent this, carefully place a drop of super-glue on the "X" formed by the crossed threads. This helps to fuse the thread to the button and the button will stay on—permanently!

Keeping moths away

Moths can wreak havoc on your wardrobe if you're not careful. One way to keep the pests at bay is to make a "moth tape". Just dust moth crystals on the sticky side of plastic tape and hang it in your closets. Moths won't *bug* you after that!

Body builders

▶ To add body to frequently washed knitted shirts, spray them lightly with starch and press with a warm iron. The shirts will keep their shape and stay cleaner longer.

▶ Give frequently washed corduroy garments more body by turning them inside out, spraying with starch, and ironing.

▶ Cheesecloth makes a great ironing cloth. It leaves no lint and retains little moisture so clothes don't get too wet.

Easier ironing

Keep these ideas in mind the next time you iron:

▶ Keep an ice cube wrapped in a thin cloth handy for dampening corners and any other small dry areas on your clothes.

▶ When not spraying houseplants, keep the plant mister on the ironing board. It sprays a fine mist that's perfect for dampening clothes before you iron.

▶ Because organdy curtains dry so quickly while being ironed, fold a damp large bath towel in half and pin each end of it to the back of the ironing board. Keep the curtain rolled up in the towel and pull it out as you iron each section of the curtain.

Ironing board protection

The long paper bags that dry cleaners use to cover cleaned clothes make wonderful ironing board protectors. Slip a bag over the folded ironing board before storing away.

Freeze frame

Freeze leftover liquid starch in an ice cube tray, label it clearly, and store it in your freezer. You'll have cubes of starch handy when a small amount is needed ironing.

Quality lasts

To tell whether you are getting quality-made clothes off the rack, look for these tailoring details:

▶ Buttonholes should be sewn on both sides of the cloth.

▶ Firm, closely woven fabric lining inside of the garment and pockets.

▶ Pinked or finished skirt seams.

▶ Seams wide enough to permit letting out.

▶ Good tape binding in hems.

▶ Even, close stitches.

▶ Collar and lapel which will snap back when rolled up and released.

▶ Pants crotch without small triangles of cloth.

▶ Smooth fabric with no puckering at the seams.

First aid for stains

Keep a home first-aid kit for stain removal handy by putting aside the following materials:
▶ Mild detergent—liquid dishwashing detergent is best as soap leaves a residue
▶ Vinegar—for tannin (vegetable) stains such as soft drinks, hard drinks, fruit juices, mustard, ketchup, coffee, tea
▶ Household ammonia—for albumin (animal) stains such as milk, ice cream, blood, urine
▶ Perchlorethylene (chemical solution available at some commercial cleaners)—for oil- and grease-based stains
▶ Terry-cloth towel

General stain removal

Before you attack a stain, test the cleaning solution on part of the garment that won't show just in case the fabric bleeds.
▶ Put a terry-cloth towel under the stain. If the stain is water-based (not oil), apply cool water to the area and blot—don't rub.
▶ If water only doesn't work, try a solution of water and mild liquid detergent (about 1 part detergent to 10 parts water). Be sure to rinse with clear water.
▶ Try a 1-to-5 vinegar and water solution for vegetable-based stains. Rinse with clear water.
▶ If a stain is oil- or wax-based (cosmetics, paints, ball-point ink, many medicines), place the terry-cloth towel under the stain, and use a solvent. Blot the area but don't rub it.
▶ If the stain has been removed from a soiled garment, a "ring" will be visible. Go back and "feather out" the stain by applying more solution along the edges of the ring and gently blending the edges. Then clean the entire garment.

Good riddance!

Here's some more help on getting rid of those bothersome stains that never seem to go away.
▶ **Mildew stain:** To remove mildew from leather bags or shoes, wipe them with a cloth moistened in a solution of 1 cup denatured alcohol and 1 cup of water. Dry carefully in an airy place.
▶ **Fruit or berry stains:** Stretch the garment over a large heatproof bowl, and pour boiling water over and through the stains. If the stains still remain, try bleaching with hydrogen peroxide or chlorine bleach.
▶ **Oil stains:** Use white chalk to remove grease or oil stains. The chalk can be rubbed onto a washable fabric before laundering.
▶ **Coffee stains:** Soak the garment overnight in a large pan of vinegar and water (heavy on the vinegar!). Hang the garment in the sun while dripping wet. Wash as usual. If that doesn't work, try one of the commercial coffee pot cleaners.
▶ **Chewing gum stains:** Put the stained garment in a plastic bag and freeze overnight. The gum should scrape off easily. Another method of gum removal is brushing egg whites on the gum stain with a toothbrush. Wash the garment as usual to loosen the gum.
▶ **Ball-point ink stains:** Saturate the spot with commercial hair spray, let dry and wash.
▶ **Crayon mark stains:** Place the stained garment between two sheets

of paper toweling. Go over the area with a warm iron, replacing the paper toweling as the crayon wax adheres to the toweling.

▶ **Felt-tip pen stains:** Soak the stain with milk, then wash as usual.

▶ **Nail polish stains:** Remove with amyl acetate nail polish remover (not acetone). Wash as usual.

▶ **Blood stains:** If the stain is on a washable fabric, wash it in cold water (hot water will set the stain) with mild soap, detergent or hydrogen peroxide.

Hang in there

Use padded hangers for fine clothing and rounded, plastic hangers for everything else. Wire hangers are too hard on clothes—they tend to ruin shoulder shapes and often are the culprits behind snags.

▶ Place slacks or knits over the bottom padded part of a hanger to save space and to prevent creasing and hanger marks.

▶ Always hang clothing up immediately after removing it. Letting things pile up over the backs of chairs creates wrinkles and wears out the fabric prematurely.

▶ Seldom-worn garments should be kept in fabric garment bags to keep them clean (the same goes for items which pick up lint and dust very quickly). Use plastic cleaner's bags for short periods of time only—they encourage mildew.

▶ Never store leather bags, boots or shoes in plastic. Leather, like silk and down garments, has to breathe.

▶ Big plastic or ceramic hooks are great for hanging nightclothes, robes and jeans. Smaller decorative hooks, grouped together, keep accessories like bags, belts, scarves and ribbons in order.

▶ Hang anything that needs cleaning or repair work on a special hook. Take clothing to the cleaners immediately so stains won't set, and make repairs as soon as possible to get the most out of your clothes.

Tip-top shape

Clothes are one category where an ounce of prevention really is worth a pound of cure. Keep your clothes in tip-top shape:

▶ Consider wearing dress shields under the arms of non-washable clothing. They're available in lots of shapes and styles—some are designed like lingerie, others you pin to the garment, and they really cut cleaning costs.

▶ Save all your care tags, extra buttons, extra mending yarn, etc., that sometimes come with clothes in a box. That way you'll know what to do when you have a stain problem or need to mend.

▶ Read care labels carefully—and seriously. "Hand wash" means just that: by hand, in a sink, with a mild soap. And, while you can sometimes get away with hand-washing fabrics like silk instead of taking them to the cleaner, be prepared for disappointments. Sometimes the luster or texture of the fabric is damaged when it is washed with water. Also, interfacings or lining fabrics will sometimes shrink differently than the garment fabric.

Good as new

Instead of throwing out your favorite outfit when it's become a bit frayed around the edges—or allowing it to *become* frayed in the first place—put a little tender loving care back into it and you'll have it looking like new again. Daily maintenance on your clothes not only extends the life on the garment, it also helps cut down on costly big repairs. Get into the habit of making minor repairs immediately with some of these helpful gadgets:

▶ **Knit-pik or Knit-fixer:** Pulls snagged threads back to the wrong side of the garment. This keeps the snag from expanding into a large unsightly hole.

▶ **Sweater combs or Sweater shavers:** Eat the little pills off of your sweaters. The combs have an abrasive metal tooth which rids your sweater of the bumpy-lumpy look. Shavers actually work like an electric face shaver to remove pills from sweaters. In a pinch, careful sanding with an emery board will remove them too. But be gentle!

▶ **Suede and leather elbow patches:** These patches not only are fashionable, they also keep the fabric on your elbow joint from wearing away quickly. Many times you can buy leather and suede scraps at smaller leather stores.

▶ **Conventional elastic braid:** Elastic is one of the first things to go in pajamas and children's clothing, and really easy to replace. Remove the old elastic, cut a piece one inch smaller than the child's waist measurement (or wrist, etc.). Attach a safety pin to one end of the elastic, and use the pin to feed the elastic through the casing by attaching it to a safety pin. Sew the ends of the elastic together.

▶ **Iron-on elbow and knee patches:** These are especially good for children's play clothing because garment joints tend to see lots of wear and tear. Remember to use a steam iron or wet press cloth to be sure the patches are properly fused.

▶ **Iron-on sock patches:** Thanks to synthetic fibers, socks don't wear out as quickly as their cotton and wool ancestors did. If a hole does develop; however, iron-on knit patches are available for socks. They are circular, cut from soft knit fabric and come in bags of assorted colors.

▶ **Fusible mending tapes:** These are great for people who hate to sew! You can do a lot of mending with just your steam iron. The best way to use these are as reinforcements. Fusible tapes are the only way to repair a large tear without leaving scars.

▶ **Fusible webbing:** Repair work is made easy with fusible webbing. Even hems easily can be ironed into place in no time at all.

▶ **Fusible fabric:** Here the fusible webbing is already attached to a soft, tricot fabric. It easily can be ironed onto the wrong side of the garment, to mend a tear or reinforce potentially weak spots (like knees, inner thighs of pants, etc.). When using any fusible fabric, remember to round the corners of the patches or they might peel off.

Rapid repairs

You can keep old clothes looking great if you take preventive action now:

▶ **Reinforcing knees:** Reinforce the knees of pants before the fabric gets too thin. The reinforcements can be made from patches of the same fabric fused to the wrong side of the pants, a patch of lining fabric or an iron-on patch.

▶ **Knitted collars, cuffs and waistbands:** Since the ribbed parts on clothing are often the first thing to go, it makes sense to replace them. They're easy to install and will prolong the life of the garment.

▶ **Pockets:** Money and keys are notoriously hard on pockets, but replacing them is easier than you would think. Just remove the torn pocket and topstitch or insert a sturdy new one in its place.

▶ **Turning a shirt collar:** Using a seam ripper, carefully open the stitching line where the collar is attached to the collar band. Remove the collar and spray the raw edges with a little spray starch to keep them from fraying. Sandwich the collar between the two layers of the collar band, keeping the good side of the collar facing the wrong side of the shirt. Pin the collar in place, baste, and stitch the collar to the neck edge through all the layers.

▶ **Turning a shirt cuff:** You can turn a shirt cuff in much the same manner as a shirt collar (see above). Remember to switch the cuffs from one side to the other so the buttonhole comes out on the right side of the cuff.

Clothing makeovers

Stretch your clothing budget and update your wardrobe at the same time by these clever makeovers:

▶ **Slimming pants or skirt:** Turn the garment inside out and take down the hem. Put on the garment and have someone pin out the excess fabric on the side seams, using rows of pins to mark the new seams. Take off the garment and place it on a flat surface; check to be sure an equal amount has been taken off both sides. Place a yardstick along the pin lines and, using tailor's chalk, mark a straight line following the line of the pins; the marked line will be the stitchline. Machine-stitch the new seams, trim the excess fabric from the seam allowances and press the seams open. Re-hem the garment.

▶ **Relining a coat:** This really makes a big difference in the life of a coat, and isn't that hard to do if you take it one step at a time. Using a seam ripper, carefully remove all the stitching that holds the lining in place. Take apart the lining, piece by piece. Press all the old lining pieces carefully; they will act as pattern pieces for the new lining. Using the old lining patterns, cut out pieces from the new lining fabric; the seam allowance is already accounted for on the old lining pieces. Set aside the sleeve pieces. Following the stitchlines of the old lining, stitch together the new body lining pieces. Turn under the edges of the new lining and pin it to the coat, matching the folded lining edges with the old stitchlines on the coat. Slipstitch the new body lining in place. Stitch two gathering rows along the cap of the new sleeve lining pieces. Tack the sleeve linings to the armhole of the coat, matching underarm seams. Gently pull the coat sleeve to the wrong side of the coat, slipping it through the new sleeve lining. Pull up the gathers to fit the lining to the cap of the coat sleeve, and slipstitch the lining in place. Hem the new lining at the wrists and along the bottom edge, and slipstitch the hems to the coat fabric 1 inch above the edges of the coat sleeves and bottom edges.

▶ **Changing necklines:**

The size and shape of a collar can make a dress or blouse look out of date. By removing or replacing the collar you can give a favorite outfit a new lease on life. Removing the collar altogether will give the garment a "jewel" neckline that can be accessorized easily with a scarf or necklace. Cut off the old collar about ¼-inch beyond the original inner edge. Fold the raw edge inside the garment, and bind the edge with the original facing, or matching bias tape. If the garment buttons up the front, create a contemporary cardigan look by removing the collar and trimming away the front neck edge to form a deep "V" shape. Bind all the raw edges with matching or contrasting bias tape. You also can replace the collar on most garments with a new, ready-made collar of fabric or lace. Just remove the old collar (and collar band, if there was one) and slipstitch the new collar in position, placing the inner edge of the new collar just inside the old collar seam line of the blouse. Bind the edges with either the original facing or with bias tape.

▶ **Shortening a coat or jacket:**

If the garment has patch pockets, remove them. Using a seam ripper, carefully remove the stitching along the lower edge of the garment lining. Open out the front facing. Turn up garment hem to the desired length, trimming away excess fabric. Tack the garment hem in place, then hem the lining over the new garment hem. The bottom edge of the lining should be 1 inch shorter than the bottom edge of the garment hem. If you have removed patch pockets, pin them in place on the garment. If the placement and proportion looks good, slipstitch them in place. If the pockets look out of proportion to the new garment length, just leave them off altogether. Another way to update a coat or jacket is to add a belt of the same fabric, a contrasting fabric or leather.

Handle With Care

Treat your clothes right and they will last longer, look better.

How to test for washability

To test a knit, stretch the fabric. If it bounces back, it is probably hand washable. Next, soak a ribbed cuff in 2 tablespoons soapy water, rinse and let dry. If the colors do not run and the cuff keeps its shape, your knit is hand washable.

To wash wool and silk

▶ Hand wash in cool water with a cold-water detergent. Soak for about five minutes. Gently squeeze suds through the garment. Rinse thoroughly and block.

▶ To remove water-soluble (most nongreasy) stains, the garment may need longer soaking. Check every three to four minutes, squeezing suds through the stain. *Do not rub.* If the stain is persistent, have the garment professionally dry-cleaned.

Keep it shapely

When hand washing head wear, such as knitted or crocheted caps, place the wet cap on a styrofoam wig stand until dry to insure shape and fit.

Acrylic knits and other synthetics

▶ Wash them inside-out in tepid water and mild soap. Squeeze suds through; do not twist or wring. Add fabric softener to reduce static electricity. Block right side out. (Acrylics will be slightly larger when wet.) To machine-wash, place the garments in a net bag and use the gentle or knit cycle.

▶ With blended knits (containing two or more fibers), care for the more fragile, natural fiber (i.e., wool or silk) or follow label instructions.

▶ To fold a sweater, lay it front side down. Fold it in half so the bottom meets the top. Cross the arms over the width of the sweater. Or use a well-padded hanger.

▶ Always block a sweater so it will dry back to its original shape: Trace an outline of the sweater on a towel. Use a laundry marker for a permanent outline; otherwise, trace with tailor's chalk or a bar of soap. Wash the sweater and roll it in another towel to remove excess moisture. Lay it flat, shape it to fit the outline and let dry.

Drying out

To dry a bulky sweater quickly and safely, place it between two fluffy bath towels and roll it lightly with a rolling pin. Remove the sweater and put a hand towel inside it before flattening and shaping it to dry. The hand towel absorbs still more moisture.

To store woolens for the summer

▶ Make sure all your woolens are clean before putting them away for the summer. Store them properly.

▶ The vapors from mothballs and crystals are heavier than air and, therefore, fall rather than rise. In order to get the utmost protection, hang a container of mothballs or crystals over one of the hanger hooks when placing clothing in a garment bag. Zip up to seal the vapors inside.

▶ Crystal-layered wool knitwear and blankets should be packed in storage boxes that can be sealed airtight. Never use flimsy plastic bags from the cleaners for storage because mothballs and crystals melt holes in them.

▶ Can't stand the smell of mothballs? Use a nonresidual spray directly on clothing. Those containing allethrin, pyrethrin or resmethrin are safe. Make sure the label reads, "For clothing moths."

Corduroy care

To keep washable corduroy looking its best—soft and wrinkle-free, with a fluffed-up nap—follow this easy advice: After washing, machine-dry for about 20 minutes using one fabric softener sheet. Remove the corduroy clothing (still damp) and hang it to finish drying at room temperature.

No wrinkles

Insert tissue paper in the long sleeves of crepe and silk dresses and blouses to preserve fullness and prevent creases during storage.

Always a fresh look

Run the cut edge of a ribbon along the brush of clear nail polish. It provides an invisible seal that keeps the ribbon from unraveling even in the washing machine.

Accessory round-up

To keep scarves, ribbons and fancy detachable collars wrinkle-free between wearings, save the cardboard tubes from foil, plastic wrap and toilet paper, and roll the accessories around them. One tube can hold several layers of "pretties," and the tiny items do not get lost in the bottom of a drawer.

Keeping scarves neat

To avoid wrinkling scarves by folding, hang them on a tie rack in the closet. You can select a dress and scarf in one motion and have no wrinkles at all.

Preventive measure

To add longer life to work shirts, press a knee-size iron-on patch to the inside of each breast pocket. Sharp screws and nails won't poke through and create holes.

Lint remover

A damp sponge is perfect for removing lint from clothes, especially when ironing. Not only is the lint easy to remove, the sponge dampens the clothes being ironed and makes wrinkles come out more easily.

Stocking savers

▶ Save fine nylons from snagging in your dresser drawer by placing them in plastic bags. Roll up the bags and slip them inside cardboard toilet paper or paper towel rolls—the size would depend on the space in your drawer. These rolls can be neatly arranged and the contents written on the outside for easy identification.

▶ Put a pair of lightweight gloves in the drawer with your pantyhose. Use them when putting on hose to prevent runs and snags caused by fingernails.

▶ Dab a bright shade of nail polish on the tag or waistband of pantyhose suitable only for wearing under slacks because of runs or snags. This simplifies finding the right pair early in the morning!

Label it

▶ Many of the labels in clothing feel uncomfortable against the skin or show through the material. To remedy this, keep a small loose-leaf notebook with a section marked Labels. Remove the labels from garments and tape each to a page alongside a description of its item.

▶ If you sew a lot of your own clothes and tend to forget the type of cleaning care necessary for certain items, clip fabric care labels out of old clothes that you no longer wear and attach them to handmade clothes of the same material. If you cannot get enough labels, make your own with smooth bias tape and an indelible marker.

Shoe shine-ups

▶ You can spruce up soiled canvas shoes with a commercial upholstery cleaner. Spray, work the foam in with a small brush, let dry and use the same brush to remove the soiled, dried-up foam.

▶ Here's another way to make dirty canvas shoes look new! Whisk a tablespoon of liquid detergent with ¼ cup warm water until suds stand in soft peaks. Stuff the shoes tightly with paper toweling to prevent suds from leaking through to the soles. With a nailbrush, apply only the suds and scrub. Rinse off the nailbrush, shake dry and use it to remove the suds. Repeat. Dry the shoes away from heat.

▶ When the wooden heels of pumps or low-heeled shoes get scuffed to the point where polish or dye won't cover the marks, smooth down the surface (an emery board will do) and cover with a strip of wood-grained self-adhesive paper. Trim with a pocket knife or safety razor and your shoes will look like new!

▶ Felt-tip pens and markers, which come in just about every color imaginable, are just the ticket for camouflaging scuffed spots on shoes, belts, bags and the like.

Bedraggled-bow blues?

Is pressing wrinkled hair ribbons part of the last-minute morning race at your house? A quick zip through the curling iron gives good results.

So-Easy Sewing

For the home sewer, tips to make your life simpler.

No more tangles

▶ Polyester thread tends to twist, snarl and knot quite a bit. Running the thread over the end of a candle before threading the needle keeps it from twisting and makes hand sewing much easier.

▶ If you always find the bobbins from your sewing machine in a tangle of threads, store them in empty prescription bottles. Using a container a bit larger than the bobbin width, you can stack five or six bobbins, depending on the height of the bottle.

For good measure

To save steps and time when you need to measure belts, elastic, seam binding, bias tape, ribbons, trim and the like, glue a tape measure to the front of your sewing machine or to the machine cabinet.

Decorative touch

Dress up a child's sweater or jumper by stitching the buttons on with embroidery floss in a floral pattern. Using four to six strands of floss, make straight stitches for the stems and leaves, French knots for the flowers.

Patch with ease

Even with a sewing machine, patching the knees in kids' jeans means a lot of maneuvering of the jeans and needle. The pins get caught on the presser foot and the jeans often slip, resulting in a patch that's crooked or bunched. Solve this problem by replacing the pins with scraps of fusible webbing. A piece the size of a dime, used at each corner, holds a patch securely in place while you zig-zag around the edges. If it's a large patch, add an inch or so of webbing at the center of each edge.

Darning do's

▶ Paint one side of your darning egg a light color, the other a dark color. This makes it easier to darn light socks on the dark side and dark socks on the light side.

▶ A more durable and attractive way to mend holes in pants and socks is to use tapestry wool or embroidery thread instead of regular thread. Not only are these materials less expensive than a patch, they can be found in almost any color to match the garment.

Quick identification

Many sewing machines have several different specialty needles that look similar. To keep from getting them mixed up, stick the needle for sewing leather into a small square of leather, the one for sewing elastic material through a little piece of elastic and so on.

Handy tweezers

Keep a pair of tweezers in your sewing kit. They will be useful for pulling threads and will come in handy to smooth out the material that is under the presser foot as you sew.

Pins and needles

▶ For a great way to keep needles and pins sharp, cover a stainless steel scrub pad with several layers of pretty fabric stitched in place. For a wrist pin cushion, do the same and add elastic to fit your wrist. The result: sharp pins and needles whenever you need them.

▶ Attach a small magnet to the side of your sewing machine. As you take pins out of the material you're sewing, place them on the magnet. They will be easy to put back in their storage box and won't be scattered around.

A button in time

When hand-me-down clothes are beyond repair, cut the buttons off and save them in a jar. On a rainy day, put your child to work matching the buttons and tying the mates together with stout carpet thread. The "sets" come in handy to use on newly sewn garments.

Tracing tactics

▶ Instead of using tracing paper for making or adjusting patterns, use the pastel-colored plastic bags many retail stores are giving out. The bags are semitransparent, easy to cut and can be written on with a ball-point pen.

▶ When using tracing paper to transfer lines from a sewing pattern to material, a pizza cutter does a much better job than the conventional wheel with teeth. It's easier to control, the pattern doesn't get torn up because of the large, smooth wheel and you get a much cleaner and clearer line on the material.

Organizing your sewing basket

▶ For quickly locating your sewing supplies, try using clear plastic multisectioned cases (the kind mechanics and carpenters use). They make it easy to separately store buttons, needles, embroidery thread by color, sewing machine disks and parts, lace, pins and elastic. Each drawer can be labeled by content for added convenience. The cases are usually available at hardware stores and in the housewares department of discount stores.

▶ To keep your sewing supplies out of reach of a curious toddler, buy an inexpensive, three-tiered hanging basket and line the bottom of each tier with printed fabric. Hang the basket over your sewing machine within your reach but too high for your child's little hands.

How To Do Your Own Alterations

With the high cost of alterations today, it pays to do them yourself. Here are the simplest ways to tackle hems, waistbands and more—and get terrific results.

Marking hems solo

To mark a hem evenly by yourself, use a table that's below the hipline but within arm's length. Pin the center front portion of the hem to the length you want. Then, wearing the garment, stand next to the table. Turn slowly and mark with pins where the skirt touches the tabletop. Take the skirt off and mark an even distance from the line of pins to the desired hemline all the way around. For bias-cut skirts, leave one inch more than you need for the hem itself and let the garment hang for a day or two unhemmed. Recheck for evenness, trim from the extra inch if necessary and hem.

Clip, don't pin

To avoid pricking your fingers on pins, hold a hem in place with paper clips.

How deep should you make a hem?

In general, the more flared the garment, the narrower the hem. Use a ¼-inch hem for a wide-cut circle skirt, a 1½- to 2½-inch hem for an A-line skirt, a 3-inch hem for a straight-cut skirt. Hemlines on bulky fabrics will be smoother if you trim the material at the seam allowances (below the hemline) to within ¼ inch on each side.

Hemming a flared skirt

To avoid excess fabric left at the side seams when hemming a flared skirt, "ease" (slightly gather) the extra fabric so it fits evenly at the hemline: Pin up the hem and press lightly. Unpin and machine-baste the hem ¼ inch from the edge. "Ease" the fabric by gently pulling in the basting stitches with a pin. Press lightly, adjust the tension (add hem lace if desired) and hem.

Need to lengthen—but there's a tiny hem?

To lengthen a dress that is 1 inch too short but has a hem only 1½ inches deep, trim the fabric to ⅜ inch. Use wide hem lace or bias tape for the hem facing or sew a narrow machine hem, found today even on designer garments.

No-sew hemming

For a no-sew method of hemming, use bonding web. (It comes in ¾-inch-width rolls, but it's easier to work with if you cut it to a width of ⅜ inch.) Position the webbing ¼ inch from the top of the hem between the garment and hem. Touch an iron briefly to the hem all around to fuse lightly. Check that the hem is smooth before permanently fusing according to package directions. If you must reposition the fabric after fusing, apply heat and moisture according to directions and pull the fused section apart. *Note:* Fusing works best on a garment that isn't constantly machine-washed and dried. The hot, moist air in the dryer will sometimes defuse a hem.

Invisible hand-sewn hems

To hand-sew a hem so stitches aren't noticeable from the outside, "blindstitch" on the inside of the hem. Pin up the hemline one inch from the top edge and press. With the wrong side of the garment facing you and the hem at the top, fold the hem over to the right side. Using a single thread and fine needle, take a tiny stitch in the garment and a larger stitch in the hem allowance. Repeat, keeping stitches loose.

No fold line

To minimize the old fold line in permanent press slacks that have been lengthened, dab the line with a solution of half white vinegar and half water before pressing. (Check the fabric for color-fastness first.) Also, try to machine-sew your new hem exactly over the previous line. This will flatten and hide it.

Pants don't fit?

To fix pants that are too big at the waist but fit perfectly at the hips, open up the center back seam, which extends through the waistband, and simply take in the required amount.

"Sam, you made the sleeves too long . . ."

For the quickest way to shorten cuffed sleeves, move the button to get a snugger fit around the wrist. Or remove the cuff band, shorten the sleeve and stitch the band back on.

Needleworks: Knitting, Crocheting and Embroidery

Helpful wisdom for nimble fingers.

Mark your place

▶ Use sheets of the stick-on note pads that are gummed only at the top to help mark your place when following a knit or crochet pattern. They stick with a touch, are easily removed and reused from line to line of the directions without damaging the paper or print and they won't fall off.

▶ To keep track of rows or stitches while knitting, keep a toy abacus close by. Each time you finish a stitch, slide a bead across the wire. If you are interrupted, you can quickly see where you left off.

Easy casting

Always cast on with both needles held together. When you have the correct number of cast-on stitches, carefully pull out one needle and the stitches will be loose enough to work with easily.

Buttonhole helper

If you're knitting a cardigan sweater or vest, work both sides of the front at the same time. When you make a buttonhole, put a purl or contrasting stitch at exactly the same place on the opposite front edge. You'll then have the place marked for sewing on or replacing a button.

Colorful blocking

When blocking a crocheted or knitted garment, use color-tipped pins. They are much easier to spot when you're ready to remove them from the garment.

Metric awareness

With the increasing conversion to metric measures, many yarn companies are repackaging their yarns in metric balls and skeins. As a result, if you haven't knitted or crocheted recently, the weight of a skein may vary slightly from the amounts you've been accustomed to. For example, much 4-ply knitting worsted is being packaged in 100 g (3½ oz) skeins, instead of 4 oz skeins. Be sure to check weights before buying yarn!

Ready, set, go

▶ When starting a needlework project, separate the various colored yarns. Thread each color on a separate needle and stick it in a pincushion.

▶ Washable needlework projects often have patterns that call for cardboard inserts to help retain the shape of the article. If you substitute plastic canvas for the cardboard, the article can be washed as needed without damage to the project.

Easy to follow

Some counted cross-stitch patterns are hard to read. Coloring a pattern with corresponding colored pencils makes the pattern easier to follow and helps avoid missing a stitch in the color being used.

Keeping thread wound

Wind embroidery thread on plastic hair curlers. Snap them shut to keep the thread from becoming unwound.

As for appliqué . . .

▶ Chintz is recommended for appliqué work because it tends not to fray when cut. In choosing chintz patterns, look for designs with well delineated shapes.

▶ Trace your appliqué motif onto fabric, leaving a ¼-inch seam to turn under.

▶ With sharp scissors, make small snips all around the edges of curved outlines to allow for neater, easier turning under.

▶ Fold raw edges ¼ inch to the back and steam iron them. Baste all around the edges following the shape of the appliqué motif. To make sewing appliqués easier, secure them with double-faced fusible bonding and sew around them.

Thread limit

When embroidering, limit thread length to about 18 inches. Working with a longer strand stretches the thread and the look of the embroidery becomes uneven.

End to loose ends

Here's a neat way to store embroidery floss and avoid a tangled mess. Purchase some plastic sheets of coin pockets, the kind collectors use, and use the pockets to store the floss. Organize the sheets in a looseleaf notebook and diagram an inventory chart on the inside cover. The chart should consist of columns that read, "color," "color number," "quantity" and so on. With the chart as a guide, it is easy to match a new project.

Dust-free macramé

Before working with macramé cords, put them in the clothes dryer on "fluff" for a few minutes. This will remove most of the dust and lint, leaving the cords much easier to work with.

Color perfect

Always check the dye lot number on skeins of wool. Even if the color looks the same, a different dye lot could produce a slight variation in the tint that will show up in the finished product.

Test run

Be sure to test your knitting or crocheting gauge before beginning a project. Make a sample swatch about four inches square and check it against the correct gauge. This will save you innumerable headaches with sizing problems.

Keeping in shape

▶ When knitting cuffs on sweaters, help them keep their shape by interweaving elastic thread throughout.

▶ If you use needles a size or two smaller than those used for the body of the sweater, cuffs and other ribbed edges will hold their shape better and longer.

Keep it clean

To keep yarn clean while you work on a project, slip the ball of yarn into a self-sealing plastic bag with a small hole cut out of a bottom corner. Slide the end of the yarn through the hole and you have an easy-to-carry yarn protector. It will also prevent the yarn from becoming entangled with other objects if you like to take your knitting wherever you go.

The eye of the needle

Most people wet the end of a thread before trying to insert it through the eye of a needle, but if you're having particular trouble, try using a little wax or hairspray to stiffen the end. This can be especially helpful with embroidery floss.

About canvas

▶ To help keep your needlework canvas clean, spray a little fabric water-proofing on it every now and again while working on your project. The canvas will wipe clean easily and resist lint.

▶ If canvas tends to fray as you work on it, cover the edges with masking tape.

▶ Remember to roll, never fold, a needlepoint canvas; it helps the canvas keep its shape.

How To Care For Your Heirlooms

Whether it's your own expertly crafted handwork or an antique quilt, here's how to care for your heirloom so you can enjoy it for years to come.

Do's and don'ts of storing heirlooms

▶ Do store heirlooms in a cool area that is clean, dry, dark and well-ventilated. Relative humidity should be about 50%.

▶ Do wrap heirlooms in acid-free tissue paper, washed muslin, washed cotton or cotton/polyester sheets. If your heirloom has a metal part attached to it, such as a bellpull, remove the metal, if possible, before wrapping.

▶ Do place wrapped pieces in acid-free boxes. Or put them in a bureau drawer lined with acid-free tissues or washed cotton or muslin sheets. For more protection, coat bureau drawers with polyurethane varnish before lining with the paper or sheets. If your home gets a lot of dust, line drawers with heavy polyethylene sheets, Mylar or fiberfill.

▶ Do fold a quilt in the following way to prevent soil buildup, discoloration and wear along fold lines during storage: Fold the quilt into thirds, placing a roll of acid-free paper along and under each fold. Fold the quilt again into thirds, toward the center. Place a roll of crumpled acid-free tissue along and under each of these two fold lines. You can substitute washed sheets or unbleached muslin for the acid-free paper.

▶ Don't store an heirloom in an attic or a basement—it will mildew.

▶ Don't wrap heirlooms in plastic, styrofoam or anything made from wood, such as cardboard or regular tissue paper.

Cleaning an heirloom

Many heirlooms over 50 years old look "dirty" because they develop brownish or rust spots. But these spots are not dirt, they're the result of a natural action in the fabric and therefore usually cannot be removed. In fact, experts say these spots enhance an article as an antique. So when should you clean your heirloom? Only if it is so soiled it can't possibly be displayed or if you've recently stained it yourself. *Note:* Never attempt to take out stains with bleaches or detergents with "brighteners added."

▶ **Washing linen or cotton with lace edging, all-linen or all-lace items:**
Always avoid wringing or scrubbing items. For a very mild cleaning of

lace or linen, soak the piece in distilled water at room temperature for a half an hour. This removes foreign matter and loosens dirt. If you are washing an all-lace item, lower the item into the water and take it out on a fiberglass screen with taped edges. For cleaning extremely fragile or very lightly soiled items, dissolve one quarter of a 3.2-ounce bar of Neutrogena or a small amount of a mild laundry detergent in 1 cup distilled water at room temperature. Add 1 ounce of this solution to a gallon of distilled water. Soak the item for half an hour, then rinse it thoroughly with distilled water.

▶ **Drying:** Spread the item on an undyed terrycloth or a plain cloth towel and let it dry at room temperature.

▶ **Ironing:** Steam-press lace on a well-padded ironing board, placing a damp undyed cloth over the lace first. For linen, start with the iron set at cool. Continue raising the heat and testing the fabric on the wrong side until you reach the setting needed. Iron the item on the wrong side, placing a damp, undyed cloth between it and the iron. To iron embroidered linen, place it on a doubled, undyed towel to cushion the threads so they won't tear.

▶ **Needlework:** Don't wash or clean needlework because the threads can be weakened and unravel or deteriorate.

Repairing a worn heirloom

To conserve the value of an heirloom, we recommend taking it to a professional who specializes in restoring fabric antiques.

On display

▶ Quilts can be displayed for three months at a time. Then "rest" them for four months by storing them as suggested on page 61.

▶ To protect needlework, cover it with glass or sheer net fabric. Leave space between the covering and the item so threads are not crushed.

▶ If you frame needlework, lace or linen, always place an acid-free mat board between it and the frame backing. (Acid-free products and other special products for heirlooms are available at crafts stores or by mail.)

▶ Never display an heirloom in direct sunlight or its reflected glare, near heat or under fluorescent lights.

▶ Never place an object on top of an heirloom, *even one under glass.*

Quilt care

▶ **Airing:** The safest method for airing a quilt 50 years and older is to place it in the shade on a nice, breezy day. Lay the quilt flat on the ground or on a table between two clean sheets. Leave it out for a half day. Never hang a quilt on a clothesline; this weakens the stitches. To air a quilt indoors, drape the quilt over a chair for half a day.

▶ **Vacuum-cleaning:** Lay the quilt flat on a bed or other clean surface. Place a piece of fiberglass screen with its edges taped (a good size to work with is a 24-inch square) on the quilt. Slowly and gently vacuum over the screen with a low-power, hand-held vacuum with a clean brush attachment. Move the screen to another part of the quilt and repeat the vacuuming. When the top of the quilt is done, turn back half of it and vacuum the bed or surface under it; repeat the vacuuming on the other side. Never vacuum a quilt with beads on it. This method should not be used more than once a year.

▶ **Dry-cleaning:** Wool, velvet or silk quilts must be dry-cleaned by an expert cleaner who specializes in antique garments. *Note:* There is no guarantee that dry-cleaning will work or that it will not damage the item.

▶ **Wet-cleaning:** Like dry-cleaning, washing a quilt should be done by an expert. It is too easy to damage it if you wash it at home.

4.
Super Money-Savers

Save Hundreds On Heating
And Electric Bills

Travel For Less

Stretch Your Paycheck

Need Cash? Ways To
Make Money Fast

Recycling: Everything Old
Is New Again

Save Hundreds On Heating And Electric Bills

Are you losing big bucks because you don't know the best ways to heat your home or run your appliances? These tips can save you a bundle.

Blanket sandwich

Keep the nighttime chills at bay by placing a quilted mattress cover or medium-weight blanket *underneath* your fitted sheets. Wool or cotton thermal blankets will keep in the heat even longer than synthetic covers for a really toasty night's sleep.

Curtain call

Make your windows work for you! Choose drapes that trap cold air, not funnel it back into a heated room. You can help your curtains keep the hot air in by attaching velcro to the sides and bottom of both the curtain and the window frame. Covering the gap between the curtain rod and window frame with a cap made from matching fabric will also cut down on cold air drafts.

Getting out of hot water

▶ If you don't have an automatic dishwasher, set your water heater no higher than 110°F-120°F. If you have a dishwasher that doesn't have a built-in hot water booster, set your water heater at 140°F-160°F. Setting the temperature any higher is not only wasteful, it can actually cause minor burns. Invest in an insulating cover for your water heater.

▶ Make a house rule that the dishwasher or clothes washer is run *only* when there is a full load.

▶ Use the cold or warm water settings whenever possible on your clothes washer.

▶ Have your family take showers instead of baths. It takes twice the amount of water to fill a bathtub as it does for a normal shower.

▶ Don't ignore a dripping faucet. One drop of water per second from a leaky tap can waste 60 *gallons* of water a week.

De-light

Get the most out of your lighting with the least amount of energy:

▶ Use fluorescent tubes whenever possible. Fluorescent tubes shed more light per watt than incandescent bulbs: a 75-watt bulb sheds 1180 lumens (the measure of light intensity); a 30-watt deluxe fluorescent tube sheds approximately 1530 lumens. Invest in compact fluorescent light bulbs that can be used in most regular light sockets — they cost more initially, but use 75% *less* electricity than their incandescent relatives, and last 10 times longer!

▶ If you use incandescent bulbs, pay attention to the wattage of the bulbs. One 150-watt bulb puts out 2880 lumens while two 75-watt bulbs shed only 2380 lumens.

▶ Clean your light bulbs, tubes and lamp shades often, using a soft cloth. Dust reduces lumen output.

Stove Saving Savvy

▶ If the flame on your gas range has traces of yellow in it, the burners may be clogged. Clean them.

▶ It's not necessary to preheat an oven for food that will be cooked for more than an hour.

▶ Use a pressure cooker or crock pot whenever possible.

▶ Open the oven door as little as possible when cooking. As much as 25% of an oven's heat is lost each time the door is opened. In the winter, leave the oven door open after

cooking (make sure the oven is turned off first); it'll help heat the kitchen.

▶ Keep pots and pans covered when heating foods to speed up the cooking time.

▶ Use a teakettle when boiling water. It brings water to a boil faster than an open pot and saves energy.

▶ Have the gas company turn off the pilot light on your stove during the summer and light your burners manually. It can saves you up to 25% on your fuel bill.

Running hot and cold

▶ If you've recently insulated your home, your furnace may now be oversized. Replace the existing burner with a smaller one—it's much cheaper than replacing the furnace.

▶ Have your heating contractor clean the combustion chamber of your oil or gas heater every year.

▶ Clean or change the air filter near your furnace every month or two. A dirty filter impedes air flow, making the furnace work harder.

▶ Clean the fan blades that move air through the system once a year.

▶ Sweep or vacuum the area around the furnace regularly. Dirt and dust can infiltrate the system, reducing its efficiency.

▶ Turn down your heating system or furnace if you'll be away for over four hours. The same goes for an air-conditioning system. Invest in an automatic timer that turns off the air conditioner/heater when you leave the house in the morning, and turns it on 15 minutes before you normally come home.

▶ In the summer, have a heating contractor turn off the pilot light on a gas furnace.

Window watch

▶ When buying a house, consider where the windows are placed. In northern climates, southern windows are very important to maximize natural light in the house. Also check out the placement of the windows for cross-ventilation.

▶ Check the insulation around your windows at the change of the seasons. Replace caulking as needed.

▶ Keep your windows sparkling clean in the winter; you'll get more solar heat that way.

▶ Dark-colored drapes and shades are great in winter; light-colored shades and drapes are best in summer. Try changing your window treatments seasonally.

"Green" landscaping

Landscaping to create a windbreak or shade is an investment which will prove financially and ecologically beneficial for many years to come.

▶ A windbreak of evergreen trees reduces heat loss considerably and helps save fuel. Cold north winds can cause large amounts of heat to be lost from a home in winter. Evergreen trees can actually block off an area that is 8 times their height. Hemlock, fir and spruce make the best windbreaks, but if you are unable to plant trees, a tall fence can provide a similar effect.

▶ Deciduous or hardwood trees lessen the need for air conditioning and fans during the heat of summer by supplying shade to cool your house. Shade trees on the west and east sides of a home can block the sun's rays before they reach the windows. If you can't plant trees, draperies and shades can be used for this purpose but they have been shown to be 7 times less effective.

▶ Vines can also absorb and reflect the sun's rays in summer and, because they lose their leaves in fall, they still allow sunlight to warm your house during the winter months. Plant deciduous vines that can be trained to grow flat against walls or trellises on the south side of your home for the best results. Avoid the evergreen vine varieties, such as English ivy, because they keep their leaves year-round and can block the sun in winter.

Travel For Less

Whether you travel by plane or by car, you can cut costs as you go.

Fly for less

To turn today's sky wars to your advantage:

▶ Ask travel agents for the most economical flights—then check other airlines yourself to make sure you really are getting the best price.

▶ Talk to people familiar with the area you want to visit. They may know about special airline deals or routings that will cut costs.

▶ Be willing to travel at off-peak times and at night, when prices are lower.

▶ Remember, flights on cut-rate airlines often involve layovers and changing planes, but usually save you money.

▶ Be on the lookout for newspaper advertisements announcing special deals.

Gasoline economy tips

▶ Always accelerate gently. Avoid the infamous "jackrabbit starts" that eat up gas.

▶ Get into high gear as soon as possible. You can "trick" an automatic transmission into high gear by simply lifting your foot off the gas pedal at about 30 mph. Then put your foot back down *gently* to continue accelerating. With a manual transmission, you can often skip a gear when accelerating on level ground or downhill. Just shift directly from *first* to *third*. Four- and five-speed transmissions provide more chances to skip gears without straining the engine.

▶ Watch traffic ahead in order to anticipate or avoid stops. Lift your foot from the gas pedal and coast up to traffic jams, rather than racing up to them at full speed and slamming on the brakes. If the traffic clears as you roll slowly toward it, you've saved even more gas: It takes 20% more fuel to accelerate to normal speed from a full stop than it does from four or five mph.

▶ Plan ahead: When you go on vacation, particularly in the summer months, plan to travel during the work week to avoid weekend traffic.

▶ Obey the speed limits. Everyone knows not to drive too fast, but driving too slowly wastes gas, too. Cars with automatic transmission get their best economy at about 35 mph. On the highway, remember that it takes 30% more gas to travel at 70 mph than 50 mph. A car with manual transmission gets its best mileage going as slowly as it can in *high* gear without lugging the engine—45 mph in *fourth* will give better fuel economy than 30 mph in *third*, because the engine is turning fewer revolutions for every mile you drive.

▶ Take it easy on long grades and climbing steep hills; pressing the accelerator all the way down only wastes gas.

▶ Don't let the car idle, whether you're stuck in traffic or just dashing into a store. An idling engine wastes about a quart of gas every 15 minutes. Shut the engine off, even for a few minutes, and you'll save gas. In the same vein, don't warm up the engine by letting it idle. Start it up and drive right off—slowly. The engine warms up faster when driving than it does when idling.

▶ Don't rev the engine just before shutting it off. That not only wastes fuel but leaves raw gasoline in the cylinders which then leaks down and dilutes the motor oil.

▶ Maintain a steady speed in expressway driving. Changing speed by as little as 5 mph can increase fuel consumption by over one gallon per mile. Stay off the brakes, except for emergencies. Whenever possible, pass slower vehicles as soon as you encounter them, rather than slowing to their pace and speeding up to pass.

▶ Keep windows closed at highway speeds. Open windows create aerodynamic drag, which increases fuel consumption.

▶ Avoid using roof racks; they can cost you dearly. Tests performed in England showed that a car traveling at 50 mph with its roof rack piled high used 17% more gas than a car with no rack. If you must pack a roof rack, make a wedge of your luggage, packing small items at the front, taller ones in the rear. That will reduce the mileage penalty by 7%.

▶ Don't use electrical accessories (radio, lighter, bright lights, rear window defroster) unnecessarily. They activate the alternator to recharge the battery, which puts more strain on the engine and uses more gas. The air conditioner is run by an engine-driven pump that really cuts into fuel mileage, so don't use that unnecessarily either.

▶ Never fill the gas tank to the brim—the attendant will usually spill some of the gas you're paying for. In addition, if you park facing uphill, some gas will drip out. If you park in the sun, the gas will expand and overflow. Both ways, it's more expensive fuel down the drain.

▶ You can stretch gas mileage 15% by maintaining your car properly: Tune the engine, adjust the wheel alignment, use the proper 10W-40 multiweight motor oil and correct tire pressure.

▶ To save more gas, don't just use the correct tire pressure (which is listed on a sticker pasted to the driver's door), but add four to five pounds more per square inch (psi). As long as you don't exceed 32 psi, it's not dangerous and it not only increases gas mileage but the life of the tire as well. Check air pressure once a week because air tends to leak out slowly.

▶ Radial tires give five to ten percent better mileage than bias ply tires. Snow tires reduce mileage by one to three miles per gallon, so get them off early and don't put them back on until the first snow.

Stretch Your Paycheck

Stop counting the days till payday. These inside moves and clever ideas will make your salary last longer.

Increase your take-home pay

Do you receive an income tax refund each year? You can get more money every payday instead of a once-a-year lump-sum refund. Here's how: Ask your payroll department for a new W-4 form. Like many people, you probably claimed zero or one exemption on this form when you first started working. To increase your weekly paycheck, simply increase the number of exemptions you claim and Uncle Sam will deduct less in taxes. There's no limit to the exemptions you can claim—just remember you don't want to end up *owing* taxes next April 15.

Stop unnecessary bank fees

Is your bank charging you monthly service fees because your checking account balance isn't "big enough?" You may be able to eliminate these extra costs. Some banks will total up the balances in *all* your accounts (including savings accounts, time deposits and Individual Retirement Accounts) so you can qualify for free checking. Therefore, if you move all your accounts to one bank rather than spread them around, you may be able to eliminate bank service fees and pocket the difference. Ask your bank for details.

Keep interest up

Try to withdraw money from a savings account *after* the interest payment date. Withdrawing beforehand makes you lose an entire month's interest.

Brown-bag it

Buying lunch every day adds up: A lunch-counter sandwich and soft drink can run $3 or more. That's $15 a week or $680 a year! A sandwich, soda and a handful of potato chips brought from home will cost you less than $1 and leave you with at least $10 more in your pocket at the week's end.

Gas up for less

Many gas stations allow you to cut your fuel costs by 3¢ to 5¢ a gallon by pumping your own gas at a self-service island. That can mean an extra dollar in your pocket every time you fill up. If you pay cash instead of using credit, many stations give you another 3¢ to 5¢ per gallon discount.

Scrimp early, spend late

Next payday spend your money like a miser at the beginning of the week so that you won't be caught short on Friday. Then, if you have money left over, you can always have a weekend splurge.

Avoid "guilty conscience" spending

Are you a working parent who leaves home many mornings feeling guilty? If so, you may be tempted to compensate by picking up a small gift for your child—a toy, a box of crayons. Don't. Remember, you work because you want to make life better for your child. If your conscience still bothers you, consider a no-cost treat for your youngster when you get home, such as reading an extra story or playing a game.

Collect "twice" on health care

If you and your spouse both work and have employee family health insurance, you can collect on both policies. "Coordination of benefits" is perfectly legal as long as you don't collect more than the actual amount of the bills. Generally it works like this: Send all medical bills first to the "primary insurer." (For you, it's the insurer at your job; for your spouse, the insurer at his or her job; for the children, it can be either, depending upon the types of coverage.) After you receive payment from the primary insurer, send copies of all bills and insurance paperwork to your spouse's insurer. In most cases this secondary insurer will pay all or part of what the primary insurer did not pay.

Put your phone bill on a diet

Sure, there's someone out there who would like to hear from you, but a letter can be even nicer than a phone call and it's certainly cheaper. If you must call, take advantage of "bargain-rate" hours after 11 P.M. on weeknights, all day Saturday and until 5 P.M. on Sunday.

Cut the coffee-cart habit

For most working people, the morning coffee break is a relaxing necessity. Keep the break but do it more cheaply. Buy an electric device (about $5) that boils water in three minutes and keep a jar of instant coffee or tea bags where you work. Add a prewrapped miniature coffee cake that you bring from home and you have your own coffee break for about 25¢, versus the 75¢ you would otherwise pay. Savings: $2.50 a week or $125 a year.

Don't blow a day's pay on kids' clothes

There are certain items that you must replace almost every year simply because the kids outgrow them. Try to find parents with children somewhat bigger or somewhat smaller than yours and suggest clothes swaps. Also consider shopping at garage sales or thrift shops, where you can often buy kids' coats, slickers, rainboots, etc., in good condition for half price or less. *For more more ways to save money on kids' clothing, see page 199.*

Weed out costly repair bills

If an appliance won't work, don't call for repairs immediately. First, check to see if it's plugged in properly. Also inspect the fuse and the on-off switch. Next, check to see if the manufacturer has a toll-free number. If you call the manufacturer for help, have the appliance model number and a description of the problem ready. If you can give a clear statement of what's not working, often the service rep can tell you over the phone how to fix it—saving you the expense of a repair visit costing $50 or more.

Slice newspaper spending

Are you a commuter who buys both a morning and evening newspaper at 25¢ or 30¢ each just so you'll have something to read on the bus or train? If you replace one of those papers with a library book, you can save $1.25 to $1.50 a week or between $65 and $78 a year.

Clip and use grocery coupons, but don't "overcoupon"

▶ Don't let coupons rule your shopping list. Make up your grocery list first and then see whether you have coupons to match.

▶ Include the cents-off value of the coupon when you comparison-shop. Don't 'impulse-buy' items just because the coupon is a good value.

Avoid birthday-gift budget busters

Don't buy last-minute presents— you're bound to pay more. Instead, keep a lookout for appropriate bargain-priced presents whenever you're out shopping. Tuck these away for emergencies, wrapped and ready. *For ways to avoid holiday overspending, see page 168.*

Need Cash? Ways To Make Money Fast

These ideas can help bring in the bucks during hours that suit your schedule.

Bazaar ideas

A bazaar is always a good money-maker for a group. These tips will help make it a success.

▶ Assign a leader for each booth you'll have. Appeal to everyone with a specialty and anyone who can devote time if not expertise.

▶ Sell items that are inexpensive to make but usually overpriced in stores (like aprons and sachets).

▶ Price all of your items at least 30% to 50% less than they would cost in stores.

▶ Work in groups at weekly workshops—it's more fun and you'll accomplish more.

▶ Encourage donations of fabrics, yarns and trims from local businesses in exchange for publicity.

▶ Concentrate on traditional best-sellers, such as ornaments, aprons, children's sweaters, cuddly toys.

▶ Think of seasonal items—stockings, ornaments and toys for Christmas; jams, dried flower wreaths and arrangements for harvest bazaars.

▶ Put someone in charge of publicity. Get notices in the local paper and put up signs in advance of the sale.

▶ The day of the bazaar, make sure every booth has a supply of change to start with. Provide a central spot where volunteers can go for help, supplies, money, etc.

▶ If your bazaar runs longer than one day, have a strategy meeting after the first day to see how you're doing. Consolidate booths so none look empty and mark down items that aren't selling.

Do you love parties?

▶ Organize birthday parties for kids. *See Party Time on page 117 for specific ideas.*

▶ Begin a catering service. Start with small groups; gradually work up to larger crowds. Catering can include just food or everything from decorations to cleanup.

For nimble needles

▶ Sew aprons for local restaurants or stores.

▶ Start a home tailoring service. Many people can alter hems, shorten sleeves, take in waists, etc.

Partial to pets

▶ Create a dog-walking service for busy working folks.

▶ Start a vacation pet-care service for your town.

Clean sweep

Start a "Clean Sweep" service. Most people could use help during spring and autumn cleaning and especially around the holidays.

Color it beautiful

If you have an artistic bent, you can create T-shirt and sweat shirt designs.

Good with numbers

Start a bookkeeping service for small organizations.

If you like kids . . .

▶ Tutor children who need help with their homework.

▶ Offer "after-school babysitting" to working parents. Kids come to your house between 3 and 6 P.M., Monday to Friday.

Plant shop

Sell small plants from a cart on weekends. Put them in pretty flower pots to attract customers.

Baby-sit a house

Offer to collect mail and papers, switch on lights, water plants, mow the lawn, etc. for vacationing families. It can provide a good safeguard against burglaries by giving a house a lived-in look.

Have typewriter, will travel

▶ Type correspondence for individuals or organizations that do not employ full-time secretaries.

▶ If you live in a university or college town, offer to type term papers and reports for students.

Recycling: Everything Old Is New Again

You can save money by finding new ways to use all the things you usually throw away. Here's how.

Window shades

When shades become torn and tattered, save the wooden roller and slat. Buy an inexpensive plastic tablecloth with a design to complement the room and cut it to the size of the shade. Hand-hem the bottom to fit the wooden slat and glue or staple the top to the roller. You now have a lovely custom-made shade for little money.

Pierced earrings

Lost the mate to a pair of pierced earrings? That lone earring can make a perfect scatter pin for cowl and turtleneck sweaters or the lapels of jackets.

Revolving tie rack

Retrieve that old tie rack and it can enjoy a new lease on life under your kitchen sink, holding brushes, measuring spoons and other small utensils.

Candle stubs

They're good for "greasing" drawer runners and as pin cushions; the tallow helps pins and needles slip through materials easily.

Display racks

Salespeople usually toss aside display racks when replacing them with new ones. Cleaned and repainted, they make great towel racks for the bathroom.

Jumper cables

Before throwing out an old set of jumper cables, cut off the alligator clips on the ends. They can be used to hold workshop projects together.

Empty jars

Empty grated cheese jars with shaker tops make excellent dispensers for baking soda when used as a cleanser for bathtub or sink.

A little squeeze

Those plastic squeeze containers that lemon and lime juice come in are handy for so many things. Pry open the top and fill with: shampoo for your children, vinegar and oil (in separate ones, of course) for picnic salads, hand lotion from larger-size economy bottles to keep by the kitchen sink or drinks for brown-baggers.

Bath mats

Worn bath mats that have lost their non-skid backing make great floor mops. Just fold one, fluffy side out, to fit your mop handle and slip it into place. No messy strings to tangle, catch or fall off and the "mop" can be washed in the washing machine to keep it fresh and clean.

Used envelopes

Save paper and time at the checkout counter: Write your grocery list on the back of a used envelope and put redeemable coupons inside.

"Junk" mail

Flyers and announcements are usually printed on one side, leaving the other side free for use as instant scratch paper. Cut sheets in half and stack them in a suitable old box. You'll always have a ready supply of paper to scribble down a phone number or an important date.

Register tapes

Save the wide register tape from the supermarket checkout and use the reverse side for the following week's shopping list.

Packing cardboards

Whether you are an accomplished cook or a budding beginner, save those 7 x 9-inch thin white cardboards used in packing women's hosiery for your own set of recipe cards. There's plenty of room for the ingredients, directions, a picture of the finished dish and the category (breads, main dishes, desserts, etc.). You can also tape recipes from newspapers and magazines onto them.

Telephone book

▶ Before you throw away an old telephone directory, flip through the Yellow Pages and cut out the local maps and ads you refer to fairly often. Place the maps in the car glove compartment for quick directions. Then alphabetize the ads and mount them in your personal telephone book, where they will always be handy.

▶ If you have young children, a slipcover will convert an old phone book into a booster seat. An overlapping side panel makes it removable for easy cleaning.

Ironing board cover

When your nonstick-surface ironing board cover begins to wear out, use the less worn areas to make potholders, barbecue mitts or hot pads. You will need to make only one side out of the nonstick coated material—the other side can be a perky print to match your kitchen decor. Scraps of flannel, cotton or other washable fabric can be used for interlining, while quilting is a simple matter of stitching all the layers together on the sewing machine in a geometric pattern. Bind the edges with bias tape and add a loop.

Bottle caps

If your children have lost some of the checkers from their game, make replacements by painting 12 soft-drink bottle caps red and an equal number black. Add a few extras of each color in case some of the new ones get lost.

Tablecloths

▶ Luncheon or dinner tablecloths, cut and hemmed, make wonderful kitchen towels. Since the tablecloths are usually linen or excellent-quality cotton, they are lint-free.

▶ When a large tablecloth becomes frayed along the edges, cut it into runners for the dining room table. For a festive touch, sew on inexpensive trim from a fabric store. The runners look so pretty on the table and are easy to iron!

Sheets

When white bed sheets wear around the edges, don't discard them to use as rags. Easily cut and sewn, they can be recycled to make pretty curtains for almost any small to standard window. Floral, pastel, striped or plaid sheets make attractive no-iron curtains as well.

Fabric scraps

▶ Save scraps of fabric from sewing projects. The prettiest ones make quilt patches, cushion covers and the like. Sew together the less pretty bits, such as scraps of pellon, plain muslin and quilt filling, for potholder padding. Covered with gingham squares and bound with bias strips, these pretty pot holders make attractive Christmas gifts.

▶ Instead of throwing away extra inches of fabric from shortened skirts, make belts, sashes, scarves, pocket handkerchiefs or headbands to match the outfits the material originally came from or to contrast with others.

Old cushions

The flat, rectangular foam cushions from discarded modern chairs make excellent extra sleeping pads for visiting children, TV-watching floor cushions, exercise floor mats or bed pillow props for those who like to read in bed. When not in use, the cushions can be stored out of the way under a bed.

Sandbox

When your children outgrow their sandbox, don't discard it—put it to good use. Remove some of the sand, fill it with rich soil and turn it into the children's first veggie/flower garden or one for yourself.

Plastic mesh bags

▶ Use a plastic mesh bag from oranges or other produce to hold baby bottle nipples and caps for washing in the dishwasher.

▶ Fold a plastic net bag and put it in the bottom of the kitchen soap dish. It keeps the soap dry and serves as a handy pot scrubber that doesn't collect the junk it scrubs off.

Plastic berry baskets

Plastic berry baskets are perfect for holding small objects, like baby bottle caps, that often end up on the bottom of the dishwasher. Put them in one basket, place another upside down on top and secure both with a rubber band. No more "lost" bottle caps!

Carpet remnants

To give your feet extra insulation from the cold, line boots or rubbers with carpet scraps. Trace your foot on a piece of paper to make a pattern and use the outline to cut the carpeting to fit. This also works well for children's snow boots.

Yogurt containers

Use yogurt containers as drinking cups for grandchildren when they visit. They are sturdy, dishwasher-safe and the children love the fruit decorations on them.

Coffee stirrers

Spatula-like coffee stirrers that you get in fast food places are great for stirring craft paints that come in tiny containers, spreading glue evenly from bottles without messy fingers and transferring small portions of face cream into travel-size jars.

Ashtrays

Since fewer people smoke these days, what do you do with all your ashtrays? Use some as spoonrests in the kitchen. Keep one on the kitchen windowsill to hold rings when you are washing dishes. Place one in the bathroom as a soap dish. Others come in handy under plants and in floral arrangements.

Fancy doilies

Do you have the old-fashioned lace doilies once popular for protecting the backs and arms of good chairs? Take them out of storage and use them as lovely placemats and table runners. You can use them alone, or with a plastic, solid-colored mat or cloth underneath to protect your table.

New life for old sweaters

▶ When your child's favorite pullover sweaters become a little too snug across the tummy, simply recycle them into cardigans. Cut a sweater entirely down the center of the front side and bind the raw edges with an attractive bias braid for a fashionable new look!

▶ Another idea: Cut off old sweater sleeves and turn them into leg warmers. The ribbed wrist sections fit securely at the ankles and the wide upper areas slip easily over the knees. Loosely whip-stitch the cut edges with elastic thread to avoid runs. Works fine for grownups in the family, too!

▶ Do you have a favorite sweater that is stretched beyond "wearability?" Grit your teeth, go to the sewing machine and remodel. Large cardigans make terrific V-necks when seamed down the center. Overcasting the new seams makes trimming possible without unraveling. Use contrasting colors to embroider or crochet to hide remodeling details and create a new look.

Worn socks

If you have a collection of knee socks with worn heels or toes, cut off the feet, fold in the cuffs and stitch. You will have great leg warmers for your small children.

Belts

A discarded leather belt (or one bought at a thrift shop), cut to size, makes a perfect dog or cat collar. Add a metal ring to the buckle to attach identification and license tags.

Soap chips

Here is a way to use every smidgeon of soap—the bits we save and never know what to do with. Take a square of nylon netting, place a handful of soap slivers in the center, fold the netting up so there are several layers of net around the slivers, tuck in the ends like a package and sew all around the edges with heavy thread. It is great for scrubbing collar stains or cleaning hands after gardening or painting.

In-jean-ious

▶ When worn-out jeans become "cutoffs," use the leftover legs to make sturdy work/gardening gloves. Trace your hands on them, allow for seams and stitch them up.

▶ For "cheap" softball bases, cut off the legs from an old pair of jeans and cut two squares from each. Sew each square together on three sides and halfway on the fourth side, fill with sand, using a funnel, and sew up the rest of the fourth side. These handy "bases" work beautifully!

Down-filled coats and vests

This may be the last winter you can wear your old down-filled coat or vest—but that doesn't mean it has outlived its usefulness. The old filling inside your now shabby coat is just as valuable (and usable) as it was when the garment was new.

▶ Old down is easy to recycle. Launder it and it's ready to use again in easy-to-make items such as pillows for your sofa or bed, a cozy lap robe, a baby bunting. You can even make a new down-filled vest for yourself (cut apart the old vest to make a pattern for the new one).

▶ Because down "settles" and loses its buoyancy, you won't know how much you have until you wash and dry it to restore its original volume. Here's how: Place the worn down-filled article in very warm water to wet the stuffing so it won't fly around. Make a slit in the garment and remove handfuls of the wet down, placing them in several zippered pillow protectors made of tightly woven, downproof fabric. Fill each protector only about two-thirds to allow for expansion and zip the pillow protector closed. Machine-wash with mild detergent and nonchlorine bleach (perhaps best done in a large-capacity washer at a laundromat). Tumble-dry at low heat. This restores the down's fluffiness so you can tell how much you actually have.

Plastic trays

Save the plastic trays from cookies, pastries and the like to be used when dividing large portions of fresh meat or poultry for the freezer. The meat pieces lie flat and slip into freezer bags much more easily. When it comes time to defrost the meat, slide the tray out of the freezer bag. The tray holds the juices until the meat is defrosted.

Pie plates

Whenever you use a ready-made graham cracker pie crust, save the plastic pie-shaped protector that holds it in place. After filling the shell, invert the protector and put it over the pie, crimping down the foil to keep it from sliding. The new "lid" fits perfectly and protects the pie when you store it in the refrigerator or take it to a friend's house.

Herbal tea bags

After you finish your cup of herbal tea, don't throw out the bag. Boil a pot of water, tear open the bag and distribute the tea leaves in the pot. Stir and allow to boil for one minute. Shut the flame and enjoy a scented and wonderful herbal facial sauna! *For more beauty ideas, see page 210.*

Bread crumbs

Bread heels, leftover pieces of toast and buns that do not split properly should be torn or cubed as soon as possible, dropped into a plastic bag and kept in the freezer. With this handy supply of bread crumbs, you will always have a head start on homemade stuffing for poultry, chops and the like, or croutons for a salad.

Pickle juice

When you finish a jar of pickles, keep the juice and add sliced cucumbers, bell peppers or other raw vegetables. This makes a flavorful low-calorie snack to reach for between meals. The juice is also a delicious ingredient in homemade salad dressings and some sauces and gravies.

Leftover cookies and candy

Use leftover Christmas cookies in place of graham cracker crumbs to make delicious crusts for cream pies. Old-fashioned hard candy melted in boiling water makes a tasty liquid for use in gelatin desserts. Leftover peppermint candy canes can be crushed in a plastic bag. The swirls of red and white candy look festive stirred into vanilla pudding or ice cream.

A chip off the old mug

Don't throw away your favorite mugs or cups just because they're chipped or cracked. They make great planters for small plants to brighten your kitchen windowsill. Or put them near your phone to hold pens and pencils for message taking.

5.
Tips
For The
Cook

Recipes For Success
Penny-Pinching Tips
Clever Ways To Liven Up Leftovers
Buying The Best Fresh Fruits
How To Get The Most From
Your Microwave

Recipes For Success

Here are cook-tested tips guaranteed to make you a hit in the kitchen. As a bonus, many of them save you time, too!

Red-dot protection

How many times have you opened the refrigerator to find a key ingredient for the next meal missing, "stolen" by some greedy snacker? To save the meal, the day and your nerves, try using red warning dots. Any food you want to save should receive one of these attention-grabbing self-sticking labels before it gets stored in the refrigerator.

Easy reminder

If you take out all ingredients at the beginning of a cooking project and put them away as used, the clean-up is easier and there's no doubt whether or not you've used an ingredient.

Stuffing the bird

Try placing turkey stuffing in cheesecloth and loosely inserting it into the bird before roasting. It can be removed intact, leaves the bird clean inside and makes it easier to store leftovers.

A "crumby" idea

▶ When you find yourself out of bread crumbs in the middle of a recipe, reach for packaged croutons and the potato masher. It is quick, saves you a trip to the store and there is no blender to wash.

▶ You can store homemade bread crumbs in an old salt carton and pour out what you need. Feed them into the carton through a funnel and store in the freezer.

Rolling made easy

To keep wax paper from curling up or slipping around when rolling a pie crust, wipe the countertop with a damp cloth or sponge before placing the wax paper on it. The moisture will keep the paper flat and prevent it from sliding.

Too old to do the job

▶ If you've had a baking disaster, the reason may be that the cans of baking powder and soda or cream of tartar were too old to do their leavening job properly. To make sure this never happens again, write the date of purchase on each can or package.

▶ Since the leavening ability of baking powder diminishes with age, always test the powder. Place ½ teaspoon in ¼ cup hot water. If the powder is fresh, the water will bubble actively.

No more bread that's a bust

When baking bread, the liquid must be just the right temperature for the yeast to work. To insure against slip-ups, use a candy thermometer to check if the liquid is too hot.

A seedy bunch

When cutting grapes for a salad, working in front of a light will make removing seeds a whole lot easier. The light shining through the grape makes the seeds more visible and quicker to remove.

Just a dot

When a recipe specifies "dot with butter," it's easier to use a vegetable peeler to shave thin curls from a frozen or very cold stick of butter or margarine.

Saving your thumb

Protect your thumb with a rubber finger tip—available in office supply stores—when peeling hot potatoes or other just-cooked vegetables in their skins.

Clean beat

To avoid splatters when using your hand-held beater, especially when whipping cream, take a paper plate and punch two holes in the center with a knife. Insert the blade posts through them before connecting to the beater. The plate will cover the bowl while the beater does its work.

Chill to beat

When whipping cream, chill the bowl and beaters so the cream will not sour while being beaten.

Stock-in-trade

When making soup stock, use a spaghetti cooker, placing pieces of chicken or meat bones in the strainer along with vegetables and seasoning. When the stock has simmered long enough, lift out the strainer along with the vegetables and bones, leaving just the clear stock in the bottom pot.

Decorating a cake

Use clean, squeeze-type catsup and mustard containers to decorate cakes. Their narrow spouts are great for writing and drawing with icing.

Crushed ice

For perfectly crushed ice every time, keep an empty, clean, half-gallon milk carton filled with fresh water in the freezer. When it's frozen, drop the carton on a cement patio floor or driveway several times, depending on how finely crushed you want the ice.

Bag it!

After you open a container of ice cream, cover it with a plastic freezer bag before you put it back in the freezer. This will help protect against freezer burn and keep the ice cream fresh much longer.

End of a messy job

Try using an electric knife the next time you prepare finger sandwiches. You'll get a neater, more appetizing sandwich, without getting the filling all over the cutting board.

No more "soggy" sandwiches

Whenever you "brown bag" lunch, wrap the lettuce for your sandwich in a damp paper towel and pack it in a separate plastic bag. At lunchtime, simply add the lettuce to the sandwich.

Quick and easy

To microwave-heat a frozen dinner that comes in a foil tray, pop the frozen food out and place it in a glass pie plate. Invert another glass pie plate over the top and heat (usually five to seven minutes on high will do). Easy, fast and delicious!

Plates to travel

The cardboards from medium-size pizzas are great giveaway cake plates. Cover one with aluminum foil and a cake, pie or batch of cookies is ready to travel to a friend or bake sale.

Varmints and victuals

▶ When you bring home a bag of flour or a box of cake mix that won't be used immediately, slip a bay leaf into the box or bag to keep the convenience food from becoming "animated!"

▶ Another idea that works well is to put all dry foods, such as baking powder and soda, rice, tapioca and flour, in jars—recycled mayonnaise jars for example. Attach the label and/or serving instructions from the original box to the outside of the jar to identify the contents.

Big batch

When cooking rice, prepare a large batch and freeze the leftover rice, two servings to a bag. The next time you want to serve rice, pull the needed number of bags out of the freezer and heat them in a steamer basket over boiling water.

A quick shake

Keep a large saltshaker full of flour near the stove for times when you need only a spoonful. This saves the time and bother of opening a big cannister and you will never have spills where you don't want them.

Double duty

Here's another use for that good old egg slicer. When you want to make a large bowl of potato salad, use the slicer to dice the potatoes. It works like a charm and saves time. It also works well for mushrooms!

Good planning

Keep at least one dated, brown-bag lunch in the freezer as a backup. You can save a few valuable minutes in the morning and a couple of dollars in the lunch line.

Freezing labels

Make your own homemade "TV dinners" from leftovers. Label them as follows: "Goulash/Date/Micro: High—one minute/Salad and Bread." By suggesting the time and menu complement, you'll find that leftovers are eaten, meals are rarely skipped and money is saved.

Souper freezing

To save time in the kitchen, freeze homemade soup in family-size portions in a bowl. When they are frozen, remove the rounds and place them in plastic bags. When it is time to reheat the soup, the frozen rounds fit perfectly into the big soup kettle.

Sauce in minutes

Quickest-of-all sauces is to deglaze a pan with a bit of wine. Here's how: When you finish browning meat or fish, remove it from the pan. Pour in a little wine while the pan is still hot and scrape up browned bits left in the pan with a wooden spoon. Reduce the wine for just a minute.

Meatballs and sauce

▶ To make meatballs that are wonderfully moist, put a small ice cube in the center of each ball before browning. Cook as usual.

▶ To prevent sauces from burning or cooking too fast, place a heat diffuser on the burner. It evens out and reduces the heat.

Oil you need to know

▶ Use peanut oil for frying. It can withstand high temperatures without burning and won't alter the taste of the food because it's flavorless.

▶ Never put oil in the pan before turning on the burner. Heat the pan first, add the oil, then add the food. This helps prevent food from sticking to the pan.

▶ Cooking with part butter and part peanut oil will give the flavor of butter with less saturated fat. The oil also helps to keep the butter from smoking.

Cutting back on oil

▶ To measure cooking oil more accurately and avoid drowning a salad or stir-fry dish in a sudden deluge, don't remove the seal from a new bottle of oil. Cut a slit in the seal and pour through that—you'll be able to measure even a teaspoonful without a spill.

▶ Try replacing the oil required in recipes for bran, whole grain or oatmeal muffins with an equal or slightly larger amount of unsweetened applesauce. You'll have a moist, low-fat variation of these mealtime favorites.

Browning basics

Don't flour meat when you're browning it for a stew or casserole. You'll end up browning only the flour and the meat won't get the color or flavor of browning. Instead, heat the pan, add a bit of oil and sear or brown the meat very quickly.

Keep covered

Keep salads, cold meat plates and hors d'oeuvres fresh on your buffet table by covering them with wet paper toweling until guests arrive.

More than one way to skin a chicken

To take the skin off a whole chicken in a jiffy and make it less fatty, remove the wings and cut the bird down the breastbone. Lay it out flat with the back up and pull off the skin.

A seasoned pan

To cure, or season, an aluminum or cast iron frying pan so it becomes almost nonstick, wash it with soap and water, using a cloth or sponge. (*Never* use a steel soap pad or steel wool.) Rinse and dry the pan. Heat the pan until quite hot and add 2 or 3 tablespoons peanut oil. Gently swirl the oil around the pan. Allow the pan to cool. Wipe out the excess oil with paper toweling, reheat the pan, add more oil, cool and wipe. Repeat the entire process a third time. The pan is ready for use. When it's time to wash it, use hot water only and no soap. If the pan is hard to get clean, rub it with a non-abrasive scouring cloth or a bit of peanut oil and salt with paper toweling.

Perfect peeling

Four quick and easy ways to peel:
▶ **Onions:** Cut off the bottom, then the top. Cut a slash in the side of the onion and remove the first outer peel, including the skin.
▶ **Tomatoes:** Turn a fork-held tomato over a gas burner until the skin begins to darken and blister. It will peel right off.
▶ **Tomatoes:** Place tomatoes in boiling water and remove the pan from the heat. Let it sit for one minute. Remove the tomatoes from the pan, plunge them into cold water and strip off the skin.

▶ **Garlic:** With the palm of your hand, crush the entire head of garlic so that the cloves fall apart. Select one clove and place the flat side of a large knife over it; hit the knife gently with your hand. The clove skin will come off immediately. *Note:* To get the smell of garlic off your hands, rub them in used coffee grounds.

Crisp lettuce

To crisp salad greens, wash, roll in a terry-cloth towel and refrigerate.

Fruit and vegetable savvy

▶ Never store carrots with apples. Apples release a gas that gives carrots a bitter taste.
▶ Slice raw tomatoes vertically so the inner pulp holds its shape for salads.
▶ Ripen avocados in a brown paper bag or dark place for a few days. Once ripe, refrigerate them until ready to use.

No stick

To avoid residue when measuring sticky liquids (honey, molasses), rinse the measuring cup in hot water first.

Sure to slice

The easiest way to slice cheesecake is with dental floss. Press a long strand of tautly held unflavored floss through the cake. Pull it out without pulling it up again.

The inside story

Favorite recipes that you use often, whether cut from magazines or written on recipe cards, can be taped to the inside of your kitchen cabinet doors. When you're ready to cook, there's no need to rummage through clippings in envelopes or boxes. Just open your cabinet door!

The dots do it

For those of you who hate searching through your cookbook collection for favorite recipes, here's a solution. Stick colorful self-adhesive dots from the dime store next to your favorite recipes on the pages of each cookbook. When you flip through the pages, the dots will catch your eye.

Helpful "heirloom"

For those times when you can't cook, prepare a small book entitled "Mom's (or Dad's) Helpful Hints," in which you record your favorite easy-to-prepare recipes. Carefully note each step for every recipe and include some special cooking tips. Your family will really appreciate it.

Just like home

Start a "hope chest" recipe card box with all the family favorites for your daughters and sons who enjoy cooking or will soon be living on their own. This truly is a gift filled with love and fond memories.

Plastic-coated recipe card

When you send a favorite recipe to a friend, copy it on a 3 x 5-inch index card and cover it with clear, self-adhesive vinyl. If you have a small picture of the dish, glue it on the back of the card.

Menu magic

If it seems like you are eating the same seven dinners every week, begin noting each evening's entrée on a small calendar near the refrigerator. This will help you vary the menus and give you a quick update on leftovers.

Foiled again

▶ Try baking apples in cups shaped from aluminum foil and placed in a shallow pan. It's a quick and easy way to serve the apples when you put them on your dessert dishes and there's no sticky pan to wash.

▶ Make a quick liner for a baking pan: Shape the foil over the outside of the inverted pan and then slip the pre-formed foil inside.

▶ When you're preparing a meal of assorted leftovers, are you fed up with trying to juggle the pots and pans? Next time, try putting each leftover into "bowls" shaped from aluminum foil. Put these bowls in one big pan, add a little water, cover and steam.

▶ You can keep rolls hot and protect your bread basket from grease stains by placing a piece of aluminum foil under the napkin in the basket.

▶ When you accidentally crack an egg, you can still soft- or hard-cook it. Wrap it in aluminum foil before immersing it in boiling water.

▶ When you have a lot of cookies to bake and are short on oven space and time, try a foil assembly line. Cut aluminum foil to fit your cookie sheets, place the cookie dough on the foil and slip the foil over your cookie sheets. You can prepare all the cookies ahead of time and just slip the foil sheet liners on as soon as the sheets come out of the oven.

Sweet ginger

Next time you make a meal that calls for fresh garlic *and* fresh ginger, try chopping the garlic first. The ginger, when chopped after the garlic, will remove the strong garlic smell from your fingers and your chopping board.

Handy Food Storage Charts

Meat	Refrigerate	Freeze
beef steaks	1 to 2 days	6 to 12 months
beef roasts	1 to 2 days	6 to 12 months
pork chops	1 to 2 days	3 to 4 months
pork roasts	1 to 2 days	4 to 8 months
fresh pork sausages	1 to 2 days	1 to 2 months
veal cutlets	1 to 2 days	6 to 9 months
veal steaks	1 to 2 days	6 to 12 months
lamb chops, steaks	1 to 2 days	6 to 9 months
lamb roasts	1 to 2 days	6 to 9 months
stew meat (any type)	1 to 2 days	3 to 4 months
ground beef, veal, lamb	1 to 2 days	3 to 4 months
ground pork	1 to 2 days	1 to 3 months
variety meats (liver, kidney, brains)	1 to 2 days	3 to 4 months

Meat keeps best in the refrigerator if it's loosely wrapped in plastic wrap or wax paper. ● *To freeze meat, wrap it in moisture/vapor-proof wrapping, such as heavy plastic wrap.* ● *Always remember to label and date your meat.*

Poultry	Refrigerate	Freeze
whole chickens	1 to 2 days	12 months
cut-up chickens	1 to 2 days	9 months
chicken giblets	1 to 2 days	3 months
whole turkeys	1 to 2 days	6 months
cut-up turkeys	1 to 2 days	6 months
whole ducks or geese	1 to 2 days	6 months

In the refrigerator, remove giblets and wrap and store them separately. Store poultry loosely wrapped in the coldest part of the refrigerator. ● *To freeze poultry, wrap it in moisture/vapor-proof wrapping. Label and date it.*
Caution: *Never freeze poultry with the stuffing inside. Stuffing may be frozen separately.*

Handy Food Storage Charts

Cooked meats & leftovers	Refrigerate	Freeze
fried chicken	1 to 2 days	4 months
leftover beef roast	3 to 4 days	2 to 3 months
leftover beef stew	3 to 4 days	2 to 3 months
leftover canned/cured ham	4 to 5 days	1 month
leftover fresh ham or pork	3 to 4 days	2 to 3 months
gravy and meat broth	1 to 2 days	2 to 3 months
meat sauce (spaghetti sauce)	3 to 4 days	6 to 8 months
meat loaf	2 to 3 days	3 months
cooked pork or lamb	3 to 4 days	2 to 3 months
cooked chicken slices or pieces, covered with broth or gravy	1 to 2 days	6 months
cooked chicken, not covered with broth or gravy	1 to 2 days	1 month
chicken salad or tuna salad	1 to 2 days	do not freeze
leftover fish	2 to 3 days	1 month
chicken and turkey pies	1 to 2 days	2 to 3 months

Always chill leftovers and cooked meats quickly. Keep them covered in the refrigerator. Separate leftover poultry meat from the stuffing when refrigerating. ● *To freeze, package and freeze quickly. Meat stuffing should always be frozen separately.*

Cured meats	Refrigerate	Freeze
ham, whole	1 week	1 to 2 months
ham, half	3 to 5 days	1 to 2 months
frankfurters	1 week	1 month
bacon	1 week	2 to 4 months
canned ham, if unopened	1 year	not recommended
ham slices	3 days	1 to 2 months
corned beef	7 days	2 weeks
luncheon meat	3 to 5 days	not recommended
sausage, smoked	7 days	not recommended

Keep cured meat loosely covered in the refrigerator. ● *To freeze, wrap it tightly in moisture/vapor-proof wrapping, pressing out as much air as possible. When freezing smoked meat, wrap extra well so its odors won't permeate other foods. Cured meats don't keep their high quality for long when frozen because the seasonings that are added in the curing process speed rancidity.*

Handy Food Storage Charts

Fish	Refrigerate	Freeze
fresh fish	1 to 2 days	6 to 9 months
shrimp	1 to 2 days	2 months
lobster, crabs	1 to 2 days	1 to 2 months
oysters, clams, scallops	1 to 2 days	3 to 6 months

Before refrigerating, rinse fish thoroughly in cold water. Pat dry with paper toweling and cover loosely with wax paper. Store in the coldest part of the refrigerator. ● To freeze fillets, wrap them well in moisture/vapor-proof wrapping. Shrimp keep best if frozen uncooked. To freeze crab or lobster, cook without any salt, cool in the refrigerator and remove the meat from the shell before freezing. To freeze oysters, clams or scallops, shell and pack them in their own liquid. ● Don't forget to label and date your fish!

Dairy products	Refrigerate	Freeze
butter, salted	2 weeks	3 months
butter, unsalted	2 weeks	6 months
eggs, whole	2 to 3 weeks	6 to 8 months
eggs, whites	1 week	6 to 8 months
eggs, yolks	2 to 3 days	6 to 8 months
milk, cream	1 week	1 month
cheese spreads	1 to 2 weeks, when opened	1 to 2 months
hard cheeses	2 to 3 months, when wrapped	6 months
soft cheeses (i.e., Camembert, Brie)	2 weeks	2 months
cottage cheese	5 to 7 days	1 to 2 weeks
cream cheese	2 weeks	2 weeks

Refrigerate eggs in their own carton. ● To freeze, eggs must be removed from their shells. For whole eggs, stir in 2 tablespoons sugar or 1 tablespoon salt for each pint of lightly beaten eggs. Pack in freezer containers, leaving half an inch for headspace. Label and date. ● Refrigerate cheese in its original wrapping, if possible, or cover the cut surface tightly with plastic wrap or foil. ● To freeze cheese, wrap it in moisture/vapor-proof wrapping or store in the original wrap with a foil overwrap. Do not freeze cheese in amounts larger than one pound.

Penny-Pinching Tips

Feeling the squeeze? Try our painless ways to trim your food budget. You'll find you can still eat well and save money.

Shop smart

▶ Check ads for sales. Do plan to go to several stores if the savings are worthwhile and you have enough to buy to make the trip worthwhile.

▶ Build menus around meat and poultry on sale.

▶ When shopping, don't deviate from your grocery list unless you find unadvertised sales, such as overripe fruit and day-old bakery items.

▶ Buy herbs and spices in bulk and store in your own bottles. You'll save as much as 70% on their cost.

Cook smart

▶ Carefully monitor leftovers. Use them as snacks or lunch, or freeze them to use another time.

▶ Try to include "filling" food on your menus for the hearty eaters in your family. Chili, stew, soup, sandwiches and slow cooker dishes are good choices.

▶ Remember that *sometimes* quantity counts more than quality. For instance, you can serve two packages of chicken franks for almost the same price as one package of beef franks. But don't substitute foods your family won't eat.

▶ Prepare hot cereals for breakfast. They're more economical and filling than cold cereals.

▶ Plan a "bake day" when all can pitch in. Assign kitchen tasks to family members and prepare inexpensive, homemade snacks to freeze or refrigerate.

▶ Recycle food scraps in soups, casseroles and omelets; even vegetable skins go into soup stocks.

▶ Substitute boneless chicken breasts or turkey cutlets in recipes calling for expensive veal cutlets.

▶ Make your own salad dressing by the bottle and keep it in the refrigerator.

▶ Save time *and* money with one-dish salad meals. Combine diced leftover meat, fish or poultry with fresh vegetables.

▶ Don't waste milk by using it for scrambled eggs or omelets. Milk makes eggs watery because it won't blend with them. Use water, which makes eggs fluffy.

▶ Create healthful, low-cost meals based on dried beans with leftover meats and fresh vegetables.

▶ Keep a pot of homemade basic brown soup stock, made of beef bones and vegetables, in the refrigerator. It's a convenient—and inexpensive— base for delicious soups and stews. Boil it up every few days.

▶ To cook a stock overnight without worrying about it, cover the pot and place it in a 225° oven until the next morning.

▶ Buy good-quality pots and pans, even if they cost more. You'll save in the long run because better equipment lasts longer.

How to save money on meat

▶ Buy meat in quantity when the price is right and the meat looks good. Then freeze it.

▶ Look over the entire meat case before choosing. Sometimes the same type of meat may be packaged in a different thickness or larger quantity, be of better quality or cost less per pound in one section than in another.

▶ Your request to have meat cut a different way than found in the meat case is called a "special order." Some markets charge more for this. Check the store's policy *before* ordering.

Beef

▶ Chuck is one of the best buys in beef, if you know how to select it properly. The most tender chuck steak is the first cut (also called blade steak, top blade steak or chuck eye steak). It is identified by a sliver of white cartilage blade bone near the top of the steak.

▶ When boneless chuck is on sale, have it ground into chopped beef. (Chuck is juicier and tastier than round or sirloin.) Ask the butcher to trim off some fat and grind the chuck *once*. You'll get better quality and less fatty meat than prepackaged

ground chuck at the same price.

▶ Chuck shoulder steak is great for broiling. Look for a 1- to 2-inch well-marbled cut on sale. For "bargain" kabobs, cut into cubes and marinate for added tenderness.

▶ Cooked chuck roast shreds if it is cut when hot. To get more servings, let it cool before slicing. Then warm it up in gravy. You can splurge on thick steaks for broiling and still save money by buying a 6-pound top round, top sirloin or eye round roast on sale and cutting it into steaks yourself.

▶ Usually the whole eye round roast is cut into two smaller roasts. Your best buy is the half in which both ends have the same diameter. It's called the "first cut" and is more tender because it comes from near the sirloin.

▶ The best buy and more tender top round steak is one that is uneven in shape. Often called "oyster cut" or "first cut," it comes from nearer the sirloin. Top round steaks cut from near the less tender heel are more evenly shaped.

▶ A grayish cast over ground beef indicates it has been in the meat case for more than a day and may have an off taste. Freshly ground meat should have no odor. Use it the same day of purchase.

▶ Don't throw away fresh bones or trimmings. Freeze them until you have enough for a hearty pot of soup. To make: Use 1 quart of water to each pound of bones. Add chopped onions, carrots, celery and seasonings. *Note:* Dark-colored bones should not be used.

Veal

▶ When you buy thick veal cutlets, get the most for your money by slicing them like a pro. Place the cutlets on a tray, cover them and freeze until semi-frozen (this makes slicing easier). Trim off any white tissue with the tip of a knife. Hold the cutlet flat and slice it in half, horizontally, with a long knife. Small pieces can be butterflied open.

▶ Don't pass up veal shoulder blade steaks or chops. They are less expensive than the rib and loin chops and are more tender, too, because they come from a very young animal.

Pork

By substituting ground pork for beef, you can serve burgers that are usually less expensive. Broil or panbroil them until brown on both sides. Peek through with a fork to see if all the pinkness is gone; pork should be well cooked.

Lamb

▶ A truly economical and tasty cut of meat is a trimmed and pocketed whole breast of lamb. Stuff it with a raw rice mixture, secure, cover with water, add 2 chicken bouillon cubes, chopped onions, carrots and celery. Simmer until fork tender, season with salt, pepper and garlic and brown in a hot oven. The leftover broth makes an excellent lentil soup.

▶ When a whole leg of lamb is on sale, ask the butcher to cut it into 1-inch thick chops. You'll get 10 tender chops for broiling and shank meat for braising.

▶ If you buy only half a leg, choose a 4-pound or more shank half. A smaller one will have a higher proportion of bone and less meat.

▶ For tasty eating, reasonably priced ground lamb is delicious barbecued, broiled or panbroiled. Make patties with bread crumbs, chopped parsley, grated Romano cheese and minced onion.

▶ When the price of rib and loin lamb chops goes sky high, use blade or round bone lamb chops from the shoulder. These are delicious, too.

Poultry

▶ There is no real difference between a chicken labeled a fryer and one labeled a roaster when each weighs 3½ to 4 pounds. Buy the fryer, since that is usually cheaper.

▶ If fowl or soup chickens are not available or are too expensive, try a frying chicken.

▶ You can save on chicken by buying a whole frying chicken or turkey on sale, cutting it into parts yourself and boning the breast for cutlets.

▶ Chicken backs, rib cages, gizzards and necks make a rich, full-flavored pot of soup for just pennies.

▶ The best value in turkey is one weighing between 14 and 16 pounds. It will have a more meaty breast than birds of lower weights. If this is too big, have it sawed in half for two meals.

▶ For an inexpensive meal with a gourmet touch, stir-fry chicken livers with bacon, peppers and white wine.

Hints for expanding dishes and meals

▶ Sautéed celery, carrots and onions can be added to most casseroles.

▶ Starches are a good way to extend servings: Add pasta, rice or potatoes to casseroles and stews or serve as a side dish.

▶ Be innovative with whatever vegetables are in the refrigerator. Try cooking several together.

▶ Include a relish/pickle platter with a meal, made up from what's on hand.

▶ Doctor up canned chili by adding canned beans and serving it over a bed of rice. Garnish with shredded cheese, chopped green onions and sour cream.

▶ Use grilled cheese sandwiches to extend soup menus.

▶ Turn a simple pasta side dish into a meal by serving it with a salad.

▶ Pizza can be made from practically anything on hand. Use Cheddar, Swiss or Monterey Jack cheese to replace the mozzarella. If you don't have cheese, use canned tomatoes, green and red sweet peppers, olives or onions to create a vegetarian pizza.

▶ Use mixed grains—rice, wheat and millet—to make a nutritious side dish. Sauté broken spaghetti with the grain before adding the broth.

▶ Use dumplings to extend soups and stews.

▶ For a quick dessert, use canned and frozen fruits for topping ice cream or sherbets.

A tasty idea

Don't toss out that last half-inch of French, blue cheese or Russian salad dressing! Transform it into a new dressing. Just add 2 teaspoons vinegar or lemon juice (or one of each if you prefer). Recap and shake vigorously. Now gradually add ½ cup mayonnaise or sour cream, shaking as you add. A brand new tasty dressing!

Wine 'n dine

No need to buy pricey cooking wine for your gourmet recipes—regular jug wine adds the same flavor for less money.

Fruit-cicles

Fruits such as melons, cantaloupes, watermelons and bananas make delicious frozen pops. Blend the fruit till smooth in a food processor or blender. Place the fruit purée in small containers and freeze till ready to use.

Pop power

Keep unpopped popcorn in the freezer to minimize the amount of unpopped kernels when you prepare a batch.

Clever Ways To Liven Up Leftovers

Don't throw out your leftovers. The following suggestions can help you recycle scraps of food as they accumulate, putting an end to waste. What's more, you'll save hundreds of dollars a year on food!

Bread

▶ Cube slices and mix them with orange juice and rind for a tasty citrus-bread pudding.

▶ Spread almost-stale or day-old slices with butter or margarine. Sprinkle with grated cheese, toast and top with a poached egg.

Pound cake or broken sponge cake layers

Soak them in sweet wine or liqueur. Top with custard or fruit sauce, or crumble them over ice cream.

Cooked vegetables

▶ Serve chilled with bottled blue cheese or Italian dressing.

▶ Slice for omelets and frittatas.

▶ Reserve the vegetable cooking liquid (rich in vitamins and minerals). Stir it into stews, soups and casseroles or substitute it for water in a basic rice pilaf recipe.

Heavy cream

Freeze heavy cream for later use in quiches, tart fillings, cream soups and sauces but remember that, once frozen, cream no longer whips.

Coffee

▶ Freeze coffee in ice cube trays. Add the cubes to iced coffee for an extra-strength brew. Or whirl the cubes in the blender with ice cream for a coffee slush.

▶ Enrich meat gravies with coffee, to taste, for a robust flavor.

▶ Use coffee in cake frostings for a luscious mocha cream.

Small pieces of assorted cheeses

▶ Shred or thinly slice them for grilled cheese sandwiches, tacos, chili, salad or potato toppings.

▶ Stir bits of cheese into fillings for stuffed vegetables.

Broken cookies

▶ Crush them into coarse crumbs. Mix with coconut and melted chocolate for a pie crust.

▶ Crumble broken cookies between layers of ice cream cakes for a surprise "crunch," or use them to top rice puddings and parfaits.

Flat beer

▶ Simmer pot roasts or less expensive cuts of meat in flat beer for a great taste.

▶ Use flat beer instead of water for tangy boiled shrimp.

▶ Make beer batter for fish fillets, clams, etc.

Fresh mushrooms going brown

▶ Sauté with garlic and parsley. Stir in thyme and wine and pour over chicken, flank steak or pork chops.

▶ Marinate mushrooms in a vinaigrette dressing for an antipasto appetizer.

▶ Incorporate mushrooms into a sherried mushroom soup.

Wine

▶ Add wine to bland tomato sauces to pep them up. Use red wine for stewing pot roasts and lamb, white wine for chicken dishes.

▶ Use wine as a marinade for tough or less tender cuts of meat.

Egg whites

Form beaten whites into meringue tarts or crusts and bake. Spoon in fruit fillings.

Egg yolks

▶ Beat extra yolks into custards.

▶ Prepare pastry cream for eclairs and cream puffs.

▶ Make cake frosting (chocolate buttercream).

▶ Beat yolks with confectioners' sugar and almond paste, and bake for incredible almond macaroons.

Potatoes

Make the most of leftover mashed potatoes. For every 2 cups of potatoes, add ½ cup buttermilk baking mix for leavening, an egg and herbs and spices, such as parsley, oregano or garlic powder, if you wish. Mix with a fork till smooth and fry in ½-inch vegetable oil till golden.

Buying The Best Fresh Fruits

Learn the secrets of selecting the very best!

Apricots

Look for a soft yellowish-orange color and firm texture. Refrigerate and use within five days.

Berries

Bright color is the best test for quality berries. Ripe berries should be stored in the refrigerator, covered, unwashed and unstemmed. Except for cranberries, which can keep for 1½ weeks, use all other berries as soon as possible.

Cherries

Cherries are sweetest when firm and dark in color. Refrigerate and eat as soon as possible.

Grapefruits

White and pink grapefruits are sweetest when their skins turn greenish-yellow. Sometimes grapefruits can dry out, appearing lighter in weight. Refrigerate and use within two weeks.

Grapes

For all grape varieties, pick ones that are plump and have flexible stems. Refrigerate and use as soon as possible.

Melons

Pick the sweetest melons by fragrance and make sure the blossom end is somewhat indented and soft to pressure.

▶ Ripe cantaloupes are yellowish, with thick, coarse veining. Avoid ones that are too soft.

▶ The best honeydew melons are those with creamy or yellowish-white smooth skin. If a honeydew melon appears dead-white or greenish-white and has a very hard feel, it will never ripen properly.

▶ When choosing a whole watermelon, pick one that is firm and smooth. The underside should be yellowish or cream-white. To test for ripeness in an uncut watermelon, gently knock or rap on the rind. You should hear a deep, hollow "thump." The inside should appear bright red, firm and juicy, with mostly black seeds. White streaks in the melon indicate a less sweet fruit.

Nectarines

Nectarines are orange, yellow and red when at their best. Store at room temperature until they soften and ripen, then refrigerate and use within five days.

Oranges

Choose oranges that are firm and heavy with finely textured skin. Valencias, Temples and Kings produce the sweetest juice. Navel oranges are good for eating. Refrigerate and eat within two weeks.

Apples

Choose those with bright color and no bruises. They should be firm or hard to the touch.

Bananas

It's usually best to choose bananas that are slightly underripe and allow them to ripen at home. Choose those that are a bright yellow, have no bruises and are slightly green at the stem end. Never store bananas in the refrigerator. If you're going to be using bananas one at a time, cut off the end of the connecting stem and separate them gently. This prevents splitting or cracking the peel of the remaining bananas when you separate one from the bunch.

Peaches

Peaches won't mature or get sweeter once picked (they only soften and wither), so choose a firm but well-colored peach for the best flavor. Refrigerate and use within five days.

Pineapples

A well-ripened pineapple can be determined by fragrance, a small compact crown, richly colored crown leaves and protruding eyes. Pineapples store best at 70°, away from direct sunlight.

Plums

Choose plums that are soft but not mushy, shriveled or brown. Refrigerate and use within five days.

How To Get The Most From Your Microwave

Probably the greatest invention ever for busy folks — but are you getting your money's worth? Read and you will!

Tips for cooks

▶ To test whether cookware is microwave-safe or not, place it in the microwave oven next to a glass measuring cup half full of water. Heat at full (100%) power for one minute. If the dish is hot, it should not be used in the microwave oven. If it is warm, use it only for reheating. If the dish is room temperature, it is safe to use for all microwave cooking.

▶ Pay attention to standing times in recipes! Internal heat finishes the cooking after the dish is removed from the oven.

▶ Make sure the cooking utensil rests on a solid heatproof surface during the standing or resting time specified in the recipe.

▶ Set your timer for the minimum cooking time called for in a recipe. Check the doneness of the food and microwave for the additional time, if necessary.

▶ When frequent stirring is necessary for a dish, leave a wooden spoon or microwave-safe utensil in the dish in the microwave oven.

▶ To prevent messy boil-overs, use a cooking container two to three times larger than the volume of the sauce, soup, drink or other liquid dish you are preparing.

▶ Recipes made with sour cream, eggs or cream should be cooked at a slightly lower setting to avoid curdling.

▶ When cooking uniform pieces of food, such as meatballs or chicken wings, arrange them in a circle in the cooking utensil for even cooking.

▶ Place tougher or thicker parts of food toward the outside edges of the cooking pan or tray.

▶ Do not use gold- or silver-trimmed dishes in a microwave oven; they could damage the oven.

▶ If there are small children in your house who might reach the controls and accidentally turn the microwave oven on, keep a glass measure or bowl containing about 1 cup of water in the oven to prevent damage to it.

▶ A microwave oven works especially well with foods that have a naturally high moisture content, such as fish, poultry, fruits and vegetables.

Meats and fish

▶ Cook clams and mussels right in their shells for an easy-to-prepare appetizer. Arrange them on a pie plate, hinged-side toward the outside of the plate, and cover loosely with wax paper. For three 5-ounce clams, microwave at full (100%) power for three to five minutes or until the shells open.

▶ If your roast beef is too rare, microwave slices right on the dinner plate until the desired doneness is reached.

▶ For one-step cooking and draining of excess fat, crumble ground meat into a microwave-safe plastic colander set in a casserole. The fat will drain into the casserole during cooking.

▶ No-fuss, fancy hors d'oeuvres: Wrap pineapple chunks or water chestnuts in bacon and fasten with wooden picks. Place on paper

toweling and microwave at full (100%) power until the bacon is thoroughly cooked.

▶ For barbecued spareribs and chicken, microwave until tender, then grill long enough for a charcoal flavor and crisp exterior.

▶ Remember: Boneless meats cook more evenly than meats on the bone because bones attract more microwave energy than meat.

Fruits and vegetables

▶ All vegetables should be cooked at full (100%) power. Remember that microwave ovens do vary in wattage output.

▶ Cooking time depends on the quantity, size, freshness and moisture content of the vegetables. Standing time is as important as actual cooking time, especially when microwaving vegetables. They will continue to cook even after the heat generated by microwaves has ceased. Overcooked vegetables turn dry and tough.

▶ Vegetables should be cooked only until bright and tender-crisp when pierced. Potatoes, yams and squash should give slightly when pressed. Test for doneness *after* the recommended standing time.

▶ In general, estimate a cooking time of about six to seven minutes per pound of vegetables. Stir or rotate after three minutes; bring the center portion toward the outside of the dish for more even cooking. After the minimum cooking time, let stand, then check for doneness. If necessary, cook in 1-minute intervals. *Note:* Dried peas and beans are better cooked in a conventional oven or on a range.

▶ To cook several large individual vegetables (potatoes or squash), place them in a circle for more even cooking, leaving about one inch between them. Arrange them in a single layer rather than on top of each other.

▶ Cut vegetables into uniform sizes and shapes. Potatoes should be placed with the thickest portions to the outside. Those with thick, tough stalks, such as broccoli, should be arranged with the tips toward the center.

▶ Stir and rotate vegetables (especially large quantities) midway through the cooking time to prevent uneven cooking.

▶ Salt vegetables only after they've cooked because salt draws liquid out of food and interferes with the microwave cooking pattern. Other seasonings may also be used.

▶ To get the maximum amount of juice from citrus fruits, microwave at full (100%) power for 15 to 30 seconds before squeezing.

▶ Peel, core or pierce whole fruit, such as apples, before microwaving to allow steam to escape and avoid spattering.

▶ When microwaving cabbage-family vegetables, such as fresh broccoli or cauliflower, cover loosely with wax paper for better flavor and color.

▶ Here's how to cook crisp frozen hash brown or French fried potatoes in half the time: Partially thaw them first in a microwave oven following package directions, then fry or bake them conventionally to finish.

▶ To plump raisins and other dried fruits, place them in a small bowl and sprinkle with a few drops of water. Microwave at full (100%) power for 15 to 30 seconds.

▶ To blanch vegetables for crudité platters or to add to casseroles:

Slightly undercook the vegetables and let stand, covered, for one minute. Place the vegetables in ice water to stop cooking. Spread the vegetables on paper toweling to absorb any excess moisture.

▶ To soften the tough skins of winter squash, place the squash on the oven floor. Microwave, uncovered, at full (100%) power for one minute. Let stand for one minute before cutting.

▶ Easy mashed potatoes: Cube the potatoes. Add a small amount of water. Microwave tightly covered, until soft. Season and mash with milk or cream.

▶ For softer vegetables, increase the amount of water and the microwave cooking time.

▶ Add butter or margarine to the water before cooking vegetables. For soft moist vegetables, such as mushroom and spinach, substitute equal amounts of butter or margarine for the water.

▶ Sprinkle vegetables with grated or shredded cheese during the standing time and toss before serving.

▶ Don't hesitate to experiment with fresh herbs. Add them to vegetables during the standing time.

▶ Substitute beef, chicken or vegetable broth for water. The result is richer-tasting vegetables.

▶ Use your microwave to dry fresh herbs. Wash and pat the herbs dry on paper toweling. Measure 1½ cups of leaves (without stems). Spread them on a double thickness of paper toweling and microwave at full (100%) power for four to five minutes, stirring several times.

▶ Shortcut acorn squash: Pierce the skin of a medium-size (1¼-pound) squash and microwave at full (100%) power for four minutes. Cut the squash in half, remove the seeds and microwave for another four minutes. Let the squash stand for five minutes.

▶ Cook broccoli or asparagus with the tender flower ends pointing toward the center and with the tougher stem ends pointing outward.

Kitchen helps

▶ Separate cold bacon in its packaging by microwaving the package at full (100%) power for 30 to 45 seconds.

▶ To soften solidly frozen ice cream for easier scooping, microwave the container at low (30%) power for 20 to 40 seconds.

▶ Soften one stick of butter at half (50%) power for 45 to 55 seconds. Remove any foil wrapping before microwaving.

▶ Use doubled muffin paper liners to microwave muffins; the liners will help absorb excess moisture.

▶ Loosen hard brown sugar by adding an apple slice or a few drops of water to the box; microwave at full (100%) power for a few seconds.

▶ To melt chocolate, microwave in a microwave-safe cup at full (100%) power for 45 to 60 seconds per ounce of chocolate.

▶ To make chocolate curls, place an unwrapped block of chocolate on a microwave-safe plate. Heat at half (50%) power for 8 to 12 seconds. Scrape off curls with a swivel-bladed vegetable peeler.

▶To "toast" one cup of shredded coconut, spread it out on a microwave-safe pie plate. Microwave at full (100%) power for two to three minutes, stirring several times.

▶ With fried or poached eggs, always pierce the yolks with a wooden pick *before* microwaving to prevent bursting.

▶ Heat pancake syrup in its own container, cap removed, or in a serving pitcher at full (100%) power.

▶ To crisp and renew the fresh flavor of day-old cookies, crackers or potato chips, microwave at full (100%) power for 5 to 15 seconds.

▶ Frozen juice concentrate can be defrosted in its container. Remove the lid from one end. Defrost at half (50%) power for 2 to 2½ minutes for a 6-ounce can, and for 4½ to 5 minutes for a 12-ounce can.

▶ Thaw frozen fish fillets right in their own packaging at low (30%) power.

Quick fixes

▶ Make your own chocolate syrup for milk: Combine 1¼ cups granulated sugar, 1 cup unsweetened cocoa powder, ¾ cup water and ⅛ teaspoon salt in a 1-quart measuring cup. Microwave at full (100%) power for two minutes or until the mixture boils. Stir. Continue cooking for two minutes longer, stirring every 30 seconds. Don't let the mixture boil over. Stir in ½ teaspoon vanilla. To serve, stir 2 tablespoons of the syrup into an 8-ounce glass of milk. The syrup will keep for up to one month when tightly covered in the refrigerator.

▶ For a quick cup of tea, instant coffee or cocoa: Heat the water directly in the cup instead of boiling a large tea kettle of water conventionally. A cup with six ounces of water microwaved at full (100%) power will be steaming after 1¼ to 2 minutes. Two cups will take 2½ to 3 minutes.

▶ Speedy toasted cheese sandwich: Toast two slices of bread (white or whole wheat) in a toaster or toaster oven. Place a slice of cheese on one piece of toast. Spread with mustard, if you wish, and top with the remaining piece of toast. Place the sandwich on a paper plate and microwave at medium-high (70%) power for 15 to 20 seconds or until the cheese melts.

Warming up foods

▶ As a general rule, to reheat foods, allow 1½ to 2 minutes for each cup of refrigerated mixture.

▶ Microwave dinner rolls in a napkin-lined straw serving basket at full (100%) power for 15 to 30 seconds, depending on the number and size of the rolls.

▶ Wrap a sandwich in paper toweling and microwave; the paper absorbs excess moisture.

▶ Heat gravy in a serving bowl or gravy boat at full (100%) power for one minute per cup.

▶ To warm a 12-ounce jar of sundae or fruit sauce topping, remove the lid and microwave at full (100%) power for 45 to 60 seconds.

▶ Reheat take-out fast food in its own paper wrapping at full (100%) power. If a container has a foil top, remove it and cover the container loosely with wax paper.

▶ Reheat a fast-food double-decker hamburger in its plastic package at full (100%) power for 20 to 40 seconds.

▶ Warm a slice of apple pie with "melty" cheese on top by microwaving at full (100%) power for 15 to 20 seconds.

▶ Popped corn can be reheated at full (100%) power for 15 to 20 seconds per cup.

▶ For hot pancakes, arrange three already-cooked pancakes, overlapping, on a microwave-safe plate. Cover loosely with wax paper and microwave at full (100%) power for 20 to 30 seconds.

Defrosting

Defrost and heat foods in boilable plastic bags right in the bag. Place the bag in a microwave-safe pie plate and cut an "X" in the bag above the liquid line for venting.

6.
Kids!
Kids! Kids!

Smart Ideas For Parents
Safety First
Housework Via Kid Power
Party Time
Play Time
Baby Care
Kids And Food
The Tumultuous Teens
"I'm Bored": Fun Things Kids Can Do
Back-To-School
Sanity-Savers For Shopping
With Children
Help For Working Parents
Easy Ways A Busy Mom and Dad
Can Say "I Love You"

Smart Ideas For Parents

Fear of the doctor, sibling rivalry, teenagers with curfews—every Mom and Dad has had to deal with these everyday calamities of raising children. You'll find this sound advice can help you through the pitfalls of parenting.

It's my week

Who will ride in the front seat of the car, which TV program will we watch, where will we stop for dinner on the road? You can find yourself constantly playing referee to your children. To simplify things, let each child make these decisions for one week. When you get in the car, for example, the child whose turn it is simply says, "It's my week," and the other gets in the back seat.

For tips on traveling in the car with children, see page 185.

Sudsy solution

Don't shock your toddler with cold shampoo. Let the shampoo bottle float in the warm bathwater until you're ready to suds up. It will be just the right temperature for your child's head.

"Watering" hair to help it grow

Is bath time a battle in your home because your kids hate to have their hair washed? Give the children a watering can to use as a bathtub toy, and after they've played with it for a while, fill it with clear water. Then wash their hair and rinse it with the watering can, pretending you are watering their hair to help it grow. There will be no more battles—just nice, clean, "growing" hair.

Baby-sitter blues

To make baby sitters more familiar to your child, take snapshots of your sitters and add them to the family album. This idea is especially helpful when there are several baby sitters involved, some of whom your child may not see for several weeks.

Making visits to the doctor and dentist fun

▶ To make going to the doctor a more enjoyable experience, carry along a couple of crayons. The paper covering the examining table is the perfect "canvas" for your child's doodles. Since the covers are thrown away after each patient's use, your child's "artistry" does no harm and it gives him something to do while waiting for the doctor. In fact, he might actually look forward to going!

▶ Whenever you have a dental appointment, take your youngster along so she can have a chance to meet your dentist and his or her staff, as well as get used to being in the office. Go one step further and ask your dentist for permission to have your child watch you being examined. Encourage your child to ask questions and, by the time the examination is over, your child and the dentist will be good friends.

Squabble buster

What do you do if your children won't stop arguing? Telling them to stop or separating them by sending them to different parts of the house won't work for long—they'll just resume the argument later. Instead hand the squabblers clean cloths and glass cleaner, put them on opposite sides of a window and tell them to get it good and clean. They are not, of course, allowed to talk while working. To get around the "no talking" rule, they will begin to make faces at each other. Soon their scowls will disappear and they will be giggling. In bad weather, each cleans half a large mirror. Watching each other's reflection does the trick, too.

Moving away

Moving to a new town can leave your child anxious about leaving his home and friends. To make the departure more festive, give him a surprise farewell party. At the party, you can read a story about friendship and about how memories stay forever in our hearts. Then give the children slips of paper and ask them to complete the following sentence: "I remember when Jeff and I . . . . " This way your child will have a collection of wonderful memories to look back on. As the children leave, give each one a packet of stationery, some stickers and a prestamped envelope addressed to your child at his new address.

Peaceful Sundays

To avoid Sunday morning hassles—when you or your spouse want to spend quiet time with the newspaper while your youngster wants attention, remove the comics section from the paper, roll and tie it, and present it to your child as his or her "very own" paper.

Just like Dad

Kids always seem to want to be in the bathroom with Dad while he is shaving. To keep little fingers and minds occupied safely, spread a washcloth on the toilet seat, fill the cap from the can of shaving cream with some of the foam, give each child a small household brush and let the little shavers have a ball!

Child's play

When neighborhood youngsters come over to visit, one problem invariably occurs: they all want to play with the same toy. Buy a portable timer with a buzzer and explain that each child can play with the favored toy for 10 minutes before passing it to the next in line when the buzzer sounds.

Mirror magic

If you can't face the daily wrestling match of getting your toddler into his winter wraps, try dressing him in front of a full-length mirror. The mirror allows him to see what is going on, making him feel like a participant rather than an unwilling victim.

No more missed phone calls

Is the telephone your child's favorite toy? Put masking tape over the two buttons on the cradle of the phone. If you need to use the phone you can easily lift the tape off, but your child can't.

Reaching across the miles

▶ To keep out-of-town grandparents abreast of their grandchild's development, start a daily calendar of "firsts" as well as family outings. At the end of each month, make copies of the calendar and send one to each grandparent and great grandparent. They will really appreciate it.

▶ To keep in touch with grandchildren, give them a tape recorder made for children (practically indestructible). By tape you can talk to them, read stories from library books and sing. Then they can record messages back to you.

The learning song

Set your address and phone number to the tune of one of your child's favorite nursery rhymes and you'll find he or she won't have any problem memorizing this important information.

The "I Wish" book

Are your children at the age where they want everything they see? Try making an "I Wish" book from a large blank notebook. When your children see something they want, help them look through old magazines and catalogs to find a picture of it. Cut it out and paste it in the book. When you go shopping for a special occasion gift, take the book along. Then you can be sure that you're buying them something they really want.
For tips on kids and Christmas, see page 162.

Accentuate the positive

If your child is preoccupied with the negative aspects of life, buy him a pretty, fabric-covered journal in which he can record happy events. Every night before bedtime, sit down together and recollect the "good" things that happened that day. He can then enter each item in his journal. This little exercise can help him to look more positively at a variety of situations.

Safe viewing

If you are concerned for your children's safety because they are sitting too close to the TV set during viewing, put tape on the floor to mark the safe distance and have them sit behind that line.

Saved by the bell

A kitchen timer can come in handy with a young child. Time your youngster's bath or those "last 10 minutes" to play before bedtime. When your child's friends come to play, avoid the constant question, "Do I have to go home yet?" by simply telling them that you are setting the timer to the time when they should stop playing.

Money management

To teach your school-age child about managing money, try this: Give her money to buy lunch at the school cafeteria. Tell her if she decides to take her lunch from home and if she packs it herself, she is allowed to spend her lunch money on whatever she wants. She will become quite adept at "planning" her lunches and deciding how she wants to budget her money.

Kids' photo albums

▶ If you can't find the time to keep family photos organized and up-to-date, let the kids do it! Buy each child an album. After sharing new photos with relatives, let your children pick out their favorites and place them in their "personal" books. Not only is this a fun project for rainy days, but family history is instantly recorded.

▶ Just about every roll of film you get developed has some pictures that you do not care to keep, either because they are poor quality or because they are similar to other pictures. Purchase an inexpensive photo album for each of your children and let them have these rejected photos. They'll love having their own picture album.

A money saver

Is your child constantly asking you to buy more of the little cake mixes that came with a play oven? Since they are expensive and often hard to find, try mixing together ¼ cup regular mix and 1 tablespoon water. The rest of the directions are followed just as if you are using a "little" mix. Store the unused dry mix in a plastic bag in your freezer for future use.

Clean catchall

Place a dish-drain tray under your child's car seat. It catches crumbs, sand and dirt from shoes and liquid from spilled drinks. The tray is easily removed, keeps the floor and seats much neater and makes cleaning easier.

Reveille

Like many adults, some children take a bit longer to get going in the morning. To help your night owl along, read aloud a wake-up story about 15 minutes before the "official" wake-up time. By the time the story is complete, your youngster will be ready to greet the morning.

"Sweet dreams" box

If it's hard for your child to get to sleep at night because he lies awake thinking scary thoughts, try a "sweet dreams" box. Cut out colorful pictures of animals, toys, children, etc. from old magazines and put them in a special box. Each night before your child goes to bed, have him select a picture and think up a story about the picture while drifting off to sleep, to promote soothing thoughts for sleep time.

Safety First

Trying to keep your child safe can cause grey hairs to pop up overnight. Check out these precautionary measures for a child-safe home.

Lowdown on safety

To child-proof your home most effectively, get on your hands and knees and crawl around your house to get a "baby's-eye view." You'll notice many potential trouble spots you might never have seen otherwise. *For ways to toddler-proof your home during the holidays, see page 167.*

Bathers beware

Child-proof the slippery edge of the bathtub by placing a bath mat with suction cups over the side.

No more tacks

A metallic stove or counter mat fastened to the wall makes a safe bulletin board for young children. Pictures can be hung with magnetic note holders (commonly used on refrigerators) instead of potentially harmful thumbtacks or pushpins. The mat also provides a terrific spot to practice spelling with colorful, magnetic letters of the alphabet!

Safe toy storage

Use laundry baskets as toy boxes. They are durable, economical and don't have lids that might fall down on little hands or heads. Sturdy boxes that small appliances (TV, stereo) come in can also be covered with colorful self-adhesive paper and used as special storage containers in your child's room.

For tumbling toddlers

Two tennis wristbands worn like kneepads keep your toddler's knees scrape-free.

Swing set

Unlike standard playground equipment, which has welded links, most retail swing sets have open links. As a result, hair can become tangled or fingers can get cut if a child tries to grasp the chain when falling. To remedy this problem, slip each chain through a 3- to 4-foot length of hose before hanging the swings.

No slip pool

Apply bathtub appliqués to the bottom of your youngster's inflatable wading pool. The appliqués have just enough grip to keep small feet from slipping.

For tips on sun sense and kids, see page 173.

Instant ice packs

▶ Save small, empty, preferably somewhat flat plastic bottles and containers from hand creams and shampoos. Clean them thoroughly, fill with water and place in the freezer to use for bumps and bruises that may need ice. Simply return the bottle or container to the freezer for the next time it may be needed.

▶ Fill self-sealing plastic bags with water and stick them in the freezer as quick ice packs for aches or bruises. Before applying, pop them in a hand-puppet washcloth or wrap in a towel.

▶ For bruised lips and tongues, try popsicles! They not only taste good, sucking on them reduces swelling and soothes the pain.

Safe seat

To prevent your baby from sliding around the seat of a wooden highchair, cut a textured plastic car floormat to fit the seat. It wipes clean easily and your baby stays securely in place.

Picture perfect

For kids who can't read yet but have been taught how to use the telephone, here's a method for easily determining whom to call in case of emergency. Put a poster board on the wall near the phone and use symbols or pictures for the people or places to be called. Then draw a line in a bold color leading to the phone number. For example, for the fire department, use a picture of firemen, for Dad's work number, a picture of him, and so on.

Housework Via Kid Power

In these days of working Moms and Dads, it's doubly important for the whole family to "pull their own weight."

Proper praise

When your children have carried out a task, praise them for a job well done and help them feel good about being part of a family effort. Praising them for "helping Mom or Dad" only gives them the idea that it is really their parents' job, not theirs.

Paired up

Have kids pin their socks together when they take them off. That way each pair stays together and you don't have to track down mates.

A perfect setup

If one of your youngster's duties at home is to set the table, he may occasionally forget where to place the fork, knife and spoon. To help him, draw a simple diagram on a 3 x 5-inch index card and tape it to the inside of the silverware drawer.

Kitchen chores

Teach kids to help out in the kitchen—even young ones can learn to set and clear the table. Add one kitchen chore on each birthday; pass on another duty to a younger child.

Toy clean-up

When your children bring their toys in from outdoors, give them old toothbrushes and let them handle the clean-up. This will help cut down on dirt and sand in the house.

Round 'em up

Tired of finding wooden building blocks scattered all over the house? Use a rope to form a circle around your child's play area. Tell her that any blocks or other toys found outside the corral will be rustled up!

Chore calendar

To make household chores more appealing to your children, borrow an idea from Christmastime. Cut a piece of poster board in the shape of a house with 30 windows, like an Advent calendar. Every day the children break a seal to open a window for their daily chores. Some days surprise them with a free day or a treat.

In the box

A "Friday Box" can help develop your children's sense of responsibility. Every night before bedtime, all toys and personal items must be picked up and put away. Anything left behind goes into the Friday Box, from which it can be retrieved only on Friday mornings after breakfast. Sometimes favorite toys, caps and blouses find their way into the box and when the children are without them for only a few days, they learn to pick up!

Neat and tidy

Enlist your children's help in sorting, folding and putting away their own laundry by purchasing rectangular-shaped plastic dishpans in assorted colors. You fold and place clothing into each child's container. It is the children's responsibility to put clothes into their closets or drawers and return the pans.

Little workers

When you need to wash the car and the toddlers want to participate, fill a small pail with soapy water and give them some old paint brushes so they can "paint" the car clean. You will be able to wash the car while having lots of fun with your kids.

Here comes the maid

▶ If you are beginning to feel like a servant in your own house, start a program called "Here Comes the Maid." Several times a day "the maid" announces unexpectedly that he or she will be coming through the house in five minutes. Everybody then has five minutes to put their things away. If someone is not at home, or ignores the warning, "the maid" will pick up anything left lying around and its owner pays 5¢ per item for "maid service." It's a humorous—but practical—reminder that no one enjoys being a maid for someone else, *unless* he or she is getting paid for it!

▶ Another technique is to give each child a chore for every item left lying around. Simply write the child a note listing the things you picked up and the jobs to be done to pay for your "services." Most kids will respond without complaint because they know they "earned" the chores.

Turns in the kitchen

All parents find themselves wondering whether they spend enough time with each child. Since there is no emptier place in the house than the kitchen at dishwashing time, why not assign each youngster a one-week stint to work with you after supper? You can regularly spend one-on-one time with a child and teach him or her about working together.

Party Time

Make the most of your children's parties—a little imagination is all it takes.

A party to remember

To make a birthday celebration really memorable, visit your local fire department. All it takes is a telephone call in advance. You'll find that community workers are eager to inform and educate youngsters, and seeing the real thing will be a big hit with the kids.

Sprinkler party for children

A sprinkler party can be almost as fun as a pool party. First set up a twirling sprinkler for the children to run through and splash in. Then attach a hose to a sliding board and you've got a small-scale water slide. Plastic sunglasses make a whimsical party favor.

Bigfoot lives!

You can turn gift-giving into a thrilling event. Tape a trail of big footprints to the floor, starting at the breakfast table, leading through the hallway and in and out of different rooms to the presents.

Half-birthday celebration

A holiday baby may often feel a little left out by the hustle and bustle of the Christmas/Hanukkah season. So why not, in June or July, have a "Happy Half-Birthday" celebration? Send invitations on half a card. Serve half a cake; wrap presents in half-birthday and half-holiday paper. Think of other ways to make the half-birthday celebration a great—and whole— success.

Puppet show

You can create your own puppet show for your child's party. Using scrap fabrics and following the themes of the characters on the party plates, sew hand puppets for each guest. Make the back of the sofa the stage and place a tape recorder behind the scene to pick up the lively dialogue that flows from your little entertainers. A floor lamp aimed toward the sofa spotlights the action and even allows enough lighting to make home movies.

Party cups

You can create edible snack cups for a party easily. With a sugar cookie as a base, use a decorating tube to outline the edge with a ridge of canned frosting. Set animal crackers on parade on top of the ridge. Filled with candy, nuts and raisins, the cups make attractive table decorations. A scoop of ice cream inside is a treat to eat, too.

Personalized toast

For a birthday breakfast treat, paint a message on your child's toast. Prepare a mixture of 2 tablespoons each of sugar and water and add 3 drops of food coloring. Paint on your message with a clean paintbrush. When it's toasted, the painted part will retain its bright color and sweetness.

Present pennies

Pennies always seem to collect at the bottom of purses, in the dresser catchall bowl and under chair cushions. Have your children start rounding them up and putting them in a special container. When a family birthday comes around, let your kids count and roll the pennies. They can cash them in at the bank and the money becomes their gift-shopping cash. The penny problem is solved and your kids have the fun of buying presents with "their own money."

Mystery trip

As your child becomes older and regular birthday parties pall, try a "mystery trip" party. Invite a small number of your child's favorite friends and "kidnap" your child. Put a blindfold on him or her and let the other children try to give your child false clues about the destination. Make the party a "doing" party centered around an activity such as ice skating, roller skating, an inexpensive matinee of a popular movie, a trip to the zoo or a picnic. For your own comfort, ask another parent to go along as a co-chaperone, with the promise to return the favor on their child's birthday.

Do-it-yourself birthday cakes

Let children decorate their own individual birthday cakes. Set out a cupcake for each child and provide frosting, raisins, nuts and colorful candies to decorate with.

Play Time

Play time can be a safe and happy time with these words of wisdom.

A weekend activity file

Have you ever found that when the weekend comes and the family wants to do something different, no one can remember what entertainment is available, but later everyone remembers something better that could have been done? To avoid this, keep a folder with clippings on movies, craft shows, restaurants and day trips in the area. Periodically update the folder with new items and remove the old.

Smart art

Save liquid shoe polish bottles with daubers; they make wonderful paint sets for small children. Fill each bottle with a different watercolor and use the daubers instead of paintbrushes.

More for less

Are you spending a bundle on art supplies for your children? White freezer/butcher paper, available at grocery stores, makes great painting paper. It costs much less than the usual craft paper, will save you a trip to the hobby store and, since there is more paper on the roll, your children can enjoy more painting sessions.

Family trivia

What can the whole family do together that's fun? Create your own "Family Trivia Game," of questions and answers about the personal achievements, special events and unique qualities of each member of the family. You can assemble your game in one evening. Make a list of questions and transfer them to index cards, putting the questions on one side and the answers on the other. To keep your game current, continue to add new questions.

Young sprouts

To start teaching children the names, characteristics and care of houseplants, give them a small, inexpensive plant of their own to keep and care for in their room.

A cleaner wading pool

Half the fun children have with a wading pool is jumping in and out, which can easily lead to a lot of grass and dirt collecting at the bottom of the pool. A simple way to reduce the amount of debris is to put an inexpensive plastic wash tub filled with water next to the pool to step into before entering.

Move to the music

Finding time to exercise on a regular basis can be almost impossible for a mother of young children. To make exercise time family fun time, go to the library and take out a few record albums for children. Set aside a time every day to dance, play follow-the-leader or exercise to the beat of the music. Not only can you get into better shape, the kids get an early introduction to the exercise habit. Best of all, it's free.

Lending library

Encourage your children to read and share their books by suggesting that they start a lending library. Make a field trip to your local public library so that they can see how it is run. Then help them make up their own card catalogue. The more friends they can get involved, the more books there will be for all.

Live theatre

Do your kids like to perform? Sing? Dance? Make-believe? Putting on their own play is the perfect outlet. You can easily turn a garage into a theatre with clothesline and old sheets as a curtain. Your local library has many books with plays written expressly for children. Or encourage them to write their own; you may be surprised at the results. This is also a way for them to make a little money if they work hard and charge a few cents for admission.

Sock it to 'em

▶ Make your own inexpensive softball that won't hurt kids or furniture: stuff an old sock with pantyhose and sew the seams together.

▶ With indelible ink, cotton balls and/or pieces of felt or yarn, create hand puppets with old socks. Then put on a puppet show!

Baby Care

Everyone agrees that taking care of an infant is hard work. These tips can help make baby care a little easier on you.

Picture perfect

When a baby arrives, so do lots of gifts, and new parents have little time for writing thank-you notes. Instead, take snapshots of the gifts in use. A picture of the baby wearing the new clothes, for example, says a lot and a quick "thank you" jotted on the back of the photo will do fine.

Freezing baby food

When preparing your own baby food ahead of time, try freezing it in ice cube trays and placing the cubes in plastic bags. They take up less space than containers or jars. You also avoid having unused leftovers from full containers by defrosting only the amount needed.

Carting baby along

Here's an easy way to take an infant to the grocery store: Place your baby, on a blanket, in an over-the-arm shopping basket and place the basket in your shopping cart. Your baby now will ride snugly in the cart.

Kid gloves

First-time parents often dread having to give their infant a daily bath, afraid that the little squirming body might slip out of their hands. Try wearing a pair of white cotton gloves while bathing the baby. The gloves give you a slip-proof hold.

Talc container

Instead of using commercial baby talc in a shaker container, keep a covered, pretty margarine tub, filled with cornstarch and a powder puff, with your baby's bath items. Controlled use of the cornstarch avoids the risk of the baby breathing possibly irritating substances.

The bell tells!

Thread a tiny bell between the two bottom eyelets on your toddler's shoes. He'll love the sound it makes as he moves about and you will always be able to locate him.

Crib buddy

To soothe a young baby who won't sleep, tape a 30-minute cassette of a cat purring and put the tape player inside a kitty pajama bag. The fabric of the pajama bag, besides being washable, is soft enough to keep him from feeling any discomfort if he rolls over on it.

Playpen pals

Babies outgrow their toys so fast. Why not buy a few brightly colored potholders in whimsical shapes and hang them around the edges of your child's playpen? They're safe, fun toys to grab and can be used in the kitchen when he or she outgrows them.

Bathtime bliss

If you have a household where only one parent is working, chances are that parent has little time to spend with a new baby while the baby is awake. Try having the working parent give the baby his or her evening bath while you fix dinner. This can be a warm, happy and relaxed time for both parent and child.

Just like new

Most clothes for infants and toddlers have color-coordinated painted snaps that often chip after the first time in the clothes dryer. To keep them unchipped and new-looking, cover the snaps with clear nail polish before the first washing.

Money-saving tip

Since safety seats come in different sizes and shapes to accomodate a child's rapid growth, borrowing instead of buying a seat can save you a bundle. Contact your local highway safety or health department to find out if a borrowing program exists in your area. If it doesn't, start a safety-seat swap yourself, placing notices in the supermarket and in your pediatrician's office.

Insta-crib

▶ If you're visiting and don't have a portable crib, you can create one. Empty a dresser drawer and line it with soft towels or a quilt. The sides give an infant a feeling of security (and parents too).

▶ Another way to make a quick "crib" is to place a baby on a regular bed and surround the child with lots of cushy pillows.

Kids And Food

Is your child all hot dog and no veggies? Try these smart ideas to get your child to eat right.

The healthful home restaurant

To rekindle a sick child's appetite, temporarily turn your kitchen into a "play restaurant." Each morning prepare an attractive menu with three or four choices for breakfast, lunch and dinner. Give this to your child and let him or her "order" from this wider-than-usual selection. If you want to add a few flourishes, set up a "restaurant table" with checkered tablecloth, linen napkin and a bowl of flowers in the center.

Breakfast cut-up

A pizza cutter quickly transforms waffles or French toast into child-size bites so you can enjoy breakfast along with the rest of the family.

Eat your vegetables

To make vegetables more tempting to a picky eater, serve finger-size pieces of fresh vegetables with a small cup of salad dressing "dip." The detested vegetables are transformed into party food!

Extra snooze

If you are concerned about your youngsters fixing their own breakfast on Saturday mornings when you want to sleep a little later, try this: The night before, fill each child's bowl with cereal and seal it with an airtight lid. Fill a thermos (with a pouring spout) with milk and store it in the refrigerator. Your kids will enjoy the morning—and you'll appreciate the extra snooze time.

"Puzzle" sandwiches

To make humdrum sandwiches more appealing to your children, cut them into several uneven pieces, making them look like a jigsaw puzzle.

Buttering up

If your child has trouble buttering an ear of corn with a knife, try spreading a thick layer of butter on a slice of bread. Have your child wrap the bread around the corn, turning the ear as he does so.

A "sweet" alternative

If you've been working hard at giving your tots "healthy" foods, what do you do when they go to a birthday party? Why not bake the birthday cake yourself and bring it to the party? Kids adore carrot-raisin cake made with just a touch of honey, banana-molasses cake or carob cake. Use lots of pineapple, apple or other fruit chunks in and on top of the cake. For frosting, try cream cheese thinned with apple juice and vanilla; add carob powder for a delicious chocolate flavor. You can rent character cakepans (Mickey Mouse or Donald Duck, for example) from a cake supply shop. You'll find most parents are delighted to have such a personalized cake for their child and pleased that you have relieved them of having to make or buy the cake themselves. The cake makes a thoughtful gift as well.

Kid-size food

Sometimes small portions can tempt fussy eaters.
▶ Make mini meatloaves in muffin tins.
▶ Scoop mashed potatoes with a melon-ball scooper.
▶ Serve cherry tomatoes, halved, instead of regular-sized ones.
▶ Make silver dollar-size pancakes.

Brown-bagging for kids

You can turn your youngster's paper lunch bag into a sturdy container to keep his or her sandwiches intact. Cut off the bottom third of a milk carton and place it in the bag. The carton reinforces the bottom and sides, yet the top of the bag can still be rolled down and closed.

Lunch box ideas

▶ To perk up your youngster's lunch box each day, use seasonal paper napkins, such as shamrocks for March, spring flowers for May or Santa Claus for December.
▶ Tuck a brightly colored washcloth into your child's lunch box. This can cushion the thermos, make a great placemat or help to quickly wipe up spills.

The Tumultuous Teens

Help your teen make a smooth transition to maturity with this wise advice.

Making the curfew stick

The problem with a curfew is knowing if your teen is meeting it without waiting up past your own bedtime. Why not let an alarm clock monitor your son or daughter? Set a clock for the agreed-upon time and place it inside the front door. If your teen comes home before curfew, she or he will turn off the alarm. If your teen is late, it will go off and awaken you. Once there is no more room for speculation about when your son or daughter gets home, your teen will become amazingly prompt.

News from home

When you send care packages of homemade cookies to children at college, use your local newspaper (neatly folded) as packing for the carton. Your kids will enjoy the news from home almost as much as they'll love the cookies!

Who gets the car?

Having more than one teenager and only one car can cause problems. Try a "reservation" system. Make a calendar chart and post it on the refrigerator door. The children write in their names on the date they want to use the car. They also write what time they need the car, where they are going and how long they'll be gone (you can also have them put the phone number where they can be reached for emergencies). The first person to reserve the car for a particular day gets it. From looking at the chart, you can tell if one child is monopolizing the car, and keep track of where everyone is! Best of all, there won't be any question about identifying the culprit who left the gas tank empty.

The barter system

As your kids get older, they need and want more responsibility. Instead of giving them an allowance, start a "barter" system: Whenever your teenagers need extra money or a special favor, such as borrowing the car for an evening, let them "earn" it by some sort of service. Find special jobs around the house, such as cleaning the oven, helping to repaint or taking younger siblings to an activity. This can help them feel more involved with the running of the household and help them learn the value of working for something they want.

News bulletin

Going off to college for the first time can be very lonely—and your son or daughter will probably miss their friends from high school. To help them "keep in touch," start a newsletter: Ask each of your son's or daughter's friends to send you a brief summary of what they're doing currently or a greeting, news of vacation plans, etc. Once a semester, type up the "news," xerox it and send it off to your freshman and his or her friends at their colleges. This can make some very lonely days a lot friendlier and provide a lasting memento of college life.

Dual-purpose packing

To help your college-bound daughter or son get ready for moving into the dorm, put clothing and small articles in a steamer trunk, rattan hamper or plastic decorator-storage crates. These items will not only streamline the large job of packing, but will give your children a head-start in furnishing their rooms.

Shopping smarts

If you're trying to teach your teenage children about family meal planning and food budgeting, try giving them the grocery allotment for one week each month. Explain to them that they have complete responsibility for planning, purchasing and preparing the family meals. As an added benefit of "good planning," they can keep any leftover grocery money to spend themselves.

"I'm Bored": Fun Things Kids Can Do

It's a long, hot summer and your kids are complaining, "I don't have anything to do!" Here are some fun activities to keep youngsters happy until the school bell rings.

Grow trees from fruit seeds

▶ Did you know there's a tree inside an orange seed, longing to get out? Plant citrus seeds (from an orange, grapefruit or lemon) ½ inch deep in peat moss and keep moist. Soon you will have a start on your own miniature orchard. (Ages 3 to 6 with help, 7 to 15 alone.)

▶ Cut off the tops of carrots and place them in a shallow tray of water. When roots form, plant them in soil. (Ages 3 to 6 with help, 7 to 15 alone.)

Create a zoo-mobile

Cut out pictures of animals from magazines. Glue or staple them to various lengths of string and hang them from a coat hanger. (Ages 3 to 6 with help, 7 to 10 alone.)

Play ace reporter

Write a newspaper containing neighborhood news, cartoons, book reviews and jokes. Pass out copies to your friends and neighbors or mail to distant relatives to let them know how you are. (Ages 7 to 15.)

Have fun with busy bingo cards

Make bingo cards with a different vehicle (car, pickup truck, delivery van, bicycle) in each space. Watch traffic from your porch and put a marker on any square that matches a passing vehicle. The first person with five markers in a row wins. This is also a good game to play on long, boring car trips. (Ages 7 to 15.)

Make a book "Starring Me, Myself and I"

Help your child start a scrapbook on himself or herself with pictures, a family tree and a list of his or her special interests, such as favorite books, movies, hobbies and foods. Add to it all year long. (Ages 7 to 10 with help, 11 to 15 alone.)

Grow Grandma's "Depression-era garden"

Place a piece of clean, wet coal (available from fuel dealers and many hardware stores) in a glass bowl. (Charcoal will also work but the results will not be as dramatic.) Generously sprinkle salt over the coal and dot it with food coloring. Pour 2 tablespoons liquid bluing to one side of the coal. Mix 2 tablespoons ammonia with 2 tablespoons water and add it to the bluing, being careful not to touch the salt. Soon colored crystals will form. (Ages 3 to 10 with help, 11 to 15 alone.)

In the bag

Use crayons to make a funny or scary mask from a paper bag. Be sure to cut holes for eyes, nose and mouth. (Ages 3 to 10.)

Memory game

Collect 20 small objects on a tray or table and spend three minutes trying to memorize what's there. (Use an egg timer.) Cover up the objects and see who can remember the most. Use fewer objects for smaller children and gradually work up to 20. Game variation: Put the objects into a bag and have players reach in and identify as many as they can by touch. (Ages 3 to 15.)

Invent fancy designs from plain potatoes

One potato, two potato, three potato, four . . . . Cut a potato in half and carve a design into it. Press it onto an ink pad and stamp it on paper. (Ages 3 to 10 with help, 11 to 15 alone.)

Starry states

Can you find Truth or Consequences, New Mexico, or Happy, Texas? Get out a United States map, put stars on all the state capitals and try to memorize them. See what other unusual town names you can find. (Ages 7 to 15.)

Be a bird watcher

Scatter bread crumbs around your backyard and count how many birds you can spot. Hide and watch different kinds of birds come to nibble. To help you identify them, check your library for bird-watching guides.

Organize a nature scavenger hunt

Each child makes a "hunt" list. For example, find five different kinds of leaves, three wildflowers, a pine cone and two different types of rocks. (All ages, with the game geared to the child's level.)

Design a personal flag

Make a flag from a scrap of material and color your own original design on it with a crayon. Put it between two pieces of paper and iron it to set the colors. Glue it to a stick and start a parade! (Ages 3 to 6 with help, 7 to 10 alone.)

ABC games

Each player takes a turn selecting a category, such as fruit, animals or cities. At the word "go," the players try to think of something in that category beginning with each letter of the alphabet. For example, *animals* could be: anteater, bear, camel, donkey and so forth. (Ages 7 to 15.)

Present a puppet show

Make hand puppets from old socks, yarn and buttons. Write a puppet show and entertain your family after supper. (Ages 3 to 6 with help, 7 to 12 alone.)

Bejeweled

String buttons on a length of string or nylon fishing line for a fun necklace or bracelet. (Ages 3 to 15.)

Lacing cards

Look through old magazines for pictures, of a puppy or pony for example. Cut them out and paste them on cardboard. Use a paper punch to make holes along the outlines of the figures. To complete, weave a very long shoelace for lacing. (Ages 4 to 7.)

Picture yourself life-size

Draw an outline of yourself on a long piece of plain shelf-lining paper. (You can help your friend, then have her help you.) Color in your face and clothes. The second time you do this, why not color in your face and clothes to look the way you think you'll look in five years? (Ages 3 to 10.)

Rainy day fun

▶ Let your children invite one or two friends over for a "Rainy Day Picnic." Set up a picnic table using a blanket on the floor and paper goods. Serve popcorn, hot dogs, hamburgers and punch. Gather around the blanket and tell stories and jokes or sing songs.

▶ Two-liter soda bottles can double as rainy day fun when empty. Save enough to set up a bowling game or as knockovers for toy bulldozers and construction trucks.

▶ Paint a hopscotch pattern on the floor of your garage or basement. It will be especially useful and appreciated on rainy days when the children are tired of playing quiet games inside.

Play astronomer for a day

Can you find the Big Dipper? The Great Bear? Draco the Dragon? Check out a book about astronomy from the library (such as *Find the Constellations*, by H.A. Rey, Houghton-Mifflin). See how many star patterns you can find at night. (Ages 11 to 15.)

Become a state scholar

What is your state's nickname? What places do tourists most often visit? Who discovered your state? Learn all this and more at the library from such books as *The New Enchantment of America Series*, by Children's Press. (Ages 7 to 15.)

Back-To-School

Smart strategies to ease the transition of starting or going back to school, plus school-bus safety tips.

"I don't want to go!" How to calm first-day fears

▶ Help your youngster look forward to school. Talk about it as a friendly place and answer all questions in a positive, reassuring way.

▶ Take your child on a tour of the school to familiarize her. Show her the classroom, the bathroom and arrange to meet with the teacher (who's usually available the week before school starts). Then go over the route to school together. Ask your child to pretend she is explaining the way to a friend.

▶ Explain what a typical first day might be like and be specific: attendance, seat assignments, lessons, rest and playtime, etc.

▶ Make sure your youngster knows his full name, address and phone number. Include a tag with this information in his lunch box. *For ways to help your child memorize this information, see page 110.*

▶ Take your child with you to shop for school supplies such as sneakers and a lunch box. She will feel more at home with things she's selected herself.

▶ Spend a few minutes a day doing school-readiness activities with your child. He will feel good if he can master some tasks—recognizing colors and shapes, tying shoelaces—right away.

▶ If your child has never been away from you for any length of time, be encouraging about the separation. It's O.K. to say, "I'll miss you," but remember to show how excited you'll be to hear her activity reports and meet her new friends.

▶ Have at least one parent take your child to school. *Don't* try to slip away; say goodbye and tell him exactly when you'll see him later.

▶ Put a picture of the family in your child's jacket pocket. It will be a reminder that home is waiting for her at the end of the day.

Listen to your child

When your child says, "The teacher hates me," don't brush off his comments or immediately blame *him*. If you react negatively, it will magnify your child's bad feelings. Instead, get the facts and discuss the situation sympathetically.

Remember, children often exaggerate

Yours might simply have had a bad day or her present teacher may be more demanding than others. Try to pinpoint the cause of her feelings and explain the true problem.

Be objective

Make certain not to foster the idea that "Mommy and Daddy will defend me." Explain that if your child did something wrong, he must take responsibility—it's part of growing up.

Monitor your child's behavior for the next few days

If she becomes increasingly negative, there may be other causes: illness, bad eyesight, she's scared or upset. In this case, speaking with her teacher may help.

The five biggest teacher turn-offs

▶ **Talking in class:** Includes a response to a reprimand and talking without being called on. The biggest don't: making a derogatory remark about another student.
▶ **Disrespect for school property:** Slamming doors, kicking garbage cans, throwing things, wasting supplies.

▶ **Messy looks, sloppy schoolwork:** Indicates lack of interest and caring about school and schoolwork.
▶ **General misconduct:** Not sitting still, running out of line.
▶ **Consistent lateness:** When a child is frequently tardy, he distracts the other students and disrupts classroom routine.

School-bus safety

To protect your youngster, review these rules with her at home:
▶ At the bus stop, line up facing the bus—not alongside it—so you aren't close to the bus as it comes to a stop. The first person in line should be *at least* an arm's length away from the bus as it pulls up.
▶ Don't play ball or tag in the street while waiting for the bus.
▶ Never go after papers that have fallen under the bus. If you must bring the papers to school, tell the bus driver. If you're going home, wait for the bus to leave and ask an older child or adult to get the papers.
▶ After getting off the bus, move immediately onto the sidewalk.
▶ When crossing the street, walk 10 steps in front of the bus so the driver can see you. *Never* cross the street behind the bus. Drivers of oncoming cars are not able to see you.

Sanity-Savers For Shopping With Children

Grocery shopping with children in tow can be hazardous to a parent's mental health. What can you do to keep them happy and out of trouble? Plenty! Read on.

Feed 'em first!

Before you go to the supermarket, make sure everyone has eaten. There's nothing worse on the wallet than shopping with hungry youngsters. If they behave well in the store, you can surprise them with a special treat.

Food games

In the car on the way to the store, make up a song about the foods you're going to get or play a guessing game involving some of the items on your shopping list: "I'm thinking of a vegetable that looks like little trees . . . " "I'm thinking of something that you put on toast and it rhymes with ham . . . "

Kids can clip

If your children are old enough (age 4 and older), appoint them your official "coupon clippers." Let them search through newspapers and magazines, clip and sort the coupons by category. If there is a special cereal they want, challenge them to find a coupon for it and buy it as a treat.

Talk and shop

Talk to your children while you shop. Tell them why you are buying certain foods. If grapes are on sale and that's why you're buying them, say so. Not only will you be providing the beginning of a consumer education, you'll be showing them by your interest and attention that they're involved participants in the family's grocery needs.

Kid say-so

Let your children make some buying decisions. Allow them to choose which flavor of yogurt to take home or figure out which fresh vegetables are the best buys.

Cart smarts

Always keep a belt in the car so that you can strap a toddler securely in the cart's child seat. (Some supermarkets have even begun to install safety seat belts on their carts.) Never let your child ride on the back of the shopping cart—it's dangerous. Keeping a very small infant balanced safely in her infant seat in the shopping cart is also tricky. Pick up items large enough, such as a sack of potatoes or onions, to support your baby's infant seat on each side (whether you buy the potatoes and onions or not).

Ain't misbehaving

Don't reinforce bad behavior in the supermarket. It might get you out of a tricky situation to hand your child a candy bar when he's demanding sweets at the store, but doing so only lays the groundwork for future bad episodes and teaches him that whining is rewarded. Although it may be inconvenient at the time, take a misbehaving child firmly by the hand (abandoning your grocery cart, if need be) and leave the store until he calms down. Teach your child that shopping with you is a treat and that he must behave well.

Add it up

Give your children inexpensive "calculator-like" clickers. Have them add up the prices of your groceries as you move through the aisles. It's an entertaining exercise in math and a good lesson in the cost of food, too.

Diversionary tactics

If you arrive home with cranky children and several bags of groceries to put away, try these diversions. First let the children participate by putting things away on the shelves, so they'll know where everything is. Then give them the paper bags to make into masks, or remove the styrofoam trays from fruit and let them make bathtub boats. The lesson here: Supermarket treats don't have to be candy, gum or coloring books.

Help For Working Parents

Just for you: some of our best ideas to help you cope with the everyday hassles and child-care crises that can wear a working parent down.

Easing the "night-out" guilts

Working parents frequently feel guilty leaving their child with a sitter for a night out on the town. But it's important for a couple to spend time together alone. When you go out for an evening, here are some fun ideas to make the occasion a treat for your child:

▶ A tape-recorded message that the baby sitter can play on a cassette recorder of Daddy and Mommy singing a silly song, reciting a funny story or reading a favorite book.

▶ A favorite treat to eat, such as cupcakes decorated with *Sesame Street* characters.

▶ A grab bag of "new" toys—not new per se, but ones you have saved or bought at garage sales and stashed away for times like these.

Finding dependable emergency sitters

▶ Trying to find child care during school vacations, on snow days or when your child or the regular sitter's child is sick can create an instant crisis. The solution? Develop a network of people you can count on in an emergency. Try your neighbors first. People who work shifts, homemakers and people with flexible work schedules may be willing to cover for you in an emergency if you'll take their children on a Saturday or Sunday. Discuss your arrangements well in advance so that no one feels imposed upon.

▶ Teachers' schedules are often the same as your child's. Some may be willing to care for children in their homes or in yours. Post notes in faculty lounges at several schools.

▶ Ask directors of local community organizations or senior citizens' centers if there are responsible people who could use extra income and would be willing to sit in emergencies or even stay with a child overnight.

▶ Students at local colleges or professional schools may be available when you need them. Out-of-town students may be as eager to have ongoing contact with a family as you are to have them on call.

▶ Try to line up several potential backup sitters. Invite them to your home so you can get to know one another and your child can feel comfortable with them. Keep in touch and nurture your relationship with each of them; they are invaluable.

Leaving without tears

▶ Kids are naturally clingy at certain stages and there will always be days when leaving the house peacefully is impossible. Try to make your daily departure smooth and predictable. A regular routine is particularly comforting to a toddler or preschooler.

▶ If a sitter comes to your house, you might arrange to have your child call the sitter before he or she leaves home and have the sitter tell your child what special activities they'll be doing that morning. Or, have the child make a special drawing for the sitter or wrap a cookie in a small bag as a present for him or her.

▶ Ask your child, "What would you like to do right after I leave for work?" If possible, make that the first activity of the day.

▶ Involve your youngster in your departure. He or she can help you find your coat in the closet, count the number of steps to the front door or even push you out the door.

▶ Leave a note for the sitter to read aloud. Mention what you're going to do when you return so your child can look forward to a good time.

▶ Offer a big hug and a kiss on the cheek. Say, "Here's a very special kiss for you to hold on to. Touch that kiss whenever you think of me. Now you give me a big kiss so that I can touch it and think of you." *Note:* If you're going to be late, make sure you call home so your child won't panic.

▶ If your child can tell time, set an unwound clock to your return time and let her enjoy comparing this clock to one that moves.

▶ Have a colleague take a snapshot of you at work and let your child keep it with him at home or take it to the day-care center and refer to it whenever he needs a little reassurance.

▶ If problems continue, ask how you might improve things: "You seem to be very sad lately when I drop you off at school. What would help you feel better?" Allowing children to help make decisions often improves the situation tremendously.

▶ Finally, make sure to really take time out for your child when you are home. Set aside specific times just for your child as you would with a client or business associate. Start having "breakfast meetings" each morning so you can talk about the day's events. When your child comes home from school, sit down to really go over her papers and discuss what went on that day. While you are preparing dinner, let your child help or practice spelling and make up word games using magnetic letters on the refrigerator.

Keeping kids safe and happy

No child under the age of 9 or 10 should be left alone regularly, regardless of how independent he or she appears. For older kids, here are some guidelines:

▶ Plan with your child how the afterschool time will be spent. A reasonable schedule can create a routine that is helpful to kids. Be sure to include some free time.

▶ Be very clear about what you expect and permit.

▶ Keys should be worn on a chain, around the neck and tucked inside a shirt, pinned to the inside of a pocket or attached to a belt loop. Leave a duplicate key with a neighbor in case your child loses his.

▶ Instruct kids *never* to enter the house if a window's broken, the door is open or a light is on that wasn't on when they left. Tell them to go to a neighbor's house for help or call the police.

▶ Leave a welcome note on the refrigerator or a taped message to pop into a cassette player. Remind the child of appointments, chores, what snacks are in the kitchen. And let him or her know that you can't wait to be together again.

▶ Call home at a prearranged time or have another adult call or stop by.

▶ Be sure to leave the phone number where you can be reached and arrange for another adult to be available in case of emergency.

▶ Find out if there's a local "Help Line," "Call-a-Friend" or similar number that kids can dial if they need help with their homework or simply want to talk to a reassuring adult.

▶ Without frightening your children, teach them what to do in case of fire, injury, crime or other emergencies. Review procedures regularly. And, of course, tell them they should never open the door to a stranger or let a phone caller know they're home alone. The proper response: "My mother (or father) can't answer the door right now (or come to the phone). May I take a message?"

▶ Don't automatically prohibit visits by friends. Say that your child can have a friend over if they both agree to abide by what is and isn't permitted in your home and if it's all right with the other youngster's parents. (Let those parents know that you won't be home.) Emphasize that you are trusting your child and that school friends can come over again if everything works out well; if not, the privilege will be revoked.

▶ If you have two or more children at home, make it absolutely clear that you expect no fighting and no hitting. Discuss the limits of older siblings' power over younger ones. You might consider paying the oldest sibling to care for the others to professionalize the relationship during that time.

▶ Ask what the toughest part about coming home alone is and what can be done to make it better. It's important to encourage children to talk about their fears and then do whatever you can to eliminate them.

▶ Have after-school snacks on hand, such as fruits, veggies (washed and cut up, stored in a plastic bag in the fridge), granola, peanut butter and crackers, cheese cubes.

Coping with before-dinner turmoil

▶ Need time to unwind? Take an extra 5 or 10 minutes at work to relax at the end of the day. It's better to come home a little late than to arrive home upset.

▶ If possible, have help for that hectic time when you get home. Ask the babysitter to stay an extra half hour or hire a neighborhood teenager to provide diversion while you collect yourself and start dinner. If there is a mismatch between your need for solitude (or a shower) and your kids' need for some time, perhaps your spouse can play a game with the children while you take a break.

▶ If you've had a rotten day or are feeling exhausted, set up the kids with an activity and tell them you'll be back to hear what they've done after you've rested a few minutes.

▶ Ask the kids to set the table and cook with you. This way they can share your company and dinner gets ready faster.

▶ Plan your evening so that you and your spouse spend some time with each of the children. Let each child choose what you're going to do during your special time together— talk, read, play a game or whatever.

Goodbye game

▶ Your young children may not understand that when you go away on a business trip you *will* come back. To help them feel more secure, try making a game out of your travels: Get out road maps and atlases before your departure to show them where you will be and how you will get there. Mark your route on a map with yellow highlighter, using stick-on stars for where you will be staying, and hang the map up for them so that they can follow your trip while you're gone.

▶ Another way to make youngsters feel secure when you must travel for a short while is to leave them something of yours to take care of while you're away. Choose something your child particularly likes or associates with you—a favorite plant, a piece of clothing that has the scent of your cologne on it, a special book—and when you call in, ask your child how they are "taking care" of the object.

Easy Ways A Busy Mom And Dad Can Say "I Love You"

Do you often feel there just aren't enough hours in a day to love and pamper your kids? These quick but loving gestures will take just minutes of your time and they'll leave your child glowing all day long.

Morning affections

▶ Hang a sign on the bathroom mirror that says, "You're going to have a great day today! Love . . ." Or draw a picture of a smiling face. Put either greeting up before you go to sleep and your child will be happily surprised by it first thing in the morning.

▶ At breakfast, raise your orange-juice glass and make an unexpected toast to your child for being an overall great kid.

▶ Surprise your child with an occasional accessory for a favorite outfit. Say it's a present just because you love him or her. It doesn't have to be expensive. A pair of colored barrettes for a special dress or a tin sheriff's star for a favorite cowboy hat are two examples of thoughtful gifts that cost under a dollar.

Lunchtime lovings

▶ For a first or second grader, add a note along with the napkin that says, "I love you. Have a good day—Mommy." Your child will be delighted just knowing you're thinking about him or her.

▶ For an older child, try including a riddle with lunch. A new joke every day can easily make your child the hit of the lunchroom. For a practically endless supply of riddles, try some of the riddle books found in the children's section of the public library.

After-school forget-me-nots

▶ Put a star chart (a piece of construction paper with the words "You're special" will do) in your child's room. Keep various-size gummed colored stars in a bowl. When your child comes home from school, say you're so glad to see her that she can pick another star and add it to the star chart.

▶ Choose one weekend afternoon or evening to make a snack together that will last the whole week long. Each day your child eats the after-school snack, he will also have a reminder of the fun time you spent making it. Cookies, brownies or colorful gelatin squares are just a few of the quick snacks you can make together.

▶ Schedule your workload so that your child can help or be with you while you work. One parent, who had an office at home, set up a mini-desk right next to her own desk. When her son came home from school each day, he sat down at his desk. He thought he and his mother were playing a game even though she was doing her work and he was coloring.

▶ Buy some cardboard picture-frame mats. Save all your child's artwork for a month and then sit down together and choose one picture to be framed and hung just like the pictures in an art gallery. The "picture of the month" can be proudly displayed; "honorable mentions" can be taped to the refrigerator.

Bedtime love notes

▶ Buy your child a notebook that will become a special secret bedtime message book for the two of you. Each night, the notebook will be on the pillow. Before falling asleep, your child can write a question in it for you to answer. After he or she has fallen asleep, take the book, write the answer and then write a question for your child to answer the next night. Not only is this an excellent way to get a reluctant child to go to bed, it will also give you some very interesting insights into your child. Thoughts that might never come up in ordinary conversation may arise through this special bedtime book.

▶ If you're off to a PTA meeting or other evening activity, tape a goodnight message for your youngster to hear. It can be your evening prayer, a lullabye, a bedtime story or poem, or just a message saying "I love you."

7.
Good Times & Special Occasions

You're Invited
Special Days And Celebrations
Valentine's Day
Easter
Halloween
Thanksgiving
Christmas

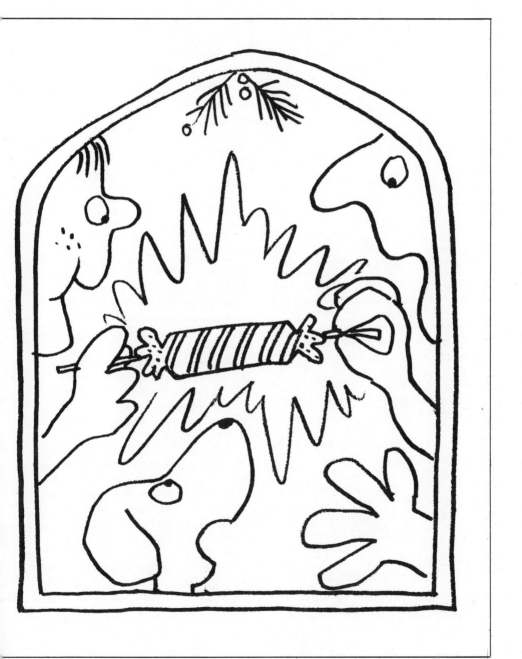

You're Invited

How to throw the perfect party? Sit back, read on — and let the good times roll!

Step-by-step party guide

This party planner will help space out your chores so you aren't too exhausted to enjoy your own get-together. Once you've decided how many people to invite and have planned your menu, it's time to make lists.

▶ List 1, Food: Include everything from snacks (mints and nuts) to "real" food (such as casseroles) and the ingredients needed for all recipes. Divide the list into two columns, non-perishables and perishables.

▶ List 2, Beverages: Liquor, mixers, juice, soda (have plenty on hand for nondrinkers), coffee, tea.

▶ List 3, Nonfood items: Cocktail napkins, plastic glasses, dripless candles, ice, flowers or centerpieces.

One week before:

▶ Order the ice, liquor and flowers.

▶ Shop for the nonperishable foods.

▶ Buy everything for List 3 except the ice and flowers.

Four days before:

▶ Select the serving dishes you'll use and set them aside in your cupboard. Need more? Ask a friend *now*.

▶ Check the tablecloths, napkins and place mats. Wash and press them, if necessary.

▶ Make sure you have enough silver, ashtrays, vases, pitchers, etc.

Three days before:

▶ Do the heavy cleaning, such as the floors and walls, and tidy up the house. Let the whole family pitch in.

▶ Decide where the guests' coats will go. If in a closet, have enough hangers on hand.

Two days before:

▶ Buy the perishables on List 1. Wash and trim the vegetables, and refrigerate.

One day before:

▶ Make extra ice, if needed.

▶ Prepare the dishes that can be reheated or served cold.

"The" day:

▶ Give the house a once-over in the morning. (If your bedroom is the coat room, neaten it *now*.)

▶ Pick up the flowers and ice.

▶ Use "kid power" to help clean. Set out ashtrays and guest soaps.

▶ Arrange the flowers and candles. Set up the eating areas and bar.

▶ Assemble the ingredients for the dishes that must be cooked that day.

Stocking the bar

▶ Set the bar *away* from the food to avoid traffic jams. If you don't have an extra pair of hands, serve the first drinks yourself and ask guests to help themselves later.

▶ To keep your budget intact, find out beforehand what your guests like to drink and buy accordingly. Most caterers recommend having Scotch, vodka, gin and blended whiskey, but you may be able to eliminate some of them.

▶ Be sure to have juices and sodas on hand for nondrinkers.

The party atmosphere

▶ Dim lighting encourages relaxed conversation, so use floor lamps and softer, pink-toned light bulbs.

▶ Place votive candles strategically around the room for a cozy feeling.

▶ Set the mood with music—use low-key classical, folk or jazz during cocktail hour and soft background music during dinner. After dessert, pick up the tempo with more lively sounds. Switch back to slower-paced music to end the party.

Icing up

▶ Allow about four cubes per drink or about 1½ lbs of ice per two to three drinks.

▶ Use blocks of ice to chill large bowls of punch and cracked ice for individual drinks.

Pretty table toppers

▶ Create visual excitement with color, texture and shapes. For a sit-down dinner, try different colored napkins and plates for each setting or mix patterned and solid-colored dinnerware.

▶ Great for a buffet table: Wrap silverware in napkins and tie with streamers.

▶ For unique centerpieces: Fill a pretty silver or glass bowl with tiny boxes wrapped in glossy paper and tied with ribbon, group crystal figurines on a mirror tile, set out fresh fruits on a gleaming silver tray.

Getting to know you

If you often have parties with guests who come from different backgrounds and occupations, and who do not know one another, break the ice with a Chinese dinner party. Guests are each given a cutting board and a knife when they arrive and are put to work chopping and cutting the various meats and vegetables that go into a Chinese meal. By the time all the preparations are done, everybody has shared a pleasant experience and gotten to know one another.

Brown-baggin' it

For an unusual invitation to a B.Y.O.B. party, print a description of the party on one side of a medium-size brown paper bag, such as "B.Y.O.B. in this bag!" Then, turning it over and folding it into thirds, write a guest's address on the outside, staple, stamp and mail it.

Easy marker

When hosting a club meeting or a party, tie a big, colorful bow onto a stake and place it at the end of your driveway. This makes it easy for everyone to locate your house. It's especially helpful at night, when house numbers are hard to see.

Balloon ice

Try this solution for keeping punch cold at a kid's party or an adult get-together. Fill balloons with water and blow them up a bit as you fill. Freeze them until party time, then float them in the punch bowl. They'll keep the liquid cold without watering it down and they'll add a colorful touch.

Thoughtful hostess

A "guest book" is a great help to a hostess. To keep one, index the pages of a notebook in alphabetical order, record the date of a visit and list the guest's likes and dislikes. If the guest returns at a later date, you can refer to the book in planning your menu and to brief yourself about his or her interests for a more enjoyable visit for both of you.

Family reunion payoff

At your next family reunion, why not hold a family auction. Ask everyone to contribute white elephants or homemade crafts, canned or baked goods. Put the proceeds in the family treasury to purchase food and beverages for next year's get-together.

The games people play

Game parties can be fun and a great way to break the ice. Follow these guidelines for a successful get-together.
▶ If you play a game that involves a special skill (drawing, spelling, etc.), try to team up players who form a balanced group.
▶ If you play a game that involves revealing morals or scruples, make sure you know the people well enough so that bad feelings will not arise from differing moral judgements.
▶ Keep an eye out for all your guests; make sure they're having a good time and feel comfortable playing whatever game is in progress.

Special Days And Celebrations

Anniversaries, bridal showers, baby showers, birthdays—here's how to make those occasions memorable as well as fun.

Freezer shower

Women with several children usually have all the "necessities" by the time the third or fourth baby comes along. It's still nice to be remembered when you're expecting, so give a pregnant mother a "Freezer Shower." Each guest brings a frozen casserole, packed in a disposable dish and labeled to indicate the contents and heating instructions. These are a great help after the latest baby arrives.

Shower favor

For practical and inexpensive favors for a baby shower, hand out old baby-food jars filled with pastel-colored candy. Wash the jars, remove the labels, decorate the lids in pink and blue felt, tie ribbon around the lips and glue plastic diaper pins on top.

Shower quilt

For a crib quilt that will be cherished for years to come, ask each guest at a baby shower to sign her name with colored sewing chalk in the middle of a small square of white cloth. Provide needles and embroidery floss and, during the party, ask each guest to embroider her name. Even those who don't know how to embroider can quickly learn to do a simple running stitch. After the shower, sew the squares together, alternating the white squares with calico squares.

A mother's best gift

As a present to a friend who has just had her second or third child, volunteer to take her older children out once a week. This gives her a chance to rest, catch up on housework or spend time alone with the baby.

Reusable baby shower centerpiece

For a baby shower, opt for a colorful and useful centerpiece instead of the usual flowers. Fill a small basket with baby notions, such as baby cream, shampoo, pins and thermometer. Decorate the basket with silk flowers and ribbons. The basket can go home with the expectant mother and become a handy caddy for her once the baby arrives.

Thoughtful gift

A personal and much appreciated shower gift is a packet of thank-you notes. Present a bride or expectant mother with a box of carefully selected thank-you cards, addressed to each of her shower guests in your best handwriting and affixed with a stamp.

Gift-giving solution

To make writing thank-you notes a breeze, write on the shower invitation: Please help out the bride-to-be by writing a description of your gift on the card.

Relatively speaking

Here's a great gift for a mother- or sister-in-law to give: a monthly calendar with notations of the names and birthdays of members of the bride-to-be's new family.

Mini toolbox

For a unique bridal-shower gift, make a mini toolbox from a black lunch pail, decorated with decals to match the bride's kitchen. Fill it with tools for the bride: a small hammer, pliers, screwdrivers, tape measure, thumbtacks, a package of screws and nails, masking tape and a paintbrush.

Anniversary special

Send a special package for a special anniversary: a photocopy of the front page of the newspaper on the couple's wedding day (get it from the library); a vintage record; a bottle of champagne and two crystal goblets; a money tree covered with crisp one-dollar bills (as many bills as years they have been married).

A year of parties

For an unusual first wedding anniversary present (paper), buy paper party items, such as plates, napkins, tablecloths for each holiday throughout the year—Halloween, Thanksgiving, Christmas, New Year's, Valentine's Day, St. Patrick's Day, Easter, Memorial Day, the Fourth of July and Labor Day. Your gift will be a year of parties. As a bonus, since you will have an entire year to collect these items, you will be able to buy most of them for half-price the day after the holiday.

Picture-perfect memories

A fun anniversary gift for good friends is to take photographs of the celebration with a Polaroid. At the end of the evening, present the anniversary couple with the instant album.

Anniversary quilt

Gather scraps of fabric from the anniversary couple's lives, such as a favorite shirt and dress, their child's baby blanket, wedding gown and bridesmaids dresses, tie, and make a patchwork memory quilt.

Traditional Anniversary Gifts

Anniversary/Gift		Anniversary/Gift	
1st	Paper	13th	Lace
2nd	Cotton, calico, straw	14th	Agate, ivory
3rd	Leather	15th	Glass, crystal
4th	Flowers, fruit, books, linen, silk	20th	China
5th	Wood	25th	Silver
6th	Sweets, iron	30th	Pearl, personal items
7th	Wool, copper, brass, bronze	35th	Coral, jade
8th	Bronze, pottery, rubber	40th	Ruby, garnet
9th	Pottery, willow, china, glass, crystal	45th	Sapphire
10th	Tin, aluminum	50th	Gold
11th	Steel	55th	Turquoise, emerald
12th	Silk, nylon, linen	60th	Diamond, gold
		75th	Diamond, gold

Photo finish

▶ Find a photo of the anniversary couple taken in their "courting" days; have it matted in a complimentary color and put it in a lovely frame.

▶ Make a collage depicting the anniversary couple's lives up to their marriage. Put photos starting with baby pictures, newspaper clippings, a high school sports letter or insignia; start putting Mom's mementos on the left, Dad's opposite and work in to their wedding picture crowning the center.

Party time!

▶ Have a "This Is Your Marriage" party and have surprise guests from the couple's past: Best Man and Maid of Honor, high school coach, college roommates, teachers, coworkers, etc.

▶ Recreate the couple's honeymoon. If they spent time in Hawaii, throw a luau; give the guests leis. If they went to the country, serve foods indigenous to the area, i.e. New England apple pie and Maine lobster. Encourage the guests to dress appropriately for the theme.

Gift acknowledgments

Writing thank-you notes for gifts—wedding, anniversary, birthday—can be a chore. It's a lot easier if you make each thank-you note a part of the festivities. As you open a gift, write out a note before going on to the next gift. Having the present in front of you will help you find something appropriate and special to say and, by the time all the gifts are opened, the chore of acknowledging will be over.

The perfect present

If you have to buy a gift for someone who is difficult to please, find a pretty bottle and insert the amount of money you had planned to spend on him or her. Attach a label, such as *In Case Of Emergency*, *Break Glass*, seal the bottle with colorful tape, wrap—and relax. Spice bottles work perfectly for this purpose.

Just desserts for the birthday dieter

Be a pal to that friend who's trying desperately to avoid sweets and make him or her a lean birthday fruit salad instead of the customary fattening birthday cake. Fill a large decorative bowl with a pleasing variety of cut-up fruits, squirt on a low-cal topping, add candle holders filled with small flowers and finish off with cherries and nuts arranged to form letters and numbers.

Kitchen keepsake

For a thoughtful gift, make a homemade recipe-and-helpful-hints book. Cover a photo album with white material and lace. Inside place favorite tried-and-proven recipes for desserts, side and main dishes, etc., and scatter household hints throughout the pages.

Remembering mama

Here's an idea to show your mother how special she is. Send flowers to her on *your* birthday—florist flowers, a garden bouquet, a silk arrangement—along with a short note or poem telling her how lucky you feel to be her son or daughter.

Gift certificate

If you have many relatives living halfway across the country, here's an idea to make gift buying easier. Starting a month or two in advance, write to the chamber of commerce in the city nearest to each relative and ask for the names of local restaurants and shopping centers. Then request information from selected places about gift certificates. Send a gift certificate for a restaurant to grandparents, for a bookstore to young adults and for a music store to teenagers. It's more personal than money.

Book dedication

A book is a wonderful gift made even more special when autographed by the author and dedicated to the recipient. With this in mind, attend "signature" parties in your area. Purchase the book with a specific friend or relative in mind and ask the author to sign it with a dedication to that person.

Birthstones and What They Signify

Month	Stone	Significance
January	Garnet	Constancy
February	Amethyst, Bloodstone	Sincerity
March	Aquamarine	Wisdom
April	Diamond	Innocence
May	Emerald, Moonstone, Alexandrite	Love
June	Pearl	Wealth
July	Ruby, Sardonyx	Freedom
August	Peridot	Friendship
September	Sapphire, Tourmaline	Truth
October	Opal	Hope
November	Topaz, Zircon, Lapis Lazuli	Loyalty
December	Turquoise	Success

Birth Flower Chart

Month	Flower	Month	Flower
January	Carnation	July	Larkspur
February	Violet	August	Gladiolus
March	Jonquil	September	Lavender
April	Sweet pea	October	Aster
May	Daisy	November	Chrysanthemum
June	Rose	December	Holly

Valentine's Day

Show someone you love him or her with these light-hearted suggestions.

Valentine tradition

You can make Valentine's Day breakfast special by using red food coloring to dye milk and pancake batter. Use seasonal cookie cutters to shape the pancakes, too.

Gifts that melt his heart

▶ A single red rose, sent to his office.

▶ A personal ad in the paper, telling him how special he is.

▶ A manual back massager, with a promise of a massage.

▶ A beautifully wrapped box with lacy lingerie inside—which *you'll* wear that evening.

▶ A bottle of champagne, with two fluted glasses.

▶ Calling up a radio station and dedicating "your song" to him.

▶ Tickets to watch his favorite team play.

▶ A night in a hotel—the best room you can afford.

Mail greeting

Did you know that Valentine's Day cards can be sent to the Postmaster of Valentines, VA 23887-9998, for a special stamp and greeting? Send a batch of your valentines—address and stamp each one—in an envelope large enough to hold them all, to the Valentines Post Office. Be sure to enclose a note telling the postmaster that you want a Valentines postmark. As many as 25,000 valentines are mailed from there each year.

Say it with flowers

Did you know that flowers have different romantic meanings? This year, present your special someone with the flower that best expresses your sentiments. *Gardenia:* I secretly love you. *Lily-of-the-valley:* Let's make up. *Rose:* I love you passionately. *Sweet William:* You are gallant and suave. *Violet:* I return your love . . . And *green leaves* stand for hope in a love affair!

Easter

These fresh ideas are a wonderful way to celebrate Easter and the arrival of spring.

Easter bonnets

▶ To delight a girl, trim a straw bonnet with brightly colored ribbons. Make small bows with several colors of narrow (⅜-inch) ribbon. Tack them to the crown of the hat with matching thread or pins.

▶ For Mom, trim a wide-brimmed straw bonnet with a garland of dried and/or fabric flowers glued to a ribbon band. Add trailing ribbon streamers for a lovely old-fashioned effect. The hat can be hung as a wall or door decoration as well.

Easter Garden

As a thoughtful gift at Easter time, present that special someone with a living Easter garden. Choose colorful spring flowers such as tulips, crocuses, daffodils and violets. They can be already in bloom, or if he or she enjoys gardening, you can simply give them the bulbs in a decorative basket, wrapped in pastel-colored cellophane.

Meaningful celebration

For an unusual Easter egg hunt, use plastic eggs and fill some with candies, others with coins and special ones with quotations from the Bible, which you read aloud together after the hunt. The activity becomes meaningful as well as fun for all the family members.

Preparing eggs for decorating

Use only fresh, clean, unbroken eggs.

▶ **To hard-cook eggs:** Place the eggs in a single layer in a saucepan; add cool tap water to cover the eggs by one inch. Heat to almost boiling and simmer, without boiling, for 10 minutes. Remove the eggs with a slotted spoon to a bowl of cold water for five minutes. Refrigerate the eggs *immediately* and use within one week. Hard-cooked eggs can be removed from the fridge and left at room temperature for up to two hours.

▶ **To empty eggshells:** Pierce the pointed end of an egg with a large, sterilized needle. Then make a bigger hole (¼-inch) at the rounder end. Carefully move the needle around inside the egg to break the yolk.

Holding the egg over a bowl, blow through the smaller hole until the egg is empty. Rinse out the shell thoroughly and let dry.

Sharing the fun

For a change, surprise grandparents with Easter baskets filled with goodies collected especially for them: small puzzle books, packets of seeds, herbal teas, recipes, blank tapes, bookmarks, magnifiers, candies and pocket-size pill totes.

Cupcake nests

To make cupcake "nests," cover cupcakes with lemon frosting. Let the kids roll them in coconut and set jelly bean "eggs" on top.

Easter tree

Make a special Easter tree for children who come to visit. Put a wrapped piece of gum or candy in a small plastic bag and place the bag inside a colorful plastic egg. Double over a piece of yarn and tape the loop to the egg. Hang the egg on a branch of an indoor tree or on a leafless branch stuck into a bucket of sand or a pot. Each child gets to select a surprise as he or she comes in the door.

Surprise packages

Instead of a basket, have the Easter bunny bring a useful goodie holder: backpacks, tackle boxes, bicycle baskets, lunch boxes, a Superhero helmet or a doll case. These fun containers, bought at a discount store, are often less expensive than baskets and your children will feel that the Easter bunny considers them extra special.

Eggs-tra fun

For some old-fashioned fun, have a traditional egg hunt. Get a group of families and friends together. Choose a date and location (preferably adjoining yards, someone has to hide all the eggs). You'll need about 100 eggs per 10 children, plus prizes, such as chocolate bunnies, nuts, storybooks. Use a combination of hard-cooked decorated eggs and plastic ones filled with jelly beans and assorted candies. Decorate the shells with nontoxic markers, stencils, and stickers or use the kits available at your local store. On the day of the hunt, hide the eggs outdoors on the property. Divide the children into groups according to age. The child who finds the most eggs within an allotted time wins the prize for his or her group. Follow up with a pot-luck party for the whole gathering. *Note:* Hard-cooked eggs should not be outside for more than two hours.

An elegant Easter

For a special Easter centerpiece, make an Elegant Easter Egg Tree. Dye unboiled eggs different colors. Make a small hole at the top and bottom of the eggs and carefully blow the insides into a bowl (use the eggs for your Easter delicacies). Decorate the colored eggs with ribbons, sequins, buttons, lace— anything you wish. Find a nicely shaped small branch without too many twigs. Spray paint it gold or silver and secure it to a mount painted to match it. Hang the eggs on the tree and you have a lovely and lasting Easter centerpiece. *Note:* Keep the egg carton to store your ornaments in.

Halloween

October 31—it's the scariest night of the year. Here's how to give your kids thrills and chills, safely.

Witches' brew: devilishly good drink for kids

Combine 2 quarts of chilled apple cider and 1 container (6 ounces) of frozen grape juice concentrate, thawed, in a 5- to 6-quart punch bowl. Scoop out 1 pint of orange sherbet and float it on top of the punch. Add 1 chilled bottle (33.8 ounces) of ginger ale. Stir gently to combine the ingredients and make the top look frothy. Makes about 20 servings.

Throw a haunted house party

▶ Have it in a basement, family room or den; someplace you can decorate without worrying about breakage or mess. Replace the regular bulbs with black lightbulbs.

▶ Hang cardboard bats and ghosts from the ceiling and place "cobweb" material (sold at variety stores) in the doorways. Tuck a skeleton in a dark doorway or closet. Touch up store-bought decorations with glow-in-the-dark paint to make them more spooky.

▶ Play a spooky record; Walt Disney's "Chilling Thrilling Sounds of the Haunted House" is a good one.

▶ Have the children plunge their hands into concealed containers of peeled grapes ("lizard's eyes"), cold spaghetti ("demon's brains") and soup bones ("from a skeleton").

▶ Shake hands with "The Thing": An adult stands in a closet with a bowl of semi-solid gelatin. As each child knocks, "The Thing" extends his gelatin-coated hand. For a more gruesome effect, tint the hand with green makeup.

▶ Create a "ghost tunnel" by covering two card tables with white sheets and have the kids crawl through. Hang furry critters and streamers under the tables so the children will feel these tickle their faces as they crawl.

▶ Afterward, listen to the haunted house album and have the kids name the sounds. Then watch a home video—*Frankenstein* or *The Legend of Sleepy Hollow*. **Note:** Some children frighten easily, so use your discretion.

Pizza face

Outline a store-bought frozen pizza with halved, pitted black olives. Use strips of sweet red pepper for the eyes, nose and mouth, sweet green pepper for the eyebrows and stem. Brush the vegetables with olive oil and bake according to directions. Easy and nutritious!

Party game

Give each child a colorful paper plate and let him or her choose from a selection of trimmings (paper cups, yarn, ribbon, pompoms, felt-tip pens) to create a paper-plate character. Give prizes for the funniest, prettiest, ugliest, scariest—enough so each child wins something.

Painted face

Instead of a mask, complete your child's costume by painting on a face. It's simple and fun to do with nontoxic makeup kits. You can even get accessories, such as vampire's fangs, to complete the disguise. For extra fun, the kids can paint each other!

Not so buried treasure

No diving or digging required—this treasure is inside a crepe paper ball that's made to be pulled apart. To create one, you need dimestore trinkets, tissue paper and lots of streamer crepe paper. (Use orange for a jack-o'-lantern, black for a cat, white for a ghost.) Place a handful of toys into tissue paper and wad it into a tight ball. Wind crepe paper around the base as you would a ball of yarn. Periodically insert more trinkets. Glue on a construction-paper face. When the kids get their hands on it, the treasures will fly out in a flurry!

Pumpkin "put-ons" with no carving

Even little kids can get in on these pumpkin decorations because you don't use a knife—just whatever materials you have at home.

▶ **Paint it:** Use neon-colored poster paints to draw a sad, happy or even scary face.

▶ **Glitz it:** Pin on sequins, glue on glitter or add glamour with a gauzy scarf.

▶ **Paper it:** Cut face shapes out of construction or tissue paper: black for eyelashes, a 3-D triangle nose.

▶ **Dress it:** Wrap a pumpkin in a scarf, add yarn hair and set it on sneakers to look like Humpty Dumpty. Or create "Groucho" with fake fur eyebrows and moustache.

▶ **Button it:** Oval, square, glass and novelty buttons give distinct "pumpkin personalities."

Jack-o'-lantern

Make a safe jack-o'-lantern for your children for Halloween. Instead of a candle, use a flashlight to light up the features. Cut a hole in the bottom of the pumpkin and insert a small pocket flashlight. The children can safely light their own pumpkin this way.

Apple treats

When you make caramel or candied apples, add "features" while the apples are still sticky. *Eyes:* M&Ms, gumdrops. *Nose:* candy corn, jelly bean. *Mouth:* candied fruit, mini-marshmallows, candy corn (fangs). *Hair:* licorice, coconut flakes. *Extras:* paper witch's hat or "Dracula" cape, Dixie cup cap for a clown.

Safety tips

▶ Make sure children can walk in their costumes without entangling their feet.

▶ Use light colors, decals or reflective tape on costumes and bags for better visibility. At night, a flashlight is a must.

▶ Since masks may obscure vision, face makeup is recommended.

▶ Be certain young ones are accompanied by an adult. A good ratio is one adult to four children.

▶ Give older children (those who trick-or-treat without an adult) coins and tell them to call if there is a problem or if they'll be late.

▶ Instruct children to walk on sidewalks, not streets. If there are no sidewalks, walk on the left side of the road, *facing* traffic.

▶ Have kids save their candy so it can be checked. Parents should examine *all* treats. Report anything suspicious to the police.

Ten things to give instead of candy

You don't have to hand out candy when the doorbell rings! Try these alternatives.

▶ Stickers, bought in sheets or rolls, scented or plain.

▶ Tickets to a movie to be shown on your VCR.

▶ Bright new pennies wrapped in shiny foil.

▶ Coupons from fast-food or ice-cream chains.

▶ Novelty items, such as funny eraser tops or pencil sharpeners.

▶ A 3 x 5-inch memo pad with a colored pencil taped on.

▶ Balloons.

▶ Plastic combs, bought in family packs.

▶ Mini boxes of raisins.

▶ Rubber creepy-crawlies.

Thanksgiving

Making Thanksgiving dinner shouldn't leave you too exhausted to enjoy it. Here's help to make your holiday truly a day of thanks.

Duty roster

If you are used to working alone in the kitchen, having a "gang" eager to "help" on Thanksgiving can really throw you for a loop. To simplify matters, sit down and compose a "duty roster." Let Grandmother butter and sugar the cake, the men carve the turkey and carry chairs. Include special directions—where to find the correct dishes, what ingredients to add.

Set a harvest table

For Thanksgiving dinner, set a homey "harvest" table. Work with decorations from nature, such as a bright pumpkin, nuts and gourds. Add autumnlike touches with leaves (you can buy artificial ones) and plaid place mats.

Napkin trick

For a fun touch, try a no-sew bow-tie napkin. Gather the napkin in the middle with a napkin ring and fan out the sides. Set it above the plate.

Plan ahead

To start, write out your menu, including the time it takes to prepare and cook each dish.

Two days before:
▶ Buy the perishables.
▶ Make the fruitcup (if you're serving it) and store it in the refrigerator. Trim the vegetables; store them in plastic bags in the refrigerator.

One day before:
▶ Bake the pies.
▶ Wash and dry the salad ingredients; refrigerate them.
▶ Set the table.
▶ Assemble the serving dishes and utensils in the kitchen.
▶ Prepare the stuffing ingredients; store dry and liquid ingredients separately in the refrigerator.

The day:
▶ Note the specific times to: make the stuffing, stuff the bird, put the bird into the oven, prepare and cook the vegetables, side dishes, first courses, salads, relishes and breads.

▶ Check that you have enough top burners to accommodate your pots. *For dieting tips on how to cope with holiday dinners, see page 246.*

Turkey Talk

Everything you need to know to make the perfect holiday turkey.

Storing

▶ **Fresh turkeys:** Refrigerate them at all times. Cook them within one to two days of purchase.

▶ **Frozen whole turkeys:** Store them in their original wrapper for up to 12 months at 0° F. or lower.

Thawing

Conventional (long) method:

▶ Thawing time: three to four days, about 24 hours for each five pounds of whole frozen turkey.

▶ Leave the turkey in its original wrapper.

▶ Place the frozen turkey on a tray in the refrigerator.

Cold Water (short) method:

▶ Thawing time: about 30 minutes per pound of whole frozen turkey.

▶ Leave the turkey in its original wrapper.

▶ Place the turkey in a sink or large pan.

▶ Completely cover it with cold water.

▶ Change the water every 30 minutes.

▶ Keep the turkey immersed in cold water at all times.

Note: Never thaw a turkey at room temperature. Once thawed, cook or refrigerate it immediately.

Stuffing

▶ When? Just before you roast your turkey is the time to stuff it. You run the risk of food poisoning if you do this earlier.

▶ How much? Allow ¾ cup stuffing per pound of bird for turkeys weighing more than 10 pounds, ½ cup stuffing per pound for smaller birds. *Note: Never* freeze stuffing that is in a cooked or raw bird. Remove all the stuffing from a cooked bird, wrap it separately and refrigerate it.

Timetable for Roasting Turkey (325°)

Bird Weight (pounds)	Stuffed (hours)	Unstuffed (hours)
6 to 8	3 to 3½	2½ to 3½
8 to 12	3½ to 4½	3 to 4
12 to 16	4 to 5	3½ to 4½
16 to 20	4½ to 5½	4 to 5
20 to 24	5 to 6½	4½ to 5½

Testing for doneness

▶ A meat thermometer inserted in the meatiest part of the thigh reads 180° F. to 185° F.

▶ The turkey juices run clear.

▶ The drumsticks move up and down easily.

Resting period

Let the turkey stand at room temperature for 20 minutes. This allows the juices to settle and the meat to firm up for easier carving.

Christmas

Sparkling spruce-ups. Last-minute gifts. Wonderful wrappings. Budgetwise advice. We've got a bundle of tips that will help you capture the spirit of the season—and make this Christmas your best one ever!

Decking the Halls

There are so many ways to bring Christmas to every corner of your home—these are just a few.

Candle magic

Gather up an assortment of thin tapers, standard-size candles and jumbos in various sizes. Roll each one in a hot towel to soften the wax and then in silver or gold glitter. Put the candles in your favorite holders and create a festive grouping on the mantel, an entry table or in the dining room. Add some greens, fresh or artificial, light the candles and you'll have a dazzling display.

Christmas in the bath

Why neglect the bathroom? Put out red and green hand towels you've trimmed with plaid ribbon; light a cinnamon-scented candle.

Kitchen cheer

▶ Heap pretty mixing bowls with glossy wooden red apples, sprigs of greenery and some pine cones.

▶ Another easy way to dress up your kitchen: put red, green and white pastas in glass storage jars and tie the knobs on the jar tops with ribbon. After the holidays, you can cook up a colorful plateful of pasta for dinner!

No muss, no fuss fireplace

A glowing fire in the fireplace is a winter treat. However, cleaning out the ashes the next day is no treat at all. Before you build a fire, remove the grate, line the bottom of the fireplace with a double layer of heavy-duty aluminum foil and replace the grate. As the fire burns, it not only reflects more heat from the foil but gives a much brighter, cheerier glow. When the ashes are cold, remove the grate again, roll up the foil and dispose of it.

Pillow presents

You can decorate pillows to look like presents just waiting to be opened. Handstitch ribbon in gift-bow patterns onto solid color velvet pillows. The fancier the ribbon the better, so look for lavish lacy plaids, candy stripes and satins.

Rosy wreath

Bright red roses turn a standard evergreen wreath into an unusual decoration. Choose between fresh flowers placed in water-filled plastic tubes and artificial blooms. Finish the wreath with pine cones and fluttery ribbon streamers.

Tabletop trees

▶ Make a pretty tree by folding layers of 4-inch pieces of ribbon and sticking them with straight pins into a 15-inch styrofoam cone.

▶ For a contemporary decor, make geometric trees by rolling gift wrap into cones, taping them and topping each with a small ball ornament.

Easy hang-ups

To hang holiday decorations on metal front and back doors without attaching permanent hooks, hot-glue large magnets on the backs of decorative items to hold them in place. Make wreaths on lightweight cardboard, cover them with colorful fabric, stuff them lightly with quilt batting and trim with lace, ribbon and silk flowers. The wreaths are held securely on doors by the large magnets and can be used indoors or out. At other times of the year make valentine hearts, Easter rabbits, etc. in the same way.

Fade no more

To keep cardboard window decorations for Halloween, Thanksgiving, Christmas and so on from fading and bending, cover them with clear plastic self-adhesive paper. It keeps the decorations clean and protected, and they can easily be wiped off and used again next year.

Old into new

You can redecorate glass Christmas tree ornaments by washing off the outside paint with a mild mixture of ammonia and water and spraying them with gloss enamel paint. After the ornaments dry, paint on the names of family members.

Snowflakes to frame

Panels of lace (like giant snowflakes) lend an old-time holiday air to any room. Cut the panels from inexpensive lace-by-the-yard and place them on green or red backgrounds in plastic box frames.

Quick touches of cheer

Give your home a warm and inviting look that says "Christmas"—quick and easy.

▶ Make plants look extra-special at Christmas by grouping them together in a straw basket that you've painted bright red.

▶ Decorate your front door like a Christmas package. Trim it with wide ribbon; add a bow, dried flowers and vines.

▶ Hang stockings along the mantel, up the staircase, on a towel bar, on the bathroom shower rod.

▶ Scent your rooms by filling bowls or baskets with cinnamon sticks, anise stars and cloves.

▶ Decorate serving trays with sprays of pine and cherry tomatoes. *Note:* Do *not* use holly—it's poisonous.

▶ Fill a silver or glass platter with Christmas balls and strings of white lights for an instant centerpiece.

▶ Tie red ribbon around the necks of vases and lamp shades.

▶ Set two miniature Christmas trees on either side of your front door with welcome signs on them.

▶ Fill an old-fashioned milk can with bunches of tree twigs sprayed with gold glitter.

▶ Bring out forgotten items from the attic—a sled, wooden shovel, pitchfork—tie them with bows and use them as foyer or fireplace dress-ups.

Window trims

▶ Transform a window into a frosty winter wonderland with paper doilies. Cut doilies into snowflake shapes and glue them (with removable glue) to an inside window.

▶ Line up a row of evergreen plants along a radiator cover or windowsill. Decorate with strings of twinkling lights and spray snow.

▶ Tie back draperies with a rope of evergreens.

▶ Drape pine garlands, wrapped with Christmas lights, around each window.

▶ Arrange sprays of evergreen along the length of windowsills; add Christmas balls, artificial berries and three-dimensional ornaments (angels, tin soldiers, Santas).

▶ For a delightful way to dress up a window in a jiffy, hang cookie cutters from bright red ribbons, using ornament hooks.

The Lights of Christmas

What would Christmas be without sparkling lights inside and outside your home? Shine safely with these tips.

Outdoor lighting tips

▶ Try floodlighting evergreens for dramatic effect. Stick to blue, green, clear white and deluxe white mercury lamps; these enhance the colors of evergreens. Avoid red, yellow, amber and pink, which turn the trees a muddy brown color.

▶ Illuminate deciduous trees as well as evergreens. Flood a tree to highlight its shape and pattern with a single spotlight. Or place shiny ornaments in the tree and light it from below with several smaller spots.

▶ Get more sparkle and glitter with transparent bulbs. Unlike color-coated bulbs, they allow the filament to show through.

▶ Set up your display at night, when you can see the effects of your illumination. You can't get the true overall picture in daylight.

Safety pointers

▶ Check your light sets for cracked insulation, frayed wires or damaged sockets. Any one of these could cause short circuits.

▶ Don't overload your string sets. Check the instructions on the package to find out how many light sets can be connected to each other.

▶ Avoid overloading circuits. Most home circuits can take 15 amps, or 1,800 watts.

▶ Cover each outdoor plug and connector joint with plastic wrap to protect it from rain, sleet and snow; seal it with electrical tape.

▶ If you use staples instead of tape to secure lights, be sure that they're *insulated* staples.

▶ Make sure that decorations pose no danger to children or pets. Don't leave cords dangling or strung loosely on the floor or stairs.

O' Christmas Tree

The highlight of a beautiful Christmas is a beautiful tree.

Tree talk

▶ Douglas firs are the most popular trees. Dark to bluish-green in color, they are noted for graceful branching and excellent needle retention. They are also the most fragrant.

▶ Norway spruces, the second favorite, are dark green with somewhat pendulous branches and moderate needle retention.

▶ Scotch pine trees are blue- or gray-green with needles up to three inches long and excellent retention.

▶ Colorado blue spruces are green to silvery-blue with inch-long needles and good retention.

▶ White pine trees are green or bluish green with flexible branches and excellent needle retention.

Want a tree you can plant?

▶ Choose a tree that isn't more than four feet tall and has fresh, not brittle, needles with signs of new growth. Also be sure you have a pot or sturdy box in which you can place it in your home.

▶ Keep the tree well watered while in the house and try not to keep it indoors for more than four or five days.

▶ Before planting, place the tree in a garage or cold basement for a day or two to gradually accustom it to the cold.

▶ If you can't plant it until spring because the ground is frozen, place the tree outdoors surrounded by a 6- to 12-inch layer of mulch. It should be located near the house or in the shelter of other trees. Be sure to plant it when the ground thaws.

Tree buying pointers

▶ If you're planning to place your tree in a corner, keep in mind that it doesn't have to be perfectly shaped.

▶ Decide in advance what height tree you need. If you have to buy a tree taller than you need, shorten it from the bottom, *not* the top. Chopping off the top will cause the tree to dry out and lose needles quickly.

▶ Before you buy, shake or bounce the tree lightly on the ground. If only a few needles fall off, you'll know the tree is quite fresh.

Once you get the tree home

▶ Until you are ready to trim it, store the tree outside in a sheltered area or cold garage. Also be sure that the trunk is cut diagonally and the tree placed in a bucket of water.

▶ Water the tree daily once it's brought indoors. A 6- to 7-foot tree needs one to two quarts of water a day.

▶ To get the most fragrance from your tree, find all the sap pockets on the trunk and break them.

For the tree

▶ Make your own interesting Christmas tree decorations from old, empty wooden thread spools. Paint them to look like small drums.

▶ Don't keep your collection of silver baby spoons, souvenir spoons from trips and demitasse spoons languishing tarnished in a drawer. Polish them up and tie them with red curling ribbon onto your Christmas tree. They make a beautiful and meaningful holiday decoration.

▶ Short on tinsel? Turn gift tie ribbons into tinsel in a jiffy. Cut 1½ yards of four colors. Holding the strands together, make a small bow at the middle. Using scissors, curl the streamers at the ends only. Open a paper clip and slip one point through the knot behind the bow. To save them for next year, store them in a long box that keeps the streamers from being crushed.

A Christmas dowry

Every year, make or buy a special ornament for each of your children. When the children grow up and establish their own homes, each will take along a box filled not only with ornaments, but with love and memories with which to decorate their first Christmas tree.

Tree-trimming guidelines

Tree Height	No. of Miniature Light Bulbs	Garland	Ornaments
2'	35 - 40	24' x 2"	15
3'	70 - 80	30' x 2"	24
4'	100-120	48' x 2-3"	36
6'	200-240	72' x 3"	48
7'	240-320	84' x 3-4"	72
8'	320-360	96' x 3-4"	96

Holiday bows

To spruce up bows for your Christmas tree that have been stored and crushed, insert a rolled up towel into the loops and press each loop with a warm iron.

"Facelift" for ornaments

To perk up frayed satin-covered Christmas tree decorations, gently push the loose threads back into place and lightly mist them with hairspray.

The Wish List

We surveyed kids and adults across the U.S.A. for the presents they loved best. And surprise! Heading almost everyone's list were gifts that require a little imagination — but not too much time or money!

Something for everyone

For kids:

▶ A recording of their most-requested fairytales—in your voice.

▶ A book to keep stickers in.

▶ A poster of a favorite rock star.

For teens:

▶ Ten "coupons" that excuse them from one chore a day.

▶ A promise for them to have a sleepover party on a specified date.

▶ Permission to use the car for a certain number of times.

For him:

▶ Something romantic: a bundle of twigs (fireplace kindling) wired with bright ribbon. Attach instant hot chocolate packets to the ends!

▶ A good book, or subscription to a special-interest magazine.

For friends:

▶ The tastiest homemade cookies you can make—with the recipe.

▶ A gift certificate for personal services, such as baby-sitting or chauffering.

▶ Beauty treats at a local salon: facial, massage, manicure or pedicure.

Christmas wishes

A month before Christmas, take your children to a toy shop and give them each a pad and pencil. Set a time limit, then instruct them to look around and write down several items they would like Santa to bring them. Take the lists home and send a letter to Santa with their requests. With this method, you can save time, avoid buying unwanted items and the children will be pleased to see that most of their wishes are fulfilled.

Gifts of Giving

Believe it or not, there are many wonderful and inexpensive gifts you can give without feeling like Scrooge. These "Santa-approved" presents are readily available and can speak volumes from your heart.

Romantic dinner for two

Whip up a batch of homemade spaghetti sauce and put it in a plastic container. Combine with a box of pasta, small bottle of red wine and a loaf of bread. Present it in a colorful shopping bag tied with ribbon. (Be sure your friends open it right away!)

Christmas in spring

If you would like to give presents from your garden but the weather in your area of the country prohibits it, give little cards reading, "Good for 6 delphiniums, 12 petunias . . . " and so on. In February or March, consult your gift list and start these presents growing in your garden.

Thoughtful gift-giving

Include your own "care labels" with the sweaters you knit as Christmas presents for family and friends. Cut heart-shaped labels and attach the care instructions from the yarn band, some strands of yarn for repairs and extra buttons.

Garage sale Christmas

If you never seem to have enough money to buy Christmas gifts for your friends, try this: Shop at garage sales all year round. Whenever you spot something you know your friends will like, buy it. When the holidays approach, gift-wrap these "used treasures," get together with your friends and exchange your garage sale goodies.

Bags full of love

A special yet affordable Christmas gift for older children to give their younger sister or brother: With colored markers, a few stickers and a lot of love and patience, they can decorate lunch bags with rainbows, unicorns and flowers, favorite cartoon heros or adventures, incorporating the younger child's name into each design. The little ones will be delighted and proud to show off their big sister's or brother's artwork at school each day.

Green-thumb gift

Depending on the price, give two or three baby plants wrapped in red or green tinfoil, along with care instructions and a small bottle of plant food.

A mix of mustards

Gift-box an assortment of imported French, German, English and Chinese mustards for the gourmet cook on your gift list.

Scrapbook starter set

Great for kids who love collecting memorabilia: Wrap up a plain scrapbook, glue, some fun stickers and photo mounting corners.

Cosmetic travel tote

Buy an inexpensive plastic cosmetic case and fill it with practical sample-size shampoos and lotions.

Mad for muffins?

A thoughtful hostess gift is a muffin pan accompanied by three small-size blueberry, corn and bran muffin mixes. Why not wrap it in a colorful dish towel?

Photographed with love

Are you a good photographer? Try this last-minute idea. Gift wrap an inexpensive 8 x 10-inch frame and attach a note promising to take—and enlarge—an adorable photo of a friend's son or daughter.

Yuletide wine wish

Select an out-of-the-ordinary wine for under $5 and top it off with a written toast for a happy holiday.

A busy cook's casserole

An ideal present for someone who has no time to cook: Give a casserole dish with three of your no-fail quick recipes. Or promise to fill it with two dinners in the next two months.

Be my guest for breakfast

For a co-worker, wrap up a mug and a box of tea biscuits with a note promising to buy morning coffee or tea for the week. What a nice way to start the day!

At-home manicure kit

Give a "nail-conscious" friend a pampering collection that includes a bottle of her favorite nail polish, emery boards, nail polish remover and a fragrant hand lotion.

Merry outing for a youngster

Treat your favorite child to tickets to the local zoo or amusement park. Wrap the tickets with a handwritten invitation to take the child on a Saturday afternoon of his or her choosing.

Holiday hair-care potpourri

Any young girl would enjoy a gift of pretty barrettes and combs for her hair. Complete by wrapping a colorful assortment in a bright bandana or pretty scarf.

Wonderful Wrappings

Don't panic when you run out of wrapping paper. The house is full of things to use.

Brown-bag it

You know all those brown paper grocery bags you have stashed under the sink to use eventually for the trash? Turn them over to your resident artists (the kids) to decorate with holiday drawings. Then drop a gift in each bag and tie with pretty ribbon or yarn. Or punch a couple of holes at the top on each side and knot ribbons through for handles.

Bandana it

They're colorful, inexpensive and make a jiffy wrap for smaller gifts. Knot the bandanna ends and you've got two gifts in one. For larger presents, make a "Santa Sack" using pieces of fabric in red, green or a seasonal print. Pull up the edges, tie with yarn and trim with pinking shears.

Basket it

Buy baskets at the dime store for a dollar, fill and tie with a bow. Basketable items include: breakfast treats (jams, teas, muffins), party snacks (cheese, pâté, crackers, cocktail napkins), fresh fruit, bath accessories, pine cones for sweet-smelling kindling.

Bottle it

Many grocery and cosmetic products come in attractive bottles. Instead of tossing them, wash them in hot, sudsy water and refill with Christmas gifts— potpourri, bath salts, Christmas candy, spices, coffee beans, your homemade spaghetti sauce. A bow at the neck and it's wrapped!

Try other clever paper substitutes

▶ Wrap a magazine subscription card in the cover of an old issue.

▶ Point your favorite jogger in the right direction with a map of the city; tie with a pair of shoelaces.

▶ Fancy up plain brown paper with gold cord and a First Prize blue ribbon.

▶ Strike the right note with sheet music for a record or concert tickets.

▶ Ask your child to draw a picture—this wrapping gets raves from Grandma!

▶ Decorate colored tissue paper with stickers for a youngster's gift.

▶ Turn on the holiday glow with wine bottles wrapped in aluminum foil; put confetti inside the foil and tie with paper streamers.

▶ Use a travel poster for someone on the go.

▶ Appeal to a lawyer with a blank legal form; close with gold notary seals. Try graph paper for an architect or engineer.

▶ Wrap up with your local newspaper. Make kids laugh with the comics; top with lollipops. Give a crossword buff a clue with the puzzle page; trim with pencil and eraser. Put a new homeowner's gift inside the real estate ads. Impress a businessperson with the stock market pages (or *The Wall Street Journal*). Top with a bag of chocolate gold coins.

Party Tips

If you have a party during the holidays, make it the easy-does-it kind.

Dessert party

Instead of serving a 4-course dinner, bake one cake from mix, brew one pot of coffee and invite a small group for a fireside get together or a VCR showing of a holiday film.

Make-your-own-sandwich party

▶ You provide the fixings plus paper plates, and your guests take it from there.

▶ Serve beverages with ice cubes shaped like trees and stars—it's a real "ice-breaker!"

Holiday fun party

This could be a caroling, ice-skating or gift-wrapping get-together. Afterward treat everyone to hot cocoa and warm cider, along with chestnuts roasted over the fire, freshly made popcorn or soft pretzels kept toasty on a warming tray.

A thoughtful touch

If you host a holiday buffet each year, why not share your recipes with the guests? On individual sheets of paper, type up all the recipes you will be serving and make photocopies of them. Roll them into "scrolls" and tie each with a red or green ribbon for a festive touch. Place them in a basket near the buffet table so that anyone who "just has to have" the recipe for a dish can take home a "scroll."

A Child's Christmas

Keep your little ones safe and happy through the holiday.

To keep kids busy at Christmas

▶ Buy prepasted, colored strips of paper at a crafts store. Children can make chains of colorful loops to wind around the tree.

▶ Let children cut out pictures from last year's Christmas cards to make this year's gift tags. A hole punch and yarn complete each tag.

▶ "Commission" Christmas drawings for specific spots—over the fireplace, in the front hall. Then cut a frame out of cardboard and let your child color it. She'll glow with pride whenever you point out her custom-made decoration to a visitor.

▶ Give children some prepackaged silver garlands to wrap around banisters or anything else you'd like trimmed. Secure them at each end with tape.

▶ Children can make holiday place cards out of folded construction paper and napkin rings from cut rounds of cardboard paper-towel rolls. Decorate them with strips of aluminum foil, crayons or colorful ribbons.

▶ For some no-hassle tree ornaments: let the kids cut out "snowflakes" from inexpensive paper lace doilies; pin colored pipe cleaners or fabric scraps to styrofoam balls.

▶ Little ones can trim their own tree if you cut a tree outline from paper or felt and tape it to the wall. Let them create ornaments from paper, yarn etc. and tape or glue them to the tree.

▶ Make up a "guest box" for young visitors with art supplies, games, books. Present it on their arrival.

▶ Staple plain paper together in book form for kids to write their own Christmas story.

▶ Have a decoration contest using small styrofoam shapes, such as balls, plus sequins, felt and gold stars. Give a prize for the best snowman, face, tree trim.

Toddler-proof your holiday home

Many favorite Christmas decorations are too fragile, poisonous or simply dangerous to have around young children. However, you can still give your home a festive look safely.

▶ Keep as many decorations as possible out of your children's reach and establish firm limits about what they can and cannot touch.

▶ Place toxic holiday plants, such as mistletoe and holly, safely out of reach.

▶ Instead of using angel hair, tinsel and glitter, which can be dangerous, try fabric, paper and wooden decorations. Don't forget edibles such as popcorn strands and candy canes.

▶ Suspend your glass ornaments from the ceiling above the tree with fishing line.

▶ Move a breakable crèche scene to the mantel and on the hearth place a straw basket filled with safe-to-handle pine cones and wooden apples.

▶ Buy a small "children's tree" and let the kids decorate it with paper chains and ornaments they make themselves. Letting them rearrange their tree now and then might discourage them from fooling around with the family tree.

The Christmas Book

To preserve your fondest Christmas memories, keep a "Christmas Book." Use a loose-leaf binder covered with Christmas fabric. In it put the children's letters to Santa, a brief description of what you did to celebrate and ideas for future Christmases.

Decorative treats

If you have candy canes left over when you take down your Christmas tree, hang the individually wrapped treats outside on the lowest branches of the trees around your house. The red-striped canes add a bit of color to the winter landscape and will be a treat for the neighborhood children on the way home from school.

Photo opportunity

Christmas trees and other holiday decorations have sprung up all over the shopping malls by the time Thanksgiving arrives. Why not take advantage of such beautiful backgrounds? Photograph your children in their "Sunday best" and you will have up-to-the-minute pictures to enclose with your holiday greeting cards for relatives and friends. You may even find a shot that's suitable for a photo greeting card.

A Budget-Happy Holiday

You can have a beautiful Christmas without going over your budget. Here's how!

Keep a running list of your expenditures

That way you'll know how well you're sticking to your budget, and you'll also be able to check bills for accuracy.

Ways to avoid overspending at Christmas

▶ Prepare a complete Christmas budget. Besides gifts, include entertaining, decorating and even party clothes.

▶ Make a list of everyone for whom you wish to buy presents. Could you make or do something for the person instead?

▶ Write an appropriate price range next to each name on your gift list. If the total is too high, revise your figures. When shopping, *never* exceed the limits you've set for yourself.

▶ Review credit card bills to see how much more you can afford to charge.

▶ Before you buy something on time, figure out how much interest you'll pay. It might be better to buy a less expensive gift and pay cash.

▶ Carry only one or two credit cards with you. Otherwise, you may think you're not spending much because the total on each card is fairly small.

▶ Wrap each credit card in a piece of paper. Every time you use the card, write down how much you're charging. Keep a running total.

▶ For unique presents at bargain prices, shop at church bazaars, garage sales and arts and crafts stores.

▶ Don't push yourself to finish shopping if you're tired. When you're exhausted, you are inclined to buy almost anything, even if it's expensive, just to get home and relax.

▶ Realize that your children will survive just fine, even if they don't get all the "must-have" toys of the season.

▶ Don't buy something just because the payment terms are easy. Eventually, you still have to pay the full cost of the item *plus* the interest.

▶ At sales, pick up "generic" presents that can be given to anyone: a basket, vase, bowl, even gourmet jam. Then you won't overspend in a last-minute panic.

▶ Consider whether you could exchange Christmas cards instead of gifts with some people. Suggest it tactfully; you may find they are delighted to have saved money themselves.

▶ Think about how much you spend on entertaining. Your warmth and caring make your party special; lavish spreads and liquors are not essential.

▶ Begin shopping in January for next Christmas. You can take advantage of sales and never have huge bills.

▶ Join a Christmas Savings Club or open a special bank account that pays more interest, into which you put money each month. Next year, you'll have the money for the gifts you want.

Holiday survival tips

▶ As early as possible, have a family meeting and set up a plan of action. Draw up a master "to do" list and divide the responsibilities— shopping, cooking and baking, wrapping presents, addressing cards—among all family members.

▶ Get the whole family to help plan the gift list. Even little ones can come up with terrific suggestions.

▶ Begin shopping as soon as possible. If you can, take off a day from work so you needn't shop on your lunch hour or at other times when the stores are crowded.

▶ Let older kids select gifts for their own friends. When you take them shopping, set time and money limits and do some shopping of your own.

▶ When planning your holiday schedule, figure out how many invitations you can accept without feeling overcommitted.

▶ Plan a shared pot-luck holiday dinner with family or friends. Repeat the same meal each year and you can start a nice—and simple—tradition.

▶ If you have brothers and sisters, take turns having Christmas dinner at a different home each year. This way no family has to assume the responsibility or expense of entertaining a large group all the time.

Practical exchange

When you have Christmas cards of the same design left over from the year before, exchange them with a friend or relative for their leftover cards. This way you will have "new" cards to send next Christmas.

Making shopping simpler

▶ Avoid the crowds. In big cities, shop very early or very late, never at lunchtime or just after work. In the suburbs, you'll do better between the hours of 10 A.M. and noon, and 2 to 5 P.M.

▶ Skip the busiest departments: accessories (belts, scarves, jewelry), men's shirts and sweaters, women's departments, toys and tree trimmings. If you can think up some imaginative gifts to buy in stationery or sporting goods, you'll save a lot of time.

▶ Consider preboxed, wrapped gifts. Departments that frequently display these time-savers are housewares, cosmetics, china and glassware.

▶ Try armchair shopping. You can stay home and still give imaginative gifts such as magazine subscriptions, tickets for the theater, ballet or circus and gift certificates from department stores, bookstore chains, salons, supermarkets or restaurants. For faraway loved ones, give a long distance call certificate (1-800-GIFT-ATT).

A valuable hint

At Christmastime, keep a 3 x 5-inch file box handy to safely file all receipts for gifts you have purchased, noting the receipts on the backs. If anyone wants to return or exchange a gift, you can easily find the sales slip!

8.
Vacation
And
Travel

Safe Fun In The Sun
Before You Leave
Pack It Up
Beauty On The Move
Traveling Tips
In The Driver's Seat
Single File: Traveling Alone

Safe Fun In The Sun

Keep your summer days action-packed and accident-free by following this smart advice.

Sunburn relief

Pain, swelling and peeling are reduced most effectively if you start treatment at the first signs of sunburn. Take two aspirin tablets every four hours to reduce inflammation and ease pain. Dissolve ½ cup baking soda in a lukewarm bath and soak for 15 to 20 minutes, or apply cool compresses soaked in 1 part milk to 3 parts water (proteins in milk soothe the skin and draw out heat). If your eyelids are swollen or burned, place cold-water compresses or cold, moist teabags over closed lids and relax for 20 minutes or so. After the skin cools down, gently smooth on a moisturizer (those containing aloe are especially soothing). Don't apply heavy cream or oil to the skin; it may trap heat. Should severe swelling and chills with high fever develop, see a doctor.

Sun sense

▶ Wear a sunscreen with a high SPF (sun protection factor) whenever you go outdoors. Apply a thin layer and repeat to avoid red burn splotches from missed spots. Pay careful attention to protecting areas particularly vulnerable to sun and to skin cancer: the nose, cheeks, hands and tops of ears.

▶ If you have a fair complexion or light-colored hair or eyes, or if you don't tan easily, wear a sunscreen with a #15 SPF and avoid passive sunbathing.

▶ Never use baby oil as a suntan lotion and avoid deep-tanning oils with a low SPF.

▶ Sun exposure while using certain products causes some people to have a photosensitive reaction: severe sunburn, rash or uneven skin pigmentation. Possible culprits are certain antibiotics, diuretics, tranquilizers, birth control pills, antihypertensives (check with your doctor or pharmacist), diet drinks containing saccharin, fragrances with citrus oils or oil of bergamot and antibacterial soaps. *Note:* Some people get a photosensitive reaction from alcohol-based sunscreens. If this happens to you, switch to a creamy, nonalcohol lotion. PABA (para-aminobenzoic acid, part of the vitamin B complex) can also cause a photosensitive reaction in some people. They should use a sunscreen with the active ingredient "benzophenone" on the label.

▶ Wear a lip sunblock (#15 SPF) on and around the lips and never sunbathe when you have a cold sore.

▶ Chronic long-term sun exposure without eye protection may damage the eyes and contribute to the formation of certain types of cataracts. Protect your eyes by wearing optical-quality sunglasses that screen out most of the sun's ultraviolet and infrared rays during peak sunlight hours (11 A.M. to 2 P.M.).

▶ Don't shave or use depilatories or other hair removers just before sun exposure or swimming. Shave at least 24 hours before or after exposure to avoid skin irritation.

▶ After sunning or swimming, slather a light moisturizing lotion all over freshly washed skin to replenish moisture and prevent peeling.

▶ Protect oily or acne-prone skin with a sunscreen formulated for oily skin. Choose a creamy, moisturizing sunscreen for dry skin.

▶ While in the sun, protect hair from dryness and other damage by wearing a brimmed hat (straw, ideally, as it allows cooling ventilation).

Children's skin-savers

▶ Use #15 sunscreen on your child. Apply it before he or she goes outside; re-apply it every 60 to 80 minutes and after swimming. Since children are in the water so much, dermatologists strongly recommend using a waterproof product.

▶ Cover delicate areas of the skin—the scalp, ears, nose, hands, shoulders and neck—with sunblock. Don't forget to tie a bonnet on a baby's head.

▶ Before using any sun protection product, do a patch test on the inside of your child's forearm.

Beware the heat!

▶ If your body is not acclimated, overexertion in hot weather sets you up for heat exhaustion (dizziness, nausea, weakness, hot skin and profuse sweating) and dehydration (weakness and cramps in the stomach or thighs). In either case, go indoors or rest in the shade. Take sips of cold water and splash cool water liberally on your skin.

▶ Overexertion after heat exhaustion can lead to heatstroke, a malfunction in the body's temperature regulating system characterized by high fever with hot, dry skin, dizziness, severe headache and even collapse and coma. (Sunstroke, with the same symptoms, is caused by direct and prolonged exposure to the sun.) To aid a person suffering from heatstroke, call for emergency medical help and, while waiting, put the victim in a cool bath or sponge him or her with cold water.

▶ To combat heat illness, avoid overexposure to the sun and be sensible about exercising in heat. Be particularly prudent about physical exertion in temperatures of 90° or days with more than 90% humidity. Drink plenty of plain water and eat lightly salted foods (if you're not restricted) to replace body fluids and salt lost through perspiration.

How to guard against insects

▶ Because mosquitoes are attracted to hot, sweaty skin, wear lightweight, airy clothing made of natural fibers. This helps draw perspiration away from the body. Always wear shoes and socks outdoors at night. Mosquitoes are most active during this time and zero in on the ankles and feet.

▶ Avoid using any fragrance, including scented deodorants, moisturizers and hair products, because they attract insects, too.

▶ You can mix insect repellent and sunscreen without altering their effectiveness as long as you let one dry for 5 to 10 minutes before applying the other.

▶ For optimum protection against insect bites, spray your skin with a repellent containing the active ingredient DEET (Diethyl toluamide). Another option is to take 100 mg of thiamine (a B-complex vitamin); it causes you to secrete an odor that is a turn-off to insects.

Itch relief

For relief from mosquito or black-fly bites, try using regular underarm deodorant. Rub it right across the bite for instant relief.

Removing a stinger

If you're stung by a wasp, hornet or bee and the stinger is imbedded in your skin, don't try to scrape or pull it out. The venom-filled bulb attached to the protruding end will release more poison if pressure is applied. To remove the stinger: Using your fingernail, gently slide the bulb away from the skin until you can grasp the "needle" of the stinger with tweezers and pull it out. Clean the skin and immediately apply ice to reduce swelling. An antihistamine will help reduce swelling, too. If you experience severe swelling or breathing problems, seek emergency medical treatment because, in rare cases, an allergic reaction to insect venom can be life-threatening. If you *know* you're allergic to insect venom, always carry an insect sting emergency kit with you when spending time outdoors.

Removing a tick

Ticks attach themselves to the skin. Apply alcohol or a hot sterilized needle to the back of a tick. When it loosens its grip, remove it with tweezers.

Poison ivy

If you come in contact with poison ivy, immediately wash your hands, change and wash your clothes and shoes, then bathe with warm water and an antibacterial or mild laundry soap. If you develop a mild rash, use cool compresses to ease swelling and dab on calamine lotion to dry blisters. For more severe rashes, apply an over-the-counter hydrocortisone cream. To soothe itchy skin, apply a paste of 3 parts baking soda to 1 part water. Let it dry and wash it off. Although poison ivy is not contagious once its sap is washed from the skin and clothes, scratching may spread the inflammation to the surrounding skin.

Water safety

▶ Swim only in areas supervised by a lifeguard. Unsupervised, unfamiliar areas are likely to be dangerous.

▶ Wait 20 minutes between eating a normal amount of food and swimming. Remember, the bigger the meal, the longer you should wait. Eating a light snack prior to swimming is safe.

▶ Never drink alcohol before swimming or engaging in any water sports.

▶ Dive only in designated areas, never into shallow or unknown waters.

▶ At the ocean, be cautious of step-offs—holes in the sand that create a sudden drop from shallow to deep water.

If you feel you are drowning

Don't panic. Float on your back or do survival floating: Lie face down in the water and, using a hands-and-feet motion, lift your head to get a breath. Put your face down again. Repeat until you feel relaxed enough to swim to shore or signal for help. When caught in weeds or debris, don't struggle; you may get further entangled. Move your arms and legs in brisk, sharp, chopping movements until you break clear. If you're caught in an ocean current, swim across the current and parallel to the shore for 15 to 20 yards until you're out of the current's pull. Then swim to shore. Don't swim against a current—you'll use energy needed to reach the shore. If you can't get out of a current, swim with it or float on your back. The current will probably dissipate within 50 to 100 yards and then you can swim in. Should you develop a cramp, tread water or float on your back while you stretch the cramped muscle.

To help a drowning person

▶ Look for a lifeguard or anyone else who might help you. Never attempt a rescue in water over your head unless you're a trained lifesaver. A drowning person could drag you under as well.

▶ If the person is within reach, hold out a stick, oar or paddle, form a human chain to grasp and draw him in, or throw a float and swim out to pull the float back in with the person hanging on.

▶ Should the person you rescue not be breathing, give mouth-to-mouth resuscitation: Clear the person's throat of any obstruction, tilt the head back and raise the chin. Look, listen and feel for breathing for five seconds. If breathing doesn't start, pinch the nostrils closed, inhale and make a tight seal over the victim's mouth with your mouth. Blow four quick, full breaths into the victim's mouth to inflate the lungs, watch the chest and listen for breathing. Repeat with one breath every five seconds for adults, one every three seconds for children. Call for emergency help.

Storm warning

Lightning strikes people most frequently in summer. For safety, follow these precautions.

▶ If you are outdoors when a thunderstorm hits, run for cover—into a house, a closed hardtop car or any large shelter. Stay clear of windows and doors and avoid small structures such as a woodshed.

▶ If it's too late to run for cover, stay close to the ground. Don't stand under tall, isolated objects such as a tree or telephone pole. Also avoid water. If you're on a boat, head for shore.

▶ Stay away from all metal objects, including fishing rods, machinery, wire fences, railroad tracks, bicycles, motorcycles and clotheslines.

▶ If you see someone get struck by lightning, call an ambulance if possible. If emergency help is not available and if the victim is not breathing, try mouth-to-mouth resuscitation. *For directions to give mouth-to-mouth resuscitation, see page 175.*

Pest-free picnics

Sites near lakes, ponds and rivers are where insect populations flourish, particularly after a rain. Picnicking in a dry, open area, away from water, means fewer insects.

▶ Place domed covers over food.

▶ Use pale-colored picnic baskets, utensils and tablecloths. Bright colors attract bugs.

▶ Eat and store food off the ground, on a table.

▶ Reduce the risk of an insect invasion by excluding from your picnic fruits that have a very high sugar content (especially grapes and melons), tuna and other high-scented fish and meats, sweet fruit drinks and desserts. Substitute milder-scented foods: vegetables, meats like ham and turkey, nonsmelly cheeses, apples, and pears, dry low-sugar snacks like pretzels, chips and nuts, drinks like iced tea and seltzer.

▶ Keep all foods in sealed containers or in self-sealing plastic bags to mask the odors.

▶ Mix 1 cup sugar and ½ teaspoon carbaryl (an insecticide available at garden centers) with sufficient water to form a thin syrup. Divide the syrup into a few pie tins placed away from but surrounding your picnic area. The pests will be more attracted to the sweet syrup than to your goodies. Or mix the sugar and water into a paste. Insects will feed on this but may still stray over to your picnic.

▶ Citronella candles emit a sharp odor that repels all types of insects. If you're picnicking at a table, place the candles on the table and under it as well. The scent rises and prevents mosquitoes from biting your legs.

Food safety

▶ Bacteria that cause food poisoning thrive in hot weather. To keep barbecue and picnic foods free from harmful bacteria, remember two things: Keep hot foods hot, serving them as soon as possible, and keep cold foods cold.

▶ Use insulated chests or thermal containers stocked with plenty of ice or sealed packs of coolant to keep picnic foods cold.

▶ Watch the dates on perishable products.

▶ Pack raw meats and poultry, salad mixtures and foods containing dairy products and eggs close to the ice.

▶ Contrary to popular belief, it is not the mayonnaise in sandwiches and salads that encourages food spoilage, but the foods you mix with it that carry bacteria. Keep mayonnaise mixtures cold.

▶ Leftover picnic food should be thrown out unless it has been continuously refrigerated.

▶ Never taste any food that looks or smells bad. Throw it out—most likely it's already spoiled.

Barbecues

▶ Always use grills outdoors.
▶ Never use gasoline or kerosene to start a charcoal fire. Use a commercially prepared firestarter or a UL (Underwriters' Laboratory) approved electric firestarter. Read and follow the manufacturer's instructions carefully.
▶ Never squirt lighter fluid on a smoldering fire to revive it. It could cause dangerous flare-ups. Instead, moisten a few pieces of charcoal separately with lighter fluid and carefully add them to the grill one at a time.
▶ Keep a bucket filled with sand nearby to smother flames that grow too big.
▶ Dispose of ashes carefully by dousing them with water, stirring and dousing them again.

Cars

▶ Never leave children or animals locked in a closed car, even for a brief time with the windows rolled down a bit. In summer, a car's interior temperature can rise to 120° within 15 minutes.
▶ Keep a 1-gallon container of water in the trunk for emergencies.
▶ If your car overheats, turn off the air conditioner, roll down the windows and turn on the heater to draw heat away from the engine.
▶ If the engine is steaming, turn on the car's emergency flashers and pull over to the side or shoulder of the road.
▶ Warning: Never unscrew the radiator cap when the engine is overheated. Wait for it to cool—about 30 minutes—and use a towel or cloth to unscrew the cap. Remember to turn your face away to avoid any escaping steam.
▶ Add water, as needed, to the radiator. Replace the cap and close it tightly.
▶ If your car has an air-cooled engine, simply pull off the road and allow the engine to cool down—about 30 minutes.
▶ Stop at the next service station to have your car checked for the cause of the overheating.

Insect protection

Spray the hood and grill of your car with nonstick vegetable oil cooking spray. The bugs will wash off easily and the car's finish won't be damaged.

Bicycles

▶ Make sure your bicycle is the right size for you. You should be able to straddle it comfortably with both feet flat on the ground. When you're riding, the ball of your foot should rest on the pedal and your knees should be slightly bent when the pedal is at its lowest point.
▶ Always ride on the right side of the road, moving *with* the traffic. Watch out for car doors that may open suddenly.
▶ Obey all traffic signs and signals.
▶ Walk bicycles across crosswalks and intersections.
▶ Use hand signals whenever you plan to change direction, slow down or stop.
▶ Ride single file when riding in groups.
▶ Equip bicycle pedals, wheels and the back and front fenders with reflectors for increased visibility at night.
▶ Always wear a safety helmet.

Fireworks

▶ Always read the manufacturer's directions before using fireworks.

▶ All legal fireworks include the words "Class C Common Fireworks" on the item or package label, the name of the particular firework, the name and address of the manufacturer and easy-to-read instructions for proper use. If these do not appear, the item may have been made illegally and could be dangerous.

▶ Avoid any firework that is leaking powder, looks old or shows signs of mishandling.

▶ Always use fireworks outdoors and keep a bucket of water nearby to douse any flames.

▶ Aim fireworks away from others.

▶ Never attempt to reignite malfunctioning fireworks.

▶ Never set off fireworks in metal or glass containers.

Easy to find

To help your children locate your spot on the beach, tie a few colorful balloons around the end spokes of your beach umbrella and a big one on the very top.

A cool idea

Sprinklers aren't just for grass and kids. When you can't get to the beach, put on your swimsuit, stretch out on a plastic chaise and let the spray refresh you.

No fuss, no muss

For thirsty kids around the house in the summer, clean and rinse small plastic bottles with twist-off caps and fill them with your children's favorite drinks. Everybody can help themselves and spills from full pitchers are avoided.

Ant barrier

To prevent ants from invading your child's playpen when it is outside, fill small containers, such as paper cups or jar lids, with water and place one under each playpen leg.

Letters home

To insure receiving letters from children away from home during the summer, let them design their own stationery on a plain, white 8½ x 11½-inch sheet of paper. They can draw borders, use fancy lettering, etc. Then photocopy the letterhead on their choice of colored paper. (The cost is small.) When you pack, be sure to include stamped envelopes. Your children won't be able to wait to use their own "brand" of stationery.

Tackling tar

Soap and water are fine for dirt and sand, but tar on bare feet is a bigger challenge. A little mineral oil on a cotton ball, applied to the tar stain with light pressure, does the trick.

Before You Leave

To insure a worry-free trip, a checklist of things to do before you go.

Alert the police

Be sure to notify the local police and leave a phone number where you can be reached in case of emergency.

Lights on!

Lock the doors and windows, but leave the shades up and the lights on or on an automatic timer.

Prep the house

Remove the food and defrost the refrigerator; store valuables in a safe place; disconnect electrical appliances; turn off all gas jets, including the hot water heater; turn off the water faucets and drain pipes in severe weather.

Pack personal gear

Remember to pack personal medicines and duplicate prescriptions, spare eyeglasses or the prescription, sunglasses, suntan lotion, a First Aid kit, insect spray, paper toweling and tissues, writing materials.

Get ready for the road

Make sure that proof of car insurance is in your glove compartment. Take along your driver's license and those of other passengers (check the expiration dates), the automobile registration, copies of birth certificates (if driving outside the U.S.) and traveler's checks. Be sure you bring a duplicate set of car keys with you.

Emergency precautions

▶ Check to see that you have a jack, spare tire, repair kit, emergency tools, flashlights, tire chains, spare fan belt, windshield scraper, auto fuses, lug wrench and work gloves. A pretrip tune-up won't hurt. Of course, be sure to "fill up" before you start out.
▶ Also check your vehicle's battery, oil and air filters, cooling system, brakes and lights.

Safety first

Buckle up your seat belt and have a good trip!

Pack It Up

You can put together a great go-anywhere wardrobe and pack it without wrinkling— all in one small suitcase.

Build a base for your clothes

▶ Pack heavy items, such as shoes and a blow-dryer, on the bottom flush with the hinged side. That way, when you carry the bag, the items won't slide and wrinkle clothes.

▶ Put jewelry into socks or stockings and tuck them into shoes. Place shoes toe-to-heel and slip them into a protective bag.

▶ Roll soft clothes, such as lingerie, and use them to cover the remaining bottom of the bag.

Interfold to prevent wrinkles

Close all buttons, zippers and snaps. Fold dresses, skirts and slacks lengthwise along their natural creaselines.

▶ Drape each garment across the suitcase, placing the top of one flush right, then one flush left. Let excess fabric hang out over the sides.

▶ Lay blouses and jackets front down with the collar toward the hinged side and the sleeves hanging out. Smooth wrinkles as you go.

Cushion folds and fill spaces

▶ Place sweaters and scarves on top of separates.

▶ Fold back ends that are hanging out, alternating from right to left, smoothing wrinkles as you go. Fasten the tie tapes. Stuff empty spaces with accessories or tissue paper. A firmly packed bag keeps clothes from sliding and wrinkling. Extra tip: To steam out light wrinkles, hang clothes in the bathroom while you shower.

How to decide what to pack

▶ Get organized. The week before your trip, check the weather reports. Then make a packing list, using your itinerary to help you figure out the very least you can get away with. A few days before your trip, put your travel clothes aside in the closet and try subtracting one or two pieces each day. As you pack, take one last, hard look at what you've selected and eliminate everything you don't absolutely need.

▶ Take mix 'n' match separates. Keep your basic pieces all in one color scheme—say, two solid, neutral colors. You can spark them up with bright, patterned accessories. Once you've decided on your colors, pick classic shapes in lightweight fabrics and layer them over each other in different ways to go from daytime to evening. A good rule of thumb: If one piece doesn't work with at least three others, leave it behind. Remember to include what you're wearing on the plane in your total wardrobe. For instance, if you're traveling in a jacket, blouse and slacks, you should pack a skirt, sweater, dress and another blouse.

▶ Plan your fabrics. The experts recommend high-quality natural fibers and synthetic blends such as knits and jerseys. They're soft and never wrinkle. For a crisper look, try lightweight gabardine; it can be worn in all but the hottest weather. Look for labels that say "wash and wear" or "drip dry."

▶ Bring a lot of accessories. Belts, scarves and jewelry take up hardly any room and give a multitude of looks. Limit your shoes to walking shoes, dressy heels and daytime pumps. If you're taking boots, wear them to save space. Carry a shoulder bag and pack a clutch.

Smart tip

When going on a trip, pack one of your outfits in your spouse's suitcase and have him or her pack a change of clothes in yours. If one bag is lost or delayed in transit, you'll both have something fresh to wear upon arrival. Or, put one lightweight change of clothes in your carry-on.

20 Things not to forget

☐ travel alarm clock
☐ small sewing kit
☐ pocket calculator
☐ travel hairdryer
☐ adapter plugs
☐ prescriptions
☐ travel umbrella
☐ nylon raincoat
☐ plastic bags
☐ clothespins
☐ hunting/fishing licenses
☐ bathing suits
☐ Swiss army knife
☐ eyeglasses
☐ small fold-up tote
☐ travel diary
☐ guidebook/maps
☐ writing supplies
☐ laundry detergent
☐ exercise gear
☐ cosmetics/mirror
☐ official papers
☐ portable radio
☐ camera/film
☐ picnic accessories

A sweet idea

If you'll be traveling for any length of time, slip a sachet into your suitcase; it keeps your clothes smelling fresh and sweet.

Check it out

When you're packing your suitcase, make a list of the contents and tape it inside the lid. Before you leave the hotel, check your list. Do you have everything? With this method you'll never leave anything behind again.

Laundry solutions

▶ When you're traveling, tuck a few medium-size plastic garbage bags into your suitcases to hold dirty laundry. This will keep your unworn clothing fresh and the bags can be emptied right into your washer upon return.

▶ Always remember to bring a few self-sealing plastic bags to hold damp bathing suits or washcloths.

▶ Laundry can be a bother on a trip but washing out underwear and quick-dry clothing can be a real space saver. So bring along some mild detergent in small plastic bottles (or in convenient pre-packaged envelopes) for your hand washables.

▶ Pack a few sheets of an "anti-cling" fabric softener that you usually toss in the dryer. They're practically weightless but, when added to rinse water, tame handwashables with ease.

All hung up

▶ Spring-type clothespins come in handy on a trip. You can use them to hang hand washed clothes to dry, or make instant skirt and pants hangers by clipping them onto the hangers most hotels and motels provide.

▶ When only wire hangers are available in your hotel room, try putting two or three together to hold heavy coats or dresses. This way the hangers won't bend or sag from the weight of the garments.

Shoe talk

Place shoes inside plastic bags to guard against soiling clothes. Then put them and other heavy items against the hinges of the suitcase so they don't shift and crush clothes and accessories.

Beauty On The Move

Check our rundown on what toiletries and cosmetics to take and how to pack them safely.

Packing toiletries

▶ When buying essential toiletries, such as toothpaste, deodorant and moisturizer, choose the smallest sizes available. Or tuck away the "ends" of toothpaste, deodorant and shampoo for travel use.

▶ Buy lightweight plastic containers in the drugstore; label and fill them with just the right amount of shampoo, conditioner, moisturizer, body lotion and astringent for your trip.

▶ Save or send away for free samples of products to use when traveling.

▶ Pick products that travel well, such as stick deodorants, solid fragrance sticks and pressed powder.

Makeup

▶ On vacations, keep makeup simple. Limit your routine to the bare essentials: a light foundation, translucent powder, blusher, one or two lipsticks, a neutral-colored eye shadow—try brown or gray—and black mascara. If you'll be working on your suntan, bring along a darker foundation for use later in the trip.

▶ Pack makeup in a tote or your handbag, not in your suitcase. If products spill or leak, they won't stain your clothing.

▶ To cut back on what you take, choose cosmetics that do more than one job. Some of the handiest are: a foundation or lipstick with a built-in sunscreen, a body shampoo you can also use on your hair. A small tube of petroleum jelly goes a long way as a great hand cream; as a moisturizer and gloss for lips; and as a conditioner for lashes. It's even a wonderful makeup remover!

▶ Airplane cabin air can be drying. Carry a small bottle of moisturizer in your purse for air travel. Smooth some on in midflight or spritz your face with water.

▶ To keep loose face powder from spilling when traveling, put it in an empty, well-cleaned spice bottle with a shaker top.

▶ Bring along diluted alcohol, witch hazel or alcohol-based skin freshener. Not only do these products remove dirt and oil from skin, they can help dry unexpected blemishes and ease the sting of insect bites or sunburn.

▶ Simplify nail care. Use a clear polish that won't show chips. Better yet, buff nails to a healthy glow.

▶ Leave your bottle of nail polish remover at home. Instead, pack a few foil-wrapped towelettes saturated in remover.

▶ An orangewood stick doesn't take up much room and is the perfect tool to help keep your unpolished fingernails clean and pretty.

▶ For hair emergencies, pack a selection of colorful barrettes, combs, ribbons and headbands. If hair goes limp, you can pin it back in an attractive style. Barrettes and combs can also hold and style wet hair prettily as it dries.

▶ Don't forget a tweezer. It will keep your brows neat and is ideal for removing splinters.

▶ Pack a handful of cotton swabs and cotton balls. Use swabs to apply and blend eye makeup; they're great for cleaning up smudges, too. Cotton balls are perfect little puffs to dab on translucent powder, swish freshener over your face or perk up makeup.

▶ To lighten your cosmetics case when traveling: Moisten cotton pads with eye-makeup remover and astringent, and pack them in small plastic sandwich bags.

▶ Never travel without a first-aid kit. Things to include: aspirin, medicated cream, antiseptic, antacid, adhesive bandages and any prescription medicine you may require.

What to leave at home

▶ Anything that's breakable. (If possible, transfer the necessary contents to a tube.)

▶ Aerosol cans that can explode under pressure or in extreme heat.

▶ Eye pencils or lipsticks with loose tops.

▶ New brands of cosmetics or toiletries you haven't tried before. A skin rash or other allergic reaction can ruin a long-awaited trip.

Traveling posts

Tiny earrings for pierced ears are easily lost during travel, when you are living out of a suitcase. Poke your favorites through the lining pocket inside the lid of your travel bag or case. Not only will they stay put, they will be easy to spot when it's necessary to make a quick change.

Traveling Tips

From how much to give your bellhop to the memories you bring back—have a great trip with these tips.

How much to tip?

When you check into a hotel, it's often difficult to determine whom, when and how much to tip. Here are some helpful guidelines.

▶ Doorman: Fifty cents for hailing a cab, $1 for help with baggage. No tip is necessary if he simply opens the door to the hotel or to a cab.

▶ Bellhop: Fifty cents per bag, or $1 per bag if there are several heavy bags.

▶ Room Service: Fifteen percent of the bill, even if there is a service charge.

▶ Maid: One dollar per room per day, to be left at the end of your stay.

▶ There's no rule that states you must leave a tip if you've been poorly treated, but good service deserves to be rewarded.

Safe car ride do's and don'ts

▶ Don't leave sharp or heavy objects loose in the car. A sudden stop or collision could turn them into lethal weapons.

▶ Do lock all car doors and teach children not to play with door handles or locks.

▶ Don't permit children to put hands or heads out of windows.

▶ Don't allow a child to suck on a lollipop while riding.

▶ Do set a good example by buckling up each time you ride.

▶ Don't leave a child alone in the car—even for a few moments.

▶ Do insist that children always use safety belts, even when they're riding in *someone else's* car.

▶ Do have children sit in the back seat whenever possible.

For tips on gasoline economy, see page 69.

Pet safety

When traveling with a pet, bring a small thermos filled with ice cubes. A few cubes put in the water dish make good "licking" and melt into cool water with no mess.

Trip tips

▶ A small surprise given to a child near the end of the day helps encourage good behavior and can also help pass the time during the last hour of traveling. Crayons or a small book would be good selections.

▶ Dress your child in comfortable clothing. Take along any favorite stuffed animals.

▶ Stop every two or three hours to let youngsters run off excess energy and use the rest room.

▶ Bring along a thermos of water.

▶ Car games help pass the time.

Travel gamesmanship

▶ When traveling by car, space is limited so your children may not be able to bring along their favorite toys. Instead, give each a notebook and pencil and encourage them to make note of all state license plates and animals they see, play old-fashioned paper games, like tic-tac-toe and hangman, and try to draw some of the scenery they pass.

▶ Another good idea: Use a felt pen to trace your youngsters' favorite board games onto a piece of stiff interfacing and roll it to fit neatly in a small bag. Take along another piece of interfacing so that the kids can make up their own game. Use an empty, plastic towelettes box to hold crayons, markers, dice and other game-playing pieces.

The better to see you with

A pair of binoculars can be a lifesaver on a long trip. It is great for reading road signs at a distance, which gives the driver plenty of time to get into the correct lane safely. It also is wonderful for keeping a fidgety child busy looking at points of interest, birds, humorous license plates and bumper stickers.

Traveling pillows

Taking along everyone's pillow in the car when traveling uses up too much space. Instead, make small pillows from an old white sheet and polyester stuffing. For the cases, use remnants of bright cotton fabrics, trims and rickrack. Choose a different color for each person. Because of their small size, the pillows can be stored easily.

Holiday travel

▶ Long trips to visit relatives for the holidays can often be trying. A novel way to make trips more enjoyable is to wrap some inexpensive gifts to be opened by the family every 200 miles or every three hours—whichever comes first. It adds excitement to the trip and gives little ones something new to play with as the trip progresses.

▶ The plastic bags with handles given out by many stores make dandy containers to stash the trash while traveling. Hang one in your car and help keep America clean!

Reading on the road

When driving long distances, borrow cassette tapes of books from your local library. Not only will they make your trip more fun, they will help you stay alert on the road.

Fast message

Before leaving for vacation, buy self-adhesive labels and write or type the names and addresses of those you know will want to hear from you. Once you're on vacation, simply write your message on a postcard, add postage and the pretyped label and off it goes.

Double-duty souvenirs

Here's a neat idea when you buy gifts for friends and relatives while you are traveling abroad. Before leaving a foreign country, buy several local newspapers. When you get home, wrap the gifts in the papers of the country where they were bought as an extra touch.

Handy carrier

If you like to pick up bargain prints or posters while on vacation, take along a cardboard tube, preferably the type gift paper is wrapped around. A rolled up print or poster will fit snugly inside the tube which, in turn, fits neatly inside your luggage. No rips or wrinkles.

Don't leave home without it

For safety's sake, pack a battery-operated smoke detector in your suitcase. When you get to your destination, hang it up so that you're sure to be alerted if there's a fire.

Vacation memories

▶ Buy each of your children an inexpensive photo album to take on vacation. At each sight-seeing stop, allow them to pick out postcards for their "vacation books." As you drive along, the children will have a great time looking at and mounting the pictures.

▶ Instead of hiding souvenirs from your vacations—tickets, menus, postcards—in a drawer, decoupage them on poster boards and hang them in the family room.

▶ Start a wonderful tradition. Whenever you are on vacation, keep your eyes open for that perfect Christmas-tree decoration—one that will remind you of a favorite time or place. This way you can relive your vacations when it's time to trim the tree.

In The Driver's Seat

Here are some tips for smart drivers to keep you—and your car—running smoothly!

Sit like a pro

▶ An expert driver sits up straight, with buttocks and back against the seat, so that he or she can "read" the messages the car sends through the seat, the steering wheel and the tires: how much side pull is being exerted in a sharp curve, whether the road is level or banked, whether the speed needs to be adjusted.

▶ Imagine that your steering wheel is the face of a clock and drive with your hands in the three o'clock and nine o'clock positions whenever you're in traffic. As long as you hold your hands on the wheel in this position, even while turning you can immediately straighten out your car without stopping to think about it. When seconds count, this can make the difference between keeping or losing control of the car.

▶ Keep your seat belt snugly fastened against your hips and chest. It will prevent your sliding in the seat and help you control the car.

Taking a curve

▶ Always slow down *before* you get to a curve.

▶ Look ahead as far as possible so that you can judge how long, sharp or gentle the curve is.

▶ If you are braking to slow yourself in advance, you should gradually release the brake pressure as you enter the curve.

▶ While you are still in the curve, begin to gradually accelerate, which will help you to steer out of the curve with more control. Simply put: Steer *into* the curve with the brakes and steer *out* of the curve with the accelerator.

What to do when you swerve

▶ *Don't brake!* The combination of an abrupt change in direction plus braking can send you skidding.

▶ The instant you spot trouble, take your foot off the gas to give the front tires better adhesion and decrease speed.

▶ Turn the wheel slightly but quickly to steer your car into the next lane or on to the shoulder.

▶ Now aim the car straight ahead, and ease on to the accelerator. (This improves rear-tire traction.) Steer carefully back into your original lane. *The whole sequence:* Take your foot off the accelerator, turn the wheel, straighten the wheel, step on the gas, then turn the wheel back. As you see, you do not use the brake at all.

How to brake

When you must stop fast, the proper way to brake is called *cadence braking*, a quick on-off braking action that helps keep your wheels from locking. "Slamming on" the brakes often locks the wheels and makes the car skid across the pavement. To cadence brake, make sure your wheels are pointed straight ahead (this will be easier if you have been driving with your hands in the three and nine o'clock positions). Squeeze the brakes on all the way, to the point of locking your wheels, then release the brake pedal about halfway up. Repeat this on-off sequence until you've come to a complete stop. If you practice somewhere safe—an empty parking lot, for example— you'll get a sense of how much effort it takes to bring your car to a sudden, straight stop.

Stopping a skid

The most common skid is a rear-wheel skid, where you feel the back of the car slide out of control. A skid can be sudden and violent; when it is, you must react quickly and aggressively to stop it. Remember: *Stay off the brakes!* Ease your foot off the gas. Then turn the steering wheel quickly in the direction the rear end is sliding. You may over-correct and have to turn the wheel in the other direction. In fact, you may have to do this several times before you straighten the car out. Keep your eyes fastened on where you want to go so that when you've corrected the skid, you can straighten out the steering wheel.

Tire talk

It's a common misconception that keeping less air in the tires improves traction in hot weather, on snow, or when you're carrying a heavy load. In fact, the opposite is true. Under-inflated tires are much more likely to blow out, come off the rims or "hydroplane" on wet pavement (ride above a thin layer of water). For better handling and mileage you should inflate tires to the maximum air pressure recommended by the car manufacturer (or even a few pounds more). *Note:* Never exceed the maximum pressure recommended by the *tire* manufacturer, which is printed on the side wall of the tire.

Eyes on the road!

▶ Focus your eyes ahead of you. This gives you warning of trouble ahead and extra seconds to react. Look through the windows of the car in front of you so you can see traffic in the distance.

▶ Check on traffic behind you every five seconds or so by glancing in your rear-view and side-mounted mirrors. The best way to eliminate the blind spot to the right rear of you is to get a right-mounted mirror installed on your car. If this isn't possible, always remember to turn your head to the right for a quick glance behind you before moving to the right-hand lane.

▶ Watch the other drivers. There's a moment when you're about to pass another driver when you can see his face in his side-mounted mirror. Check to see if he's spotted you coming up on him; this is especially useful when passing a truck, whose driver often cannot see you once you pass the truck's rear bumper. By doing this, you minimize the chance that a driver may suddenly swing into your lane because he didn't see you coming.

▶ When entering a freeway, be sure to watch the acceleration lane as well as the oncoming traffic. People sometimes stop in these lanes—and get rear-ended by drivers who weren't looking ahead.

▶ Help others to see *you*. Put your headlights on when it's snowing or raining. *Always* turn them on at dusk.

Stormy weather

▶ When rain begins to fall, particularly after a dry period, a slick film of oil and grease forms on the road; it takes 20 or 30 minutes of hard rain to wash it away. Slow down and remember to be especially cautious during that first half hour.

▶ On ice, a skid is an ever-present possibility no matter what your speed. Slow down and keep any action you make—steering, braking, accelerating—slow, smooth and steady. Any abrupt action can initiate a skid in icy conditions. Keep in mind that you may find ice where the road is above ground level; bridges freeze first. If possible, stay off icy roads until they've been sanded or salted. Even if you're extremely careful, somebody else may skid into you.

Tailgating

▶ Always follow the "two-second" rule for judging your distance from another car. When the rear bumper of the car in front of you passes some stationary object, count "one thousand and one, one thousand and two." When you finish, your front bumper should reach the stationary object. Remember: When you're driving at 55 mph and you suddenly have to stop, your car will travel 60 feet before you can even get your foot on the brake. And it can take yet another 225 feet to get the car to stop. Leave yourself enough room.

▶ If someone is tailgating you, put on your turn indicator and pull over as soon as you can to let the tailgater go by. If you try to keep him from passing you, you just increase the possibility that he'll try something more foolish. If you are constantly being tailgated or passed by other cars, you may be going too slowly. Keep up with the flow of traffic as long as that doesn't require driving above the legal speed limit, and always keep right except to pass.

When you turn the key and nothing happens

Turn the key off—you need to check the battery.

▶ If the two cables attached to the metal terminals are loose, use a wrench to tighten them.

▶ If the battery has caps on top that open, check to see if the liquid inside covers the metal fins in each chamber and, if it doesn't, add *distilled* water.

▶ If the battery is sealed, leave it alone.

▶ If the cables look very corroded, the electrical current may not be getting through to the battery. Force the point of a screwdriver (be sure that it has an *insulated* or *wooden* handle) between the cable connector and the terminal, and have someone start the car. If that works, you probably need to replace the cables.

▶ If you left the lights on when you parked the car, the battery has run down and you'll need to jump start the car.

Jump starting a car

Jump starting is quite safe *as long as you hook the jumper cables up in the proper order*. Check your owner's manual to be sure you can use battery cables with your car.

▶ Be sure that both cars are in *park*, that their ignition switches are *off* and their emergency brakes *on*.

▶ Remove the caps of the batteries on both cars. (If the batteries are sealed, leave the caps alone.)

▶ Each set of jumper cables has a pair of red clips and a pair of black ones. First, attach one of the *red* clips to the positive terminal of *your* battery. (That's the terminal that has

a *POS* or " + " sign on it, and/or is larger than the other one.) Attach the other red clip to the positive terminal of the other car.

▶ Now, attach one of the *black* clips to the negative terminal of your car's battery and then the other black clip to an unpainted metal part of the other car, away from the battery and carburetor.

▶ Start the helper car first and let it run for several seconds. Then get into your car and turn on the ignition. Your car should start.

▶ *Without turning off your engine*, disconnect the cables and go on your way. It's important to drive your car around for at least 15 minutes to recharge the battery before you shut it off again.

▶ If the alternator light stays on, or if the gauge continues to point to *discharge* or "-" (a minus sign), the fan belt may be too loose to run the alternator.

My car is making clicking noises!

If you hear a clicking when you turn the key in the ignition and the battery isn't dead, the cable that runs from the battery to the starter may have a loose connection. Follow the cable from the positive terminal to make sure it's properly connected at the other end.

Single File: Traveling Alone

No one to travel with? No problem!
Just follow this guide to safe soloing.

Driving smarts

▶ Always keep the car doors locked. If you're driving in questionable neighborhoods, police suggest that you also keep the windows rolled up, with the air conditioner on when it's hot. If your car doesn't have air-conditioning, open the windows partway but roll them up when you stop for a light.

▶ Place your purse and packages under the seat. This keeps temptation out of a purse snatcher's sight. If you need your purse handy, loop the strap onto your safety belt.

▶ Don't use dark side streets even in your own neighborhood.

▶ *Never* pick up hitchhikers—men, women or youngsters. An Arizona survey recently showed that out of 100 hitchhikers, only 4% had no previous or current problems with the police!

▶ Always fill up when the gas tank is half full. Treat the halfway mark as if it were the empty mark.

▶ If you travel a lot by yourself, install a CB in your car—it's your emergency hotline to the police.

Parking insurance

▶ Park in well-lit streets or parking lots. Be observant: If the diner where you planned to stop is surrounded by a bunch of hot rods or motorcycles, find someplace else to eat.

▶ Always check for loiterers wherever you park, even if it's by your friend's house. When you return, check the back seat before you get in.

▶ Have keys ready before reaching your car. Fumbling in pockets and purses makes you extremely vulnerable to attack.

Emergency procedures

▶ When you have a breakdown, lift the hood of the car and attach a white handkerchief or cloth to the antenna or left door handle to signal for help. Get back into the car and lock the doors. At night, leave your lights and emergency flashers on. If a stranger stops, lower your window slightly and ask him or her to call for assistance.

▶ If it's only a minor problem or a flat tire, drive to a well-lit area before you pull over. It's better to ruin a tire rim than risk your life. Keep your flashers on to alert police.

▶ Never stop when a stranger tells you something is wrong with your car. Instead, drive to a service station and check the situation there.

▶ If you think someone is following you, go to the nearest police or fire station. When that isn't possible, drive to a well-lit service station or supermarket and pump your horn in short blasts. In the event that you can't do any of the above, just *keep moving*. If you must jump a curb to get away, do it. Should you come to a red light, go through it if the way is clear. These maneuvers also increase your chances of attracting the attention of the police—which is exactly what you want.

▶ When you see a car in trouble, do your part. Drive to a public telephone (choose a well-lit area at night) and call the police.

A good night's sleep

If you find yourself staying in a hotel room that only has a simple knob lock—don't take chances. Wedge a chair against the door to insure against intrusion. There are also portable door alarms that are movement-activated. You can buy them in travel and novelty shops.

The educated traveler

If you have always dreamed of going to Europe or one of the larger American cities but were always too nervous about going alone, check out the nearest university. Many of them sponsor "summer school." The classes cover a wide range of topics, from English literature to art appreciation. Generally, housing and two meals a day are provided. So if you have a yen to see Paris, New York or San Francisco, try going back to school for the summer.

9.
Shopping Sense/ Fashion Savvy

Off-Price Shopping Tips To
Save You Bundles
Kid's Clothes: How To Get
The Best Buys
Dress Thin Tactics
Look Great Whatever Your Shape
Color Yourself Beautiful

Off-Price Shopping Tips To Save You Bundles

You can make shopping for clothes less costly and less confusing. The end result: You and your family will look great!

How to get the best buys

▶ Shop early in the day, before crowds have had a chance to pick through the merchandise.

▶ Make friends with a salesperson who'll give you inside information on new shipments, special merchandise and clearance sales.

▶ To get the best selection, find out when a shipment is due. Give the store a few hours to get the clothes unpacked and on the racks.

▶ Some stores are constantly receiving new merchandise, so check back every week or so.

▶ To make room for new arrivals, many stores "age" merchandise with weekly markdowns of up to 30%. Look for tags with multiple reductions for the best buys.

▶ Check out special clearance racks, where prices may be slashed up to 90%. In May you will find big end-of-season clearances on spring merchandise; in August, you'll find great summer markdowns.

▶ To get advance notice, add your name to the store's mailing list and check newspaper ads.

▶ Compare prices among off-price stores. One may have better buys on swimwear, another on suits or dresses.

▶ Learn to recognize brand names so you'll know what kind of quality you're getting. Also make note of the labels that consistently have the look and fit that is best for your figure.

▶ If your kids can't come along to try clothes on and the store has a cash refund policy, take your picks home and return what doesn't fit.

▶ Stick to the styles and colors you usually wear. Off-price stores are not the place to start experimenting; they don't have the displays or personnel to show you how to put pieces together.

▶ Don't buy something just because it's a bargain. Make sure you need it and be certain it looks good on you. A $20 dress may sound like a good deal, but if you don't love it, you probably won't wear it and you'll wind up wasting your money. If you realize you've made a mistake, take it back.

▶ If you're looking for something specific, a department store is your best bet. You never know what off-price stores will have in stock at any given time.

▶ Decide what departments you want to cover and go through all the racks before you start trying clothes on.

▶ If you're shopping with your husband, he can start trying on clothes while you finish looking through the racks closest to the men's dressing room. You save time and stay close enough to help make a decision on style or fit.

▶ Different categories of clothes—shirts, slacks, skirts—will be hung on separate racks and organized by size rather than color or label, so you may have to search for pieces that mix 'n'

match. Be flexible in putting together a look. Don't expect to find it all in one label.

▶ A sure-fire way to match something you already own: Take a clipping from an inside seam. Then, when faced with five blouses in shades of blue, you can make a critical choice and avoid a return trip.

▶ If you can't find the right size, check the racks with clothes two sizes larger and smaller than the one you're looking for. Shoppers often stick clothes back in the wrong place.

▶ Always check the care labels. If they say "dry-clean only," you can end up spending more than you saved. Kids' clothes should always be "wash and wear."

▶ Check for quality fabrics and durable construction, especially for work and school clothes. Crush fabrics, pull at seams, see how they hold up.

▶ Irregulars and seconds are rare but not always clearly marked. Check carefully for ripped seams, snags and pulls, broken zippers, missing buttons. A decent discount may make up for certain minor repairs you can do yourself.

▶ Examine collars and cuffs for stains. Lipstick and other makeup can be removed but heavy soil and pen marks mean you should probably pass. Look for fading or discoloration around the shoulders—a definite no-no.

▶ Some off-price stores still have community fitting rooms so, if you're modest, wear a full slip, body stocking or leotard.

▶ To get the best fit, try everything on and study yourself in the mirror, front and back.

▶ Minor alterations are definitely worth the time and expense. With what you've saved, you can afford to have them done and still come out ahead. Consider moving the buttons, taking in a waist or back seam or raising a hem to get a custom-tailored fit.

▶ When you're looking for simple pullover sweaters, don't ignore discount men's clothing stores. The prices are often lower than for women's clothing and the quality is just as high.

Smart shopper

Whenever you have a garment you want to match and cannot take a swatch of the fabric itself, take a crayon of the same shade and color a small patch in a little notebook. Carry the notebook in your purse when you shop, so you can easily compare colors. No more guesswork and no more trips to the store to return mistakes.

If the item fits . . .

Carry your family's clothing sizes with you when you shop off-price. Include accessories, too; hat and glove size, sock and stocking preference, etc., so you'll always be prepared for an unexpected bargain.

Good fit

Good-quality used clothing is often available at substantial savings in many resale and thrift shops and at yard sales. However, there is usually no place to try the clothes on so, before you go shopping, draw a pattern on waxed paper or newsprint by tracing around a garment that fits well. Carry the pattern with you to make certain you purchase the correct size.

Mail-order smarts

▶ Order pantyhose, sleepwear, socks and panties in bulk.

▶ When buying items that need to be tried on, use only reputable mail-order firms with 800-numbers and easy return policies.

▶ Use carbon paper when ordering by mail or from a TV ad so you can keep track of what you ordered.

Keep the receipt

Sometimes you won't notice a flaw until you try a garment on again at home. Always keep the register receipt so you'll be able to return the garment.

Kids' Clothes: How To Get The Best Buys

Calling all parents! We've got just what you want—shopping guidelines, what to look for in identifying quality clothing and nifty ways to get more mileage out of those clothes.

Shop with your kids

▶ Encourage your kids to make the initial selection; they'll be happiest in clothes they like. Then together choose what satisfies both of you.

▶ Don't do all your shopping in one day. Limit shopping time with young children to two to three hours.

▶ Discuss with your child what other kids are wearing before you go shopping. This will sidestep temper tantrums and outbursts of "But, *everybody's* wearing it!"

Shopping smarts

Take inventory of what fits and what needs replacement. Make a list and stick with it; you'll avoid extra hours in the store and impulse-buying.

How to "shop for quality"

▶ **Stitching:** Small, regular stitches are recommended. About 10 to 12 stitches per inch is ideal. Stitching should be reinforced at points of strain (elbows, knees and underarm seams).

▶ **Fabric:** Preshrunk cotton blends with a wrinkle-resistant finish, denim, seersucker and corduroy are all durable and easy-care. Avoid flimsy, very light-weight materials for everyday wear, and stay away from heavy, stiff or rough fabrics that most children would find uncomfortable. A loosely woven or knitted fabric is more likely to shrink than one that is firmly knitted or woven. Some lesser-quality fabrics are starched to look better. To check, run your fingernail over the material to see if starch flakes off.

▶ **Pattern:** If the material has a pattern, check the reverse side to see that the pattern is woven into the fabric and not just printed on—a sign of poor quality. Keep in mind that fabrics printed with small designs or patterns don't show soil or wrinkles as quickly as those printed with large designs.

▶ **Seams and buttons:** Look for wide, carefully finished seams. Narrow or unfinished seams may unravel. Pocket seams ought to be reinforced. Buttons should be sewn on securely.

Ways to get more mileage out of kids' clothes

▶ Choose clothes with stretch or "grow" features. A-line or wrap skirts, raglan or kimono sleeves, wide underarm and leg seams that can be let out and wide hems or tucks in dresses all allow room for growing. Loose, straight-hanging dresses, without a defined waistline, and empire-waist dresses usually "fit" longer. While you generally shouldn't buy clothes that are too large, a roomy coat does trap the heat better and loose-fitting sweaters can be layered over blouses.

▶ Two-piece garments can usually be worn longer than one-piece garments. Both parts can be lengthened and, if the bottom no longer fits, the top can be mixed and recycled with other clothes.

▶ Buy pajamas in the same color, style and pattern so that you can match up tops and bottoms from various pairs as the child's dimensions change. Also look for pajamas with two sets of snaps on the waistline. Turn winter pajamas into summer nightwear by cutting off the legs and sleeves. Let T-shirts double as pajama tops in warm weather.

▶ For infants, buy the double-breasted undershirts that fasten with snaps because they will grow with the child. As a bonus, they're easier to put on than over-the-head styles.

▶ Buy a two-piece snowsuit that's roomy. It's more versatile, too, since it can be mixed and matched with other outdoor wear. The snowsuit jacket can also be worn alone in warmer weather. Don't buy a coat that is double-breasted or fitted at the waist. Chances are it won't fit next year.

▶ Buy mittens and socks in two or more identical pairs so that odd partners can be re-matched. Tube socks without pre-shaped heels will "grow" with the child.

Sewing tricks that make clothes last

▶ If a shirt starts to come untucked because your youngster outgrows it, sew an 8-inch-wide strip of material around the bottom of the shirt. The shirt will stay in place and the material will not show.

▶ When you let the hem down on a pair of jeans, you can get rid of the unsightly white line by coloring it in with a nonwashable dark blue marker.

▶ At the end of a season, before you send a coat to the dry cleaner, remove both the sleeve and bottom hems. Store the clean coat with the hems hanging. Next year try the coat on your child and make a new hem without crease lines.

▶ Extend the life of a long-sleeved shirt by making it short-sleeved without sewing. Just cut off the sleeves and fold the cut edges under. Attach the edges to the inside of the shirt with iron-on tape.

Double purposes

Long underwear sets serve a double purpose: Not only do they keep out the chill during those romps in the snow kids love so well, they also make long-lasting, warm pajamas on chilly winter nights.

The Big Top

Today's oversized looks are a godsend when shopping for children. Those extra-large sweaters and shirts can be used as long as they stay in one piece. As the child gets older, either the garment becomes a more form-fitting model or it is passed down to younger sisters or brothers to wear.

Pretty nightshirts

You can purchase men's small-size undershirts on sale and embroider them for girls to use as nightshirts. They can also be worn as pretty (and practical) coverups with bathing suits.

Dress-Thin Tactics

Unbelievable, but true! Wearing the right clothes and accessories can make you look ten pounds thinner.

Color yourself slim

▶ Use bright colors, not basic colors, as accents. Build your wardrobe around the "new neutrals" such as teal, burgundy, tobacco, navy and black.

▶ When choosing a bright article of clothing, select one in a cut and texture that elongates your shape— an oversized vest, a long, slouchy sweater.

▶ Keep your silhouette long and lean by wearing separates in the same color family. Try solids or small prints. To make your legs appear sleek, harmonize your skirt, hose and shoe color.

Shape up your shape

▶ Starting at the top, place shoulder pads in all your jackets, sweaters, dresses, coats, etc. This little extra works miracles by making your shoulders appear wider, your waist and hips smaller.

▶ Give your torso extra length by choosing jackets, cardigans and tunics that fall below the hips. Straight, unconstructed styles are more flattering than fitted; opt for single-breasted over double-breasted.

▶ Forget tent dresses and dirndl skirts; they only add pounds. Your best bets are shapes that skim your body but bypass trouble spots.

▶ In skirts, keep to the straight and narrow (no pockets) or A-lines. No matter what the current fashion is, below-the-knee length is always more flattering.

▶ Straining seams and buttons will make you appear overweight. A good fit is a must to look thin so always buy your correct size.

▶ Draw attention *upward*, with bold earrings, a pretty scarf, hair accessories. The idea is to place the focal point at the neck level or above. Try wearing long strands of pearls and/or a man's tie to create a lean, vertical line.

Select flattering fabrics

▶ Clingy fabrics may feel sexy but they may also play up any little bulges you have. Stick to fabrics that have more substance, such as wool jersey and gabardine.

▶ Nubby knits or fuzzy wools add bulk to your figure. Go for flat-textured fabrics (linen, cotton blends) instead.

Create slimming optical illusions

▶ Warning: Not all stripes are flattering. Too many vertical stripes actually make you appear wider. A small number of vertical or diagonal lines in a related color will pare you down.

▶ A longer neckline visually lengthens your upper torso. Try wearing V-necks or leaving the top few buttons of your blouse open.

▶ Think vertically. A single line of buttons down a dress, braid trim or vertical ribbing on a knit dress will slim you down.

Trim down with trousers

If buying pants depresses you, you may not be choosing the right styles.

▶ Trousers that are straight, uncuffed and tapered are the most slimming.

▶ Avoid pleats on the side, patch pockets (on jeans) on the rear or extra "fussy" details.

▶ To conceal a tummy bulge, pants with pleats in *front* can be slimming, as can some yolked styles that form a "V".

▶ Slip on a pair of control-top pantyhose under pants for a smooth silhouette.

Make accessories work for you

▶ Don't shy away from belts; play it loose. A double-wrap belt or one that's cinched an inch or two *below* the waist will whittle both waist and tummy.

▶ Dark textured hose minimizes calves, knees and ankles.

▶ Steer clear of chunky-heeled shoes. A classic pump with a medium tapered heel will play up your legs to advantage.

▶ To camouflage heavy calves, stick to straight-silhouette boots.

▶ Points of pizzazz: Go for bright gloves, interesting watches, bold jewelry and snazzy scarves.

Look Great Whatever Your Shape

So what if you don't have a perfect figure! With just a few fashion tricks up your sleeve, you can almost look like you do.

Dressing to conceal a disappearing waistline

A thick waist can be troublesome at any age but as you get older, a "disappearing waistline" becomes more of a problem. Luckily, you can camouflage it easily. Wear one-tone combinations with tops that go over the waistband. Try using long vests, tunics and overblouses. Wear soft fabrics (silk, jersey, etc.). Don't wear short jackets or anything that cuts the waistline.

Lengthening a short-waisted figure

While a short waist is not a major flaw, it can make you look awkward if proportions are off-balance. (To shorten a long waist, do the opposite of what we suggest below.) Wear dropped-waist styles and skirts that ride low on the waistline. Wear tunics, longer jackets and sweaters outside of skirts and pants. Don't wear dresses with obvious waistlines, wide waistbands or belts. Steer clear of high-rise waistlines.

How to camouflage large hips

▶ Wear combinations that direct the eye upward and watch hips disappear! Wear vertical lines, stripes and A-line dresses. Try unfitted jackets and tunics, but make sure the fabric in the jackets and tops doesn't cling to your hips. Wear skirts that fit smoothly and fall straight over the hips.

▶ Don't wear large prints, plaids or horizontal stripes.

▶ When choosing pants, make sure the pleats are in front. Side pleats emphasize the hips.

▶ Avoid below-the-waist accents such as back pockets, side pockets, fancy stitching and hip belts.

▶ Keep accessories above the waist to draw the eye upward: earrings, a pretty necklace, a scarf.

▶ Choose pants in smooth fabrics that skim over you.

Adding height if you're under 5'3"

▶ Avoiding a "little girl" look is a major concern of petite women. By creating vertical lines and wearing fashions designed especially for the petite figure, you can seemingly add inches to your height.

▶ Wear vertical stripes and small prints.

▶ Wear straight, tapered skirts.

▶ Keep dress lengths just below the knee and jackets and sweaters in shorter lengths as well.

▶ Wear sling-backs and sleek pumps with matching stockings.

▶ Don't wear billowy sleeves, large ruffles, prints or horizontal stripes.

▶ Beware of pants that "sag," making your legs look shorter, and avoid cuffs.

Flattering looks for a large bosom

▶ Playing up vertical lines is the key to balancing a top-heavy look. Wear soft, drapy fabrics; stick to vertical lines and tucks, single cables. Buy separates to accommodate larger top and smaller bottom sizes. Try V-necklines and simple collars. Wear long vests, cardigans and tunics. Add small shoulder pads to blouses and dresses to prevent a slumped-shoulder look. Wear a good support bra.

▶ Don't wear large, loud prints or horizontal lines. Avoid tight, clingy tops and sweaters or bulky fabrics.

Tips for skinnies

▶ Opt for color! Wear vibrant brights, the palest pales and don't be afraid of original or offbeat combinations. Your thin figure can carry them.

▶ Consider weightier fabrics such as corduroy, velvet and velveteen, any weight of wool and the heavier knits.

▶ Be daring. Wear bold plaids, horizontal stripes, exciting and exotic flower and animal prints.

▶ Layer! Use shawls, scarves, big belts, loose blazers; you can wear almost any look and get away with it.

Color Yourself Beautiful!

Everyone has certain colors that he or she looks great in—and others that are only so-so. But how do you figure out which to wear, which to avoid? Read the descriptions for the four color types, or seasons, following. Beneath each season, you'll find the color cues that make that season a stand-out. (We also have some great tips for men, so they can look their best too!)

What season are you?

▶ To find out, ask yourself this question: Which lipstick color—bright pink, soft pink, terra cotta or peach—flatters you the most? If the answer is bright pink, this means you are probably a Winter; soft pink indicates a Summer complexion; terra cotta looks best on an Autumn; and peach flatters a Spring.

▶ Another good test: Your true skin color is that on the underside of your forearm. Use it to determine skin coloring and to match foundation.

▶ Puzzled about which blusher color is most flattering? Pinch your fingertip: the color you see is a marvelous choice for blusher!

Can you be more than one season?

No. Even though you may look good in a couple of season's colors, you'll always look better in one particular palette.

What if you love colors that are not in your palette?

Sometimes the colors you like—and think look good on you—really don't. They have been determined by fashion and taste, not by fact. The colors in the palettes, however, are selected objectively and tested with positive results. The idea here is to try some of the colors in your palette and see the reactions you get. It may surprise you!

What if you already own clothes that are not in your season's palette?

Don't throw them out! Just use them in combination with colors that are in your palette. A good rule is to always put your season's colors near your face—a scarf, perhaps, or a blouse or some jewelry.

The Winter Complexion

Dramatic colors belong to Winters, who dazzle in clear tones, sharp contrasts.

▶ Skin: An incredible variety—from subtle blue or pink undertones (milky white through taupe beige) to olive, Black, Oriental.

▶ Hair: Usually dark, from light brown to charcoal; red-black; blue-black.

▶ Eyes: Brown, black, hazel, deep blue, gray-green.

Winter Color Cues

▶ Your best colors are true and primary—red, emerald, sapphire—as well as their darker counterparts: royal blue, royal purple, magenta.

▶ Winters look great in pure black, stark white, cool grays.

▶ When wearing pastels, go 'icy,' not powdery. Think of white, with a drop of color.

▶ Avoid browns, beiges and the rust/gold/peach family. The only yellow you *can* wear: clear, bright yellow. Dull, muted tones are out.

▶ You're the only season that can wear pure black—so go for it! Nothing is quite so dramatic or so striking. (For fair-skinned Winters, you may want to let a bit of skin show by the neck.) You can also carry off brights that are unrelieved by neutrals.

▶ High-contrast accessories are for you: silver and black; white or gray pearls; rhinestones or diamonds.

▶ Contrast works in makeup, too. Red lipstick and blusher plus black liner can be one combination that works well. As with clothing, steer clear from muted or frosted makeup shades.

▶ Some famous Winters you'd recognize: Cher; Elizabeth Taylor; Sally Field.

The Spring Complexion

Delicate coloring with golden undertones—that's the Spring woman, who looks best in clear colors.

▶ Skin: Creamy ivory; peach-beige; freckles.

▶ Hair: Blonde to dark brown with golden tones; strawberry or carrot red.

▶ Eyes: Blue, green, aqua, golden brown, golden hazel.

Spring Color Cues

▶ Clear, fresh colors are what to look for; smoky or muted shades will make you look washed out.

▶ Some pinks *are* for you, as long as they're "warm." Try peach, salmon, coral.

▶ "Warm" blues look great on you: aqua, turquoise, periwinkle, violet.

▶ Milk chocolate is the darkest brown you should wear. But do try beiges: golden tan, camel, buff, ivory.

▶ Steer clear from too many darks (touch up with lighter accents); try darks plus brights and color combinations of equal intensity.

▶ For jewelry, opt for gold tones, blonde wood, and creamy pearls.

▶ Instead of rosy makeup, (which can make you look ruddy), choose blusher, lipstick and highlighter in shades of peach, cinnamon and gold. These will add color without overpowering a delicate complexion.

▶ Some famous Springs you'd recognize: Shirley Jones; Debbie Reynolds; Julie Andrews.

The Summer Complexion

The Summer woman's fair complexion is flattered by soft brights and cool pastels.

▶ Skin: Fair, with blue undertones; visible pink.

▶ Hair: Blonde to dark brown with ash tones; blonde-gray.

▶ Eyes: Usually blue, green, aqua or hazel; sometimes cloudy coloring.

Summer Color Cues

▶ Think vibrant, feminine tones— such as raspberry, plus the whole family of lavender, orchid, mauve and plum.

▶ Practically all blues and blue-greens look super on you—just remember to avoid those with yellow undertones.

▶ "Winter white"—a soft shade with no yellow—is your best white.

▶ Pastels with blue undertones flatter very fair Summers; darker-haired Summers perk up in brighter hues from their palette.

▶ Make the most of your coloring by choosing soft contrasts, medium tones and monochromatic schemes. Try not to choose stark combinations, such as jet black and pure white.

▶ Accessory picks: All silver-toned jewelry; rose pearls; rosy ivory.

▶ Rosy makeup brings out the pink in your face—and you'll find you will need less to look your best. Some makeup with blue undertones also looks good on you, such as lilac, lavender and mauve.

▶ Some famous Summers you'd recognize: Candice Bergen; Cheryl Tiegs; Farrah Fawcett; Nancy Kissinger.

The Autumn Complexion

Autumns look sensational in the fiery splendor of golden, spicy, earthy colors.

▶ Skin: Golden undertones— ivory, peach, warm beige, copper.

▶ Hair: Brunette, with gold or metallic-red highlights; golden blonde, red or auburn; occasionally black.

▶ Eyes: Brown, green, hazel, possible turquoise (for redheads).

Autumn Color Cues

▶ Autumns can wear bright *and* muted colors with golden undertones. Brown and oranges—bronze, coffee, terra cotta, rust—are fabulous on you; yellow- and earth-greens (like lime and olive) also look great.

▶ You can wear red, but make it a dark tomato or bittersweet shade.

▶ Your best blues are teal, turquoise, deep periwinkle.

▶ What not to wear: pinks and colors with pink undertones (purple, lilac); navy; gray; black.

▶ Very fair Autumns look best in muted tones; those with darker complexions glow in brighter, more intense shades.

▶ Avoid very pale tones.

▶ For accessories, go with gold, brass or copper; wood or tortoise shell jewelry.

▶ Most Autumns have colorless cheeks, so blusher is essential. Warmer makeup tones make the most of your complexion: peach, brown, brick-red, ochre, toasty caramel. Don't be afraid to experiment with vibrant tones.

▶ Some famous Autumns you'd recognize: Vanessa Redgrave; Katharine Hepburn; Shirley MacLaine.

Special note for black complexions:

You can find your color type by considering your skin's undertone. If you have a golden undertone, you're a Spring; a brown-black undertone makes you an Autumn; a pinkish-rosy tone is a Summer; and if you are light-skinned, with ivory tones, or dark with blue-ish tones, you're a Winter.

Color For Men

Men can benefit from color strategies too. Check out these tips for men to look their best.

For the Winter man

▶ Black, navy and gray suits all look good on you. *Note:* Gray should be pure, not muddy, without any brown undertones.

▶ Your Number 1 shirt is pure white. Icy tones of blue, yellow and pink are good choices, as is clear gray.

▶ If you prefer shirts of a different color, such as peach or golden yellow, select ones with white collars.

▶ Best ties are dark blue-red, bright burgundy (solid or patterned) or dark navy with red accents.

▶ If you wear glasses, go for silver-toned, black, burgundy or navy frames.

▶ For leisure wear, don't be afraid to try emerald green, deep purple, or cobalt blue in your shirts.

For the Spring man

▶ A bright light navy, gray or blue suit is the most flattering.

▶ Ivory, light beige, buff, light periwinkle and warm pink are ideal for shirts.

▶ The word in ties: Go for orange-red or clear red, patterned or solid.

▶ In eyeglasses, gold frames look wonderful, as do dark blue, beige-brown, and chocolate brown.

▶ On weekends and after hours, try aqua, camel, coral and violet.

For the Summer man

▶ Select suits in grayed-navy, medium brown, dark blue-gray, light blue.

▶ Shirts in soft white and pastel shades of blue, yellow and rose-beige are good bets.

▶ In ties, think burgundy, blue-red and all blues—either solid or in prints.

▶ For eyeglass wearers, opt for silver-toned frames, or frames in plum or teal. Tinted lenses are an option, too; just avoid yellow or brown lens tones.

▶ Leisurewear colors can include anything in the blue/green, or mauve/raspberry family.

For the Autumn man

▶ Try subtle business tweeds, especially in browns and greens.

▶ In shirts, aim for oyster white, beige, buff.

▶ Your perfect ties are bittersweet red and brown red, dark green, browns.

▶ Frame yourself (in glasses!) with tortoise-shell, brown, cinnamon or gold tones.

▶ In non-working hours, try teal, brick, rust, olive or lime green.

10.
Beauty
Secrets

Head To Toe: Tips For A
More Beautiful You
Cosmetics: What's In There?
7 Days To A Younger-Looking You
Looking Lovely—After 40
Stop-The-Clock Beauty Products
Sun-Lovers Guide To Looking
Your Best
On-The-Go Beauty
Look Great In Glasses

Head To Toe: Tips For A More Beautiful You

Here's everything you need to know to look like a million, from head to toe.

Shampoo how-to's

▶ Take a minute to rinse your hair before you shampoo to loosen the dirt.

▶ Massage shampoo into the scalp with your fingertips, not your nails.

▶ Don't equate lots of lather with cleansing efficiency. Lather comes from the shampoo's sudsing agents, which do nothing for cleanliness.

▶ Always shampoo in warm or tepid water, never very hot.

▶ Finish off your shampoo with a cold-water rinse to flatten down the cuticle of the hair shafts and make your hair look shinier. It will also close scalp pores.

▶ To cleanse the scalp and eliminate shampoo buildup, rinse with equal parts lemon juice and water.

▶ No time to shampoo? Wet your hair and blow-dry. This will get rid of some of the oil and make your hair bouncier.

▶ Another no-shampoo tip: Rub a small amount of cornmeal into your scalp, bend over the sink and brush it out. Your hair and scalp will feel much cleaner.

▶ To counteract the drying effects of dandruff shampoo, alternate it with a regular shampoo.

▶ On long hair, apply shampoo to the scalp and work through to the ends with your fingers. You'll get out collected dirt on the scalp and reduce tangles in the hair.

Dry shampoo

If friends phone to say they're dropping by unexpectedly and your hair needs washing, a dry shampoo will do the trick. Dust your hair with dry oatmeal, cornstarch or baby powder and brush the hair thoroughly. Grime and oil disappear, and your hair has more volume.

Color tips

▶ If hair is colored, wear a swim cap in chlorinated water. Chlorine tends to discolor processed hair.

▶ Hennaed hair should not be exposed to sunlight for long periods of time because it could turn orange. Wear a hat or scarf.

▶ Too-pale highlights make your complexion look faded. Warmer shades are more flattering.

▶ Red highlights are an easy way to subtly change the look of brown hair without constant touchups.

▶ If you get your hair professionally colored, bring along a picture of the hair color you'd like. The colorist may not be able to match it perfectly, but you'll end up with a closer approximation than if you just ask for an ash or golden tone.

Conditioning

▶ For a deep conditioner you make yourself, mix 1 egg white, 1 tablespoon olive oil and 1 tablespoon mayonnaise. Comb the mixture through your hair. Wrap your head in a towel and leave the conditioner on for 20 minutes. Rinse well.

▶ Mix a tiny drop of lanolin-based hair "finisher" with water and run it through your hair with your hands for some shine. This is especially great for dry, curly heads.

▶ If you use hot rollers, curling irons or blow-dryers often, use an instant conditioner every time you shampoo. Deep condition your hair about once a month.

▶ If you have oily hair, alternate balsam-type conditioners with body-building formulas.

▶ Conditioners that contain sodium hydroxide can straighten hair; avoid them when you have a perm.

▶ Whenever you color, be prepared to condition using a deep treatment once a month and instant conditioners more often.

Blow-drying

▶ **For straight hair:** Blow-dry the hair completely, concentrating air on the roots to build body. Bend forward and blow-dry underneath for a fuller, softer look.

▶ **For curly hair:** Blow-dry in a continuous circular motion to avoid straightening curls. Leave the hair slightly damp.

▶ **To straighten curly hair:** Brush from the roots to the tips, following with the nozzle of the blow-dryer. Dry the hair thoroughly.

Beat the heat

Using a curling iron is the most efficient way to put bounce and curl in your hair. But it's hard to avoid singeing your fingertips, even with rubber-tipped wands. To prevent this, wear a glove on your left hand. A snug-fitting garden glove with a latex palm gives your fingers complete flexibility and protection when you curl your hair.

Setting specifics

▶ If your hair doesn't hold a set well, curl it with a curling iron but pin each curl to the head as you remove the iron. Spray lightly with hair spray, unpin and brush.

▶ Setting lotions with alcohol listed *before* water will be more drying but hold longer.

▶ With long hair, apply setting lotion to the roots only. Too much lotion weighs hair down.

▶ Use some setting lotion in hair when it's oily and there's no time to wash. It will make hair look less limp.

▶ Don't try to set hair in the opposite direction of its natural wave pattern. The set won't last.

Tips for black hair

▶ Avoid sponge rollers that contain fiberglass. The rollers expand as hair is wrapped around them and pressure can cause fiberglass to cut the hair.

▶ Do not use hot rollers or curling irons every day. Alternate with mesh rollers placed in your hair right before showering. The steam will speed the setting time.

▶ Since black hair is fragile, use a pH-balanced shampoo.

▶ Massage a small amount of cream rinse into your hair after shampooing. Leave it on.

▶ Use semipermanent colors, not those with peroxide.

▶ Moisture, not oil, is recommended for dry hair. The best conditioner is water. Shampoo and mist often.

▶ A small amount of pomade adds a finishing gleam.

Skin care

▶ Use a mask twice a week to tighten pores, smooth out the complexion and rev up circulation. Splash on cool water to close pores and apply moisturizer.

▶ For normal to dry skin, use a richer moisturizer at night. While you sleep, your skin is more receptive to the richer emollients found in night creams.

▶ If you have oily skin, avoid heavy night creams, which can clog the pores.

▶ Always apply moisturizer when the skin is slightly damp.

▶ Dot and dab moisturizer, blending it gently and evenly.

▶ Since undereye skin is fragile and shows age quickly, use eye cream sparingly. Lightly pat it on from the outer corner in; never rub it on.

▶ Moisturize before making up. It helps makeup last, keeps colors truer and protects the skin.

▶ You'll save a step, and protect your skin, by using makeup products with sunscreen.

▶ Keeping makeup on overnight clogs pores and can cause blemishes to appear, so cleanse *thoroughly* each night.

▶ For healthy skin from within, drink six to eight glasses of water daily, eat lots of fresh fruit and vegetables and get seven hours of sleep nightly.

▶ For good skin circulation, use an exfoliating scrub once a week. More frequent use can cause the skin to thicken.

▶ When you wash face cloths, add fabric softener. You'll protect your skin from the fabric's abrasive surface.

▶ Since body skin tends to be drier than facial skin, use an emollient body lotion daily. Apply it right after bathing, while the skin is still damp.

▶ If you use petroleum jelly as a body moisturizer but have often had difficulty smoothing it on evenly, try microwaving a small amount of the jelly before applying it. Not only does it go on smoothly, it feels and acts like an expensive oil. Microwave the jelly in a glass cup on full (100%) power for about 30 seconds or until it melts; watch it closely.

▶ Give rough feet an overnight treat. Rub off dead skin with a pumice stone, apply petroleum jelly in a thin layer and put on a pair of cotton socks. In the morning, gently remove the excess petroleum jelly.

Help for oily complexions

▶ Before applying makeup, make sure the skin is properly cleansed. Don't aggravate your condition by scrubbing or overdrying the skin. Wash it with a gentle, creamy cleanser.

▶ Keep breakouts to a minimum with a benzoyl peroxide medication. It clears up blemishes and prevents new ones from forming. Apply it to existing pimples and acne-prone areas.

▶ Choose a water-based foundation and lightly dust translucent powder over it. This will fight shine and prevent foundation from turning "orangy."

▶ Use a lightweight, nongreasy moisturizer to encourage elasticity and smoothness.

Facts on foundation

▶ Always try on foundation before buying it; the color in the bottle may look different on your skin. Smooth it onto your jawline in natural light. If there is a noticeable line, choose a different shade.

▶ Always apply foundation lightly, with a damp sponge or clean fingertips. Heavy coverage only emphasizes lines and wrinkles.

▶ Always blend foundation downward. Stroking upward causes the downy hairs on your face to stand up. Stroking downward helps to flatten them out.

▶ Never apply foundation to your neck. You'll only end up with a "ring around the collar."

▶ Stay away from orange-toned foundations; they tend to be aging. Choose a sheer base that most nearly matches your dominant skin tone.

▶ Use a primer under foundation to even out skin tones. Use green if your skin is ruddy, mauve for sallow tones.

▶ Set foundation by "dusting" translucent powder over it with a soft, large brush.

▶ Three-in-one bonus: Mix your foundation with a bit of moisturizer and sunblock. You'll get a smooth base that protects you, too.

▶ Under your foundation, you can use concealer for more than just hiding circles. Carefully stroking concealer on nose-to-mouth lines and forehead furrows helps make them disappear.

Holiday glow

You can brighten your foundation by mixing a bit of liquid rouge into it. This gives your complexion an instant lift during the hectic holidays.

Basics about blush

▶ To find your best color, use your skin tone as a guide. If you have yellow undertones, go for warmer colors: peach, coral, cinnamon. If your skin has bluish undertones, choose cooler shades: pink, raspberry, plum, burgundy.

▶ The best way to apply powder blush: Place two fingers (index and middle) under the eyes. Stroke on blush just below the fingers out to the ears. Blend it well so there are no obvious lines of demarcation.

▶ Stroke blush on the browbones and continue it out to the temples. It gives your face a pretty, even glow.

▶ Apply blush high on each cheek. It makes eyes look bigger and wider.

▶ Add moisturizer to cream blush and smooth it on.

▶ For dry skin, apply a cream rouge, then powder blush.

▶ For blush with staying power, dip the brush into loose translucent powder, shake off the excess and add cake blusher. Brush on the two together.

Focus on beautiful eyes

▶ Cover up dark circles with concealer that's one shade lighter than your foundation. Undereye circles vanish when you use a concealing cream with a pale blue tint. The reason? Blue casts shadows away from your face. (Blend your foundation over the concealer to avoid "raccoon" eyes.)

▶ Apply harmonizing eye shadow colors: the darkest shade in the eyelid's crease, a medium color on the lid and the lightest on the outer half of the browbone.

▶ Avoid matching shadow and eye color. Use contrasting shades: rose or pink with blue eyes, blue or green with brown.

▶ For lasting eye shadow, apply foundation, brush on the shadow and blot with a dry sponge.

▶ If you have crepey lids, avoid creams and liquid shadows. Use a brush (not a sponge tip) to apply matte powder shadow.

▶ To make eyes look more wide-set, use a paler shade of shadow on the inner half of the lid, a deeper shade on the outer half. Then blend.

▶ Use an eyelash curler before applying mascara to emphasize the lashes.

▶ Use a tissue to blot up excess mascara on the wand. This eliminates clinging bits of mascara.

▶ Apply mascara to the bottom lashes first. It's easier to do them before the top lashes become heavy with mascara.

▶ To make lashes look thicker, brush fragrance-free talc over the lids before applying mascara. The powder coats the lashes and helps build them up.

Quick tricks for tired eyes

Use these exercises to relieve eyestrain:

▶ Blink and yawn three times.

▶ Every hour, look up from your work and focus on an object 20 feet away.

▶ Rub your hands together briskly, then cup your palms and place them gently over your eyes for 30 seconds.

Red eyes?

Colds, allergies and smoke can rob eyes of moisture, creating irritation. To the rescue: artificial tear solutions that supplement the natural tear film to moisturize and soothe the eyes.

Makeup do's and don'ts for contact lens wearers

▶ Put your lenses in before applying eye makeup and take them out before removing makeup.

▶ Use a cotton swab dipped in soap and water to remove eye makeup. Avoid makeup removers; they may leave a residue that can end up on your contact lenses when you put them back in.

▶ Don't use waterproof mascaras, which require removers. Try a brand that does not contain fibers and comes off easily.

▶ Don't put liner inside the lid. It could stain the lens.

Natural looking brows

▶ If your brows are naturally sparse or overplucked, use an eyebrow pencil one shade lighter than your brow color. Feather in bare spots with light, upward strokes. To avoid an artificial look, do not extend penciling beyond your natural browline.

▶ Keep eyebrows full and natural; don't over-tweeze. If you want darker eyebrows, feather on eyebrow powder.

▶ To make your brows appear thicker, use hairspray or mousse on an eyebrow brush and brush the brows straight up.

▶ Tweeze under the browline only and alternate plucking hairs from one brow to the other to ensure a better balance.

▶ The best time to tweeze is after a shower, when pores are open and hairs are softer. Always tweeze in the direction the hair grows.

▶ Always apply an astringent when you are through tweezing.

▶ To tame bushy brows, brush the brows down. Cut off any parts that overhang your natural brow contour. When you brush the brows up again, you'll find you've gotten rid of lots of scraggly ends without having to tweeze hairs and leave a sparse area in your brow. Another technique is to apply a bit of hairspray or wave-set lotion on an eyebrow brush and brush it on the brows for more control.

▶ To find your natural browline: Hold a pencil next to your nose, pointing toward the forehead. The brow should begin at the outside of the pencil. Slant the pencil so that it forms a diagonal from the side of your nose to the outer corner of your eye. The brow should end at the inside edge of the pencil. The arch should be above the center of your iris.

▶ To groom all brows, use an old, thoroughly cleaned mascara brush. Brush the brows up, then sideways.

The lowdown on lipstick

▶ Prepare your lips for color with a lip conditioner or foundation. Lipstick, like makeup, wears better with moisturizer underneath.

▶ Outline lips with a lip pencil to prevent color from bleeding.

▶ For perfect lips, outline the lips with a lip brush and fill in with lipstick. Dust with translucent powder and apply a second coat of the same color.

▶ Get the most out of your lipsticks. Try gloss to brighten matte shades, gold over brown tones or a lighter color on the upper lip.

Makeup dos and don'ts

▶ Buy small quantities of makeup and fragrance.

▶ Don't buy a package that has been opened or appears tampered with.

▶ Wash your hands and face before applying makeup.

▶ Don't apply makeup to sunburned or windburned skin, or to skin that has broken out in a rash.

▶ Don't borrow makeup or share yours with friends.

▶ Don't moisten makeup with saliva.

▶ Don't rim your eyes by applying liner inside the lash line.

▶ Don't overdo mascara. Excess can flake off and irritate your eyes.

▶ Close your makeup containers securely after each use.

▶ Don't keep your makeup in sunlight, near hot radiators or air conditioners, or in unventilated bathrooms.

▶ Don't use a product if it looks dried out, has changed color or has a disagreeable odor.

▶ Don't mix leftover products.

▶ Don't try several new products at the same time. Test them individually so that if you have a reaction, such as redness, itchiness or swelling, you'll know which product to suspect.

▶ Don't put on makeup in a moving vehicle.

Nail niceties

▶ File nails in one direction, from the side toward the center, working on the undersides of the nails. This helps keep nails from splitting.

▶ Buff nails before polishing them. It gives a smooth base to work on and makes the nails healthier, stronger.

▶ Use two thin coats of polish rather than one heavy coat. Polish wears better, lasts longer and is less susceptible to chipping.

▶ Using basecoat under polish reduces nail discoloration. By itself, it protects nails from the elements and from dishwashing detergent.

▶ To give nails a longer, more streamlined look, leave a bit of each side of each nail free from polish.

▶ When polish gets raggedy and there's no time for a complete redo, add a darker color and finish off with a topcoat.

▶ For double strength, apply nail hardener in two directions: side to side, let dry, then up and down. The nylon fibers form a lattice "mesh" that makes a tougher bond.

▶ Nail stains? Insert your fingertips in half a lemon and "swish" around. This whitens under and around the nails and cleans the cuticles.

▶ "Break in" a new emery board by running the coarser side over another emery board. The new emery will be less rough on nails.

▶ For ragged cuticles and hangnails, wear protective gloves when washing dishes and keep cuticles well-lubricated by applying hand cream several times a day. Push cuticles back regularly with an orangewood stick. Also try this once-a-week cuticle "bath": Warm a little olive or almond oil and soak your nails for 15 minutes; the cuticles are instantly softened.

How Long Do Most Cosmetics Last?

Product	Opened	Unopened
Eye Makeup		
Mascara	2 to 3 months	2 to 3 years
Liquid eyeliner	3 months	2 to 3 years
Eyeshadow (powder)	3 months	2 to 3 months
Eye pencil	about a year	3 to 4 years
Face Makeup		
Liquid foundation	6 months	2 to 3 years
Face powder	1 year	3 to 4 years
Powder blush	1 year	3 to 4 years
Cream or gel blush	6 months	2 to 3 years
Lipstick	6 months	2 years
Lip gloss	6 months	2 to 3 years
Fragrance		
Perfume	1 year	3 to 4 years
Toilet water/cologne	1 to 2 years	2 to 3 years

Fragrance pointers

▶ Don't overwhelm everyone by putting on too much fragrance—a dab of perfume or two to three seconds' worth of spray on each pulse point is enough. Remember that sometimes you can't smell your own fragrance because you've grown so accustomed to it. Reapply perfume after eight hours, cologne after four.

▶ To make your fragrance last longer, use soaps, powders and lotions in the same scent. Apply fragrance to your pulse points: the insides of wrists and elbows, backs of knees, behind the ears. This gives a lingering but not overpowering effect.

▶ Before you buy, test the perfume on *yourself*; the same scent varies from person to person.

▶ Don't make a final judgment on a scent until at least 10 minutes after application. Never try more than two scents at a time. You'll confuse your nose!

▶ During the course of the day, stroke the area where you first applied the fragrance. The warmth of your fingertips releases more scent.

▶ If you have dry skin, it will not retain fragrance for as long as oily skin. Apply perfume generously. Fragrances containing rich essential oils like jasmine and tuberose are excellent for dry skin.

▶ Make your house smell as nice as you do. Dab some of your favorite bath oil on a small area on light bulbs. The heat of the bulbs will spread the scent.

▶ Heat intensifies scents. Wear lighter forms of fragrance in the summer (eau de toilette or cologne); a more intense form (perfume) in colder weather.

▶ If you put on too much perfume, you can take some of it off by saturating a cotton ball with alcohol and dabbing it over the perfumed area. It will dissipate the strength of the fragrance without altering the scent.

▶ In summer, avoid wearing fragrance on parts of your body that will be exposed to direct sunlight. The strong sun rays can stain and leave a ring. Instead, dab perfume on unexposed areas such as pulse spots: the hairline, the nape of the neck, under the breasts, the inside of the wrists and on the sides of the ankles. In addition to being hidden from the sun, these are points where blood vessels that lie close to the skin's surface generate heat to prolong your perfume's fragrance—an added benefit.

▶ Don't let your fragrances fight each other. When wearing perfume, stick to unscented soaps and deodorants. Always wait at least six hours before switching scents.

Cosmetics: What's In There?

Most of us apply makeup without ever looking at the label. Knowing the "inside story" will help you be a smarter consumer.

Learn the ingredients in your cosmetics

▶ **Botanical extracts:** ingredients derived from plants and used chiefly for their cooling and soothing properties. Examples: cucumber, cornflower, rosemary, aloe vera, kelp.

▶ **Carbohydrate:** a compound of carbon, hydrogen and oxygen; used for thickening and moisturizing.

▶ **Collagen:** a natural body protein that is part of the connective tissue in the dermis that gives the skin firmness. For cosmetic products, collagen is usually derived from cows. Claims are that it helps skin regain firmness; most doctors believe that it does not penetrate the dermis. On the plus side, collagen is a good moisture binder.

▶ **Elastin:** with collagen, elastin is part of the connective support tissue of the dermis. It gives skin elasticity and, as an anti-aging ingredient, is supposed to help restore this quality.

▶ **Emollients:** oil-based ingredients that help prevent moisture from evaporating from the skin. Examples: cetyl alcohol, glyceryl stearate, hydrogenated vegetable oil, isopropyl myristate lanolin, mineral oil, petrolatum.

▶ **Glycoprotein:** a combination of carbohydrate and protein thought to enhance the cell-renewal process.

▶ **Moisture binders** *(also called humectants)*: water-trapping and water-sealing ingredients that hold moisture in the skin. Examples: hyaluronic acid, biohyaluronic acid, cholesterol sorbitol, glycerol, plyethylene glycol, propyleneglycol, sorbitol, urea.

▶ **Placental protein:** cells taken from the placenta of sheep and other animals. Nutrient rich, they help skin look fresher and smoother, supposedly by speeding up cell renewal.

▶ **Protein:** a combination of amino acids vital to all living cells. Used in anti-aging products as a skin conditioner.

▶ **Retin A (or retinoic acid):** a vitamin-A derivative, successfully used to treat acne. Thought to promote collagen production and increase blood flow for more youthful-looking skin.

▶ **SPF:** sun protection factor. A number indicating amount of time you can safely stay in the sun without burning. The higher the number, the more protection offered. For example, an SPF of 15 means that you can be in the sun 15 times longer than if you used no protection at all.

▶ **Thymus extract:** taken from the thymus gland of animals. Known as the youth gland because it is present in younger animals and tends to disappear with aging. Used for rejuvenation purposes.

▶ **Tocopherol:** an alcohol form of vitamin E, an antioxidant. *See* "Vitamin E," *below.*

▶ **Tocopheryl:** a form of vitamin E, an antioxidant. *See* "Vitamin E," *below.*

▶ **Vitamin C:** vital to collagen production.

▶ **Vitamin E:** an antioxidant. Hampers an oxidation process that leads to the formation of molecules called free radicals. Free radicals are aging because they can damage other cells, such as collagen and elastin.

7 Days To A Younger-Looking You

Whether you're in your twenties or your eighties, better-looking skin will be yours when you follow this daily regimen.

Daily skin-care routine

The basis for better skin is a faithful regimen.

▶ **Morning:** Cleanse your face and neck with soap or a cleanser designed for your skin type. Rinse with lukewarm water. Apply a toner and light moisturizer.

▶ **Night:** Take off eye makeup with a tissue. Cleanse your face thoroughly as in the morning; use eye cream and moisturizer where needed.

Day 1: Steaming

Steaming helps rid the skin of impurities. Cleanse your face thoroughly. Holding a towel over your head to form a "tent," stand over a basin of steaming hot water for five minutes. Keep your face at least 12 inches from the basin; intense heat can break capillaries. Finish with splashes of lukewarm water and apply a toner.

Day 2: Massaging

Massaging boosts circulation, tones muscles and reduces puffiness. Cleanse your face. Apply moisturizing cream to your fingertips. Add more cream to your fingers for each new massage step.

▶ Using a firm movement of the fingertips, stroke upward and outward from your mouth to your cheekbones. Do 10 times.

▶ Sweep your fingertips from the center of your forehead outward with long, extended strokes. Do 8 times.

▶ Make a fist and, using your knuckles, knead the skin from ears to chin along the outer part of your face. Remember: While your motions should be firm, you should never stretch your skin. Do 10 times.

▶ Form a "V" with the index and middle fingers; stroke them from the outer corners of your mouth to the top of your ears. Do 8 times.

▶ Keeping your fingers in the "V," go from the outer sides of your nose to the top of your ears. Do 8 times.

▶ Make circular motions with your fingertips all over your face. Starting from the chin, work up, always moving in an outward direction. Do 5 times.

▶ End the massage by tapping your face lightly and quickly with your fingers from chin to temples.

▶ Remove the cream from your face and cleanse.

Day 3: Dry-zone treatment

Dry-zone treatment moisturizes and smooths areas prone to extra dryness. Look at your lips, eye area and brow in a makeup mirror; run a finger lightly over these spots. If you see or feel wrinkles, cracks or tautness, try these anti-dryness strategies.

▶ **Lips:** Dab on a lip softener (such as petroleum jelly), making sure you smooth it into the corners of the mouth. If your lips are very dry, use a lip softener under your regular lipstick during the day.

▶ **Eyes:** Apply a nonoily eye cream, patting it on from the outer eye corner to the undereye area. Always pat perpendicular to the wrinkles; any motion that moves the skin in the same direction as the wrinkles or lines makes them worse.

▶ **Furrows in the brow:** Pat on a moisturizing cream, starting at the bottom of each furrow and working upward.

Day 4: Mask

A mask cleanses the skin and/or absorbs oil, helps to trap moisture, refines pores and boosts circulation to give the skin a glow. Use this guide to choose the right mask for your skin type.

▶ **Normal/dry skin:** gel-type (moisturizing) masks with vegetable or mineral oils, placenta, aloe vera, panthenol, carotene or collagen. Avoid oil-absorbing ingredients such as kaolin, talc and oatmeal.

▶ **Normal/oily skin:** clay (cleansing) masks with ginseng, yeast, calamine, clay. Avoid masks with oils and fragrances.

▶ **Combination skin:** a clay mask for your oily T-zone, a gel mask for everywhere else.

▶ **Sensitive skin:** non-irritating masks with rose hips, panthenol, allantoin or chamomile. Avoid silicates, alcohol, kelp and sulfur.

▶ To use, cleanse your face and remove any residue with a toner. Apply the mask evenly with upward motions. Leave the mask on and remove as directed on the package. While the mask is doing its work, lie down, feet elevated, with cool compresses or damp tea bags over your eyes.

Day 5: Neck beautifier

A neck beautifier massage combats dryness, helps prevent wrinkles and keeps the skin smooth. Since your neck contains fewer sebaceous glands than your face, it has a tendency to become dry, which can cause wrinkles and age you before your time. After cleansing your neck and applying a toner, try this.

▶ Put some moisturizing cream on your hands. Cross them slightly so that the right hand will stroke the left side of your neck, the left hand the right side.

▶ Keeping your fingers and palms extended, stroke the neck upward and outward with quick, smooth motions. Do 15 to 20 times.

▶ Remove the cream from your neck. Cleanse and follow with a toner.

Day 6: Exfoliating

Exfoliating sloughs off dead dry cells, which dull the complexion.

▶ Cleanse your face with a granular scrub such as oatmeal or almond.

▶ Massage your face gently with circular motions of your fingertips, moving in an outward, upward motion. Start from the chin and work up to the forehead.

▶ Rinse the scrub off thoroughly. Pat your face almost dry and apply a moisturizer.

Note: The more sensitive your skin, the more water you should add to the scrub and the more gently you should massage your face. If your skin is ultra-sensitive, do a patch test with the scrub before using it.

Day 7: T-zone corrector

T-zone corrector treatment gets rid of blackheads and fights oiliness. If you have an oily T-zone, you probably have blackheads in this area. Although some experts do not believe you should treat blackheads yourself, you can use this emergency treatment once in a while.

▶ Cleanse your skin. Splash your face with warm water 20 times to open the pores.

▶ Using a tissue (never your bare fingers), press on either side of the blackhead with even pressure. Don't force.

▶ Cleanse your face again and rinse with cool water.

▶ Apply an astringent with a clean cotton ball.

▶ Follow up with a drying acne medication such as benzoyl peroxide.

Looking Lovely After 40

You're not really getting older—and you are definitely getting better! Here are some tips to help you look as great as you feel.

Blushing beauty

Because your skin loses pigment and gets paler, try this for an allover vibrant glow: After applying foundation, blend cream blush in a soft peach or rose under your eyebrows. Blend it out to the hollow of the temples. Then apply the same blush along your cheekbones. Complete the look by smoothing a little over the front of your ears.

Skin

▶ Use a lightweight skin moisturizer during the day, a night cream when you sleep. Pay extra attention to the throat and undereye areas.

▶ Brighten the complexion by sloughing off dead surface skin with a washcloth or abrasive sponge.

Makeup

▶ Since complexions fade with age, choose a sheer oil-based foundation with a hint of pink or peach.

▶ Choose subtle blush for cheeks and soft, bright lip colors.

A touch of color

▶ Women of all ages look better with color on their lips, but after 40, it's a must. To keep lipstick from fading, set it with one of the new primers. Apply the primer, blot, pat on translucent powder and apply your lip color. Primer also prevents lipstick from bleeding into the fine lines around your mouth.

▶ Avoid iridescent lipsticks and blushers; they only spotlight lines and wrinkles. Matte finishes are the most flattering makeup choices.

The eyes have it

▶ Rose-tinted lenses can turn your eyeglasses into a beauty asset. They cast a healthy, pinkish glow on cheeks and can even disguise tired eyes.

▶ Your lashes do get sparser. To make them appear fuller, dot brown eye pencil along the upper lashline and smudge. This fills in lashes at the lid. Then apply mascara in brown/black, brown or navy.

▶ Stick to neutral matte eye shadows such as taupe, brown and gray. Iridescents emphasize wrinkles.

Undereye wrinkle aid

Undereye wrinkles are aging no matter how pretty your eyes are. Ordinary creams or moisturizers can make the area puffy. Instead, use intensive spot-treatment formulas that firm and smooth the skin, helping it look younger.

Hair talk

▶ Any above-the-shoulder length goes as long as it's softly swept off the face for lift.

▶ Hair tends to get drier with age, so use a shampoo for dry hair plus instant conditioner. A monthly deep-conditioning treatment helps, too.

▶ If you want to use color, go a bit lighter than your natural shade. Play down the yellow tones in gray with a platinum, silver or white rinse.

▶ Thinning hair? Try mousse to add body.

Hide 'n seek

▶ Fill in fine lines around the mouth with an eyeliner brush dipped in concealer.

▶ Play up your assets. If your cheeks are chubby, emphasize your eyes or lips instead.

▶ Play down loose fleshy skin under the jawline: Apply foundation, then dust light brown contour powder along the jawbone from the earlobes to the chin. Blend until you have a faint shadow and dust on translucent powder.

▶ As you get older, less makeup, with an emphasis on lighter cosmetic shades, is usually more flattering.

▶ Apply makeup in the same light you'll be seen in. Bathroom light can be dim and you may use too much for fluorescent or daytime lighting.

Stop-The-Clock Beauty Products

The newest skin helpers are anti-aging products. Many promise a lot—smoother, healthier, younger-looking skin. But do they deliver? Check out this mini-guide for some no-nonsense answers.

Eye creams: a wrinkle in time

Because the area around your eye has fewer oil glands, it is usually the first to show signs of sun damage and aging. Eye creams are specially formulated for this delicate area. They have a stickier base than all-purpose moisturizers, so they won't spread into the eye and irritate it. They contain no water-sealing ingredients that would make the eye area puffy. Most are also fragrance-free. The new eye creams plump up surface cells to camouflage wrinkles. Many also contain sunscreens. Remember, like moisturizers, eye creams give *temporary* results.

Moisturizers: the inside story

The skin's outer protective layer consists of dead cells. Live cells beneath this layer keep it supplied with moisture. But, as you get older, or if you have dry skin, water evaporates from the skin surface faster than it's supplied from below. As a result, your skin becomes flaky, drier and looks older. Moisturizers attempt to prevent this evaporation from the skin's surface; that's why it's best to apply them after bathing when the skin is moist. They also contain ingredients that help to trap the moisture from the atmosphere. By plumping up dead surface cells, smoothing over fine lines and making them less noticeable, moisturizers can help temporarily. Although they may reduce the appearance of lines and wrinkles, moisturizers cannot prevent them. However, many new moisturizers contain sunscreens, definite anti-aging protection against the sun's harmful rays. Do you have sensitive skin? Check the label for potentially troublesome ingredients such as: fragrance, lanolin, propylene glycol and some preservatives — methyl paraben, propyl paraben.

Cell renewal products: magic or malarky?

Skin cells develop in the inner (basal) layer of the epidermis and travel up to the skin's surface where they become drier and flatter until they eventually die and drop off the skin. In a younger person, this can take about three or four weeks, but as you get older, the cycle takes longer. The longer the journey, the drier the cells when they reach the surface. Cell renewal products are designed to give nature a boost by increasing the rate at which the skin naturally renews itself. The idea is: if older cells on the skin surface are shed faster, fresher ones can rise more quickly, making skin appear younger and smoother. Exactly how these products work isn't clear, but some experts suggest that they cause a low level of irritation to the skin surface. This stimulates the skin to produce new cells to replace ones that have been sloughed off. (Some dermatologists will remind you that washing gently with a facecloth also stimulates cell renewal.)

Sunscreens: not for summer only

Within the dermis, a network of connective tissue containing collagen and elastin helps support the skin and give it resiliency. The sun's ultraviolet rays break down this network, thereby weakening the skin's underlying support. As the skin's support system weakens, the skin sags — and wrinkles. Once collagen is broken down, the body cannot produce new collagen. By filtering out the sun's harmful rays, sunscreens prevent the breakdown of collagen. Visible proof of the sun's effect is evident when you compare the skin of your inner thigh, which receives little sun exposure, with your facial skin. The thigh is smooth and unlined; the face is not. For long-term anti-aging benefits, dermatologists unanimously recommend wearing sunscreeens daily year-round. The most effective products have an SPF of 15 or higher; SPF's go all the way up to 34.

Guidelines to smarter cosmetic shopping

▶ A higher price does not necessarily equal better results. In fact, a published study of moisturizers showed that some inexpensive products (as little as 10¢ an ounce) rated far better than the most expensive ones (as much as $70 an ounce).

▶ It is not essential to buy an entire treatment line. Many companies would have you believe that you won't get optimal results by mixing products from different firms. But you *can*. For instance, you could use your present moisturizer with a cell-renewal product from another line.

▶ Special packaging is tempting, but it raises the cost. Scientific-looking bottles do give convenient premeasured doses, but these are primarily packaging gimmicks — and you are paying for them.

▶ Always sample a product before buying it. Testers are usually available; if not, ask the salesperson to open a product for you.

▶ If you have sensitive skin, avoid trying several new products at once. That way, if you develop an allergic reaction, you'll be able to identify the source.

Cold-Weather Beauty

Cold, windy weather and dry, overheated houses are murder on your hair, face and skin. All three need a little extra TLC from you.

Bath basics

▶ Take lukewarm baths and showers. Hot water strips the skin of its natural oils.

▶ As the skin gets drier, it gets more delicate. Put away your abrasive loofahs and stiff-bristled brushes and wash instead with a soft cloth or very soft-bristled brush.

▶ Don't wait until your skin feels dry to use a moisturizer. Prevention is the best cure, so make moisturizing after a bath or shower a regular part of your routine. Apply a cream or lotion to the skin while it is slightly damp to help trap moisture.

▶ Bathe or shower at night rather than in the morning. This way your body has the entire night to replenish its natural, protective oils.

Turn your bath into a spa

Make your bath extra-special with ingredients from the kitchen.

▶ Add a cup of vinegar to eliminate dry-skin itching.

▶ A handful of Epsom salts soothes aching muscles.

▶ Herbs and spices make everything nice. Tie cinnamon, cloves and basil in cheesecloth and hang under running water. Other herbal relaxers: lavender, elder flower, comfrey, rose.

▶ Sweet-dreams milk bath: Make 3 quarts hot milk from dry-milk powder and add 1 cup honey and 1 cup chamomile tea. Mix and add to the bath.

Skin

▶ Cleanse your face at night with soap or a cleanser and follow with an alcohol-free toner. In the morning, splash lukewarm water on your face. If you have oily skin, you may also want to use a toner in the morning.

▶ Try plain milk as a cleansing lotion when your skin gets flaky. Apply it with a cotton ball, follow with a splash of lukewarm water and rinse the face thoroughly with cold water.

▶ Switch to an oil-based moisturizer, richer than the one you use in summer. Massage it thoroughly, but gently, into your face.

▶ Don't forget about sunscreens! Even though it's not summer, you still need protection from the sun's ultraviolet rays. Mix a sunscreen with your moisturizer before applying it, or use a product with a built-in sunscreen.

▶ Don't wash your face for at least half an hour before you plan to go outdoors. The water plus the cold winds have a drying effect on the skin.

▶ Coming in from the cold and warming yourself immediately by the fire may sound wonderful, but it can cause broken capillaries to appear on your face. The cold outside causes blood vessels to contract, and when there's a sudden change to a hot temperature, they expand and can burst. To avoid this, head straight for the sink. Splash your face with cool water, gradually increasing the temperature to warm, *not* hot. Then enjoy the fireside!

▶ Go easy on caffeine; it tends to dehydrate the skin. Try a cup of herbal tea or even plain hot water with a slice of lemon as a substitute— very refreshing!

▶ One way to avoid the all-over itchy feeling from winter-dry skin is to use mild soaps and bleaches on any clothing that will be next to your skin. The chemical residue left by strong detergents and bleaches can strip oils from the skin, leaving it prone to irritation.

▶ Humidity is vital for the skin as well as the hair in winter. To raise the humidity level in your home, purchase a humidifier or place a pan of water on the radiator. Fill your bedroom with plants that require lots of water. Bamboo, ferns and large-leaved plants, such as begonias, give off moisture that benefits the skin.

▶ To keep lips from chapping, use lipstick with moisturizer or lip balm.

▶ Avoid irritating the skin when shaving. Shave while you're in the bath—the water softens the hair. Lather on shaving cream to lubricate. Never use soap; it clogs the razor.

▶ Avoid using an alcohol-based lotion when shaving your legs. It only adds to dryness. Check labels to see if they mention alcohol (or ethanol, another commonly used term for alcohol).

▶ Guard against chapped hands by moisturizing them regularly.

▶ Here is an at-home hand-softener treatment: Massage a hand cream into your hands and nail beds. Cover each hand with a plastic bag and wrap the hands in a towel warmed from the dryer. Leave on for 15 minutes. Remove the towel and bags and massage the remaining cream into the hands and nail beds.

▶ Don't neglect your feet in cold weather months! A soothing warm soak, followed with rich moisturizer, will keep feet looking and feeling their best.

▶ In the shower, use a washcloth all over your body. This helps exfoliate dead skin and keeps the skin feeling smooth. After the shower, follow with a rich moisturizer.

Hair

▶ If your hair tends to get dry during the winter, change to a shampoo formula for dry hair or don't use as much of your regular shampoo. Instead, dilute your shampoo with water before applying.

▶ Do you have flyaway hair? Winter's dryness causes static electricity. Condition your hair regularly to make it more manageable.

▶ To cure flyaway hair caused by static electricity, try this at-home conditioner. Mix ½ cup of any creamy conditioner, 1 egg yolk and 2 teaspoons sesame oil in a blender for one minute. Massage this into your hair. Cover your head with plastic wrap or aluminum foil and leave on for 20 to 30 minutes. Shampoo your hair thoroughly.

▶ Another destatic trick: Before brushing, dip your hairbrush into a solution of conditioner plus water to coat the bristles.

▶ If your scalp starts flaking, it may be dry scalp rather than dandruff. Switch to a milder, castile-type shampoo for a few washings and see if it makes a difference.

▶ Be gentle with heat. Use your blow dryer on a warm-to-cool setting only and stop blow-drying when your hair is slightly damp. This avoids overdrying the hair. Don't use curling irons or hot rollers on damp hair—they can cook it!

▶ Give your hair a hot oil treatment once a month for extra deep conditioning. This will tame brittle ends and make the hair softer.

▶ Use wooden or metal combs and brushes, not plastic or natural-fiber ones, which create more static. To "de-static" a brush, slip a nylon stocking over the bristles.

Makeup

▶ If your face feels drier in the winter, you may want to use an oil-based foundation if you're presently using a water-based one.

▶ Try a cream rouge instead of a powder blush; dust translucent powder over the rouge to "set" it.

▶ Pay careful attention to your eyes. Slick on an undereye protector (SPF 15) before going outdoors. It will protect the delicate undereye area from sunlight and wind.

Sun-Lover's Guide To Looking Your Best

Here's how to deal with summer's special beauty problems and look great all season long.

Skin

The summer sun may bring you a luscious glow, but it also makes your oil glands work overtime and that calls for a change in skin care.

▶ Cleanse more frequently and use a mild astringent to unclog pores.

▶ Instead of using foundation, switch to a tinted moisturizer—all the better to show off a tan. If your skin is oily, try one that's oil-free.

▶ Change concealers. Your winter version is probably too light, accentuating undereye circles and uneven skin tones.

▶ Two skin savers to tote to the beach: a cotton ball soaked in refrigerator-cooled water to refresh your face and remove excess oil, and a spritzer bottle of water to rinse away saltwater and chlorine that can dry out the skin.

▶ The best thing for your face in summer is deep cleansing. The easy way is to add chamomile tea to a basin of boiling water. Hold your face over the basin and at the same time apply a granular scrub. Massage your face in a circular motion. This will loosen debris in the pores so impurities are freed and your skin will look more radiant. Do this once a week for dry skin, twice weekly for oily/normal skin.

▶ Once or twice a week when showering, apply a grainy scrub with your fingers or a washcloth. Concentrate on flaky areas—the elbows, knees, feet—but give the entire body, except for sensitive areas, a gentle once-over for best results.

▶ To neutralize perspiration odors, soak in tepid water mixed with ½ cup baking soda. An afterbath dusting of baking soda on the feet and underarms helps keep you fresh.

Makeup

▶ To set foundation and keep it from streaking, brush loose powder on oily areas, making sure you shake the excess off the brush before applying. Repeat as needed. To look sun-kissed, choose a slightly warmer shade of powder than your own skin color.

▶ To prevent makeup from running in the sun, use waterproof eye makeup and choose lipsticks labeled "long-wearing" or "long-lasting."

▶ The best colors to wear with a tan are bronzy-golden shades. Look for them in eye shadows, lipstick, blush.

Shaving

▶ Don't dry-shave. This irritates the skin. Instead, lubricate the skin before shaving by splashing on warm water, or rubbing in baby oil or a body lotion.

▶ Use an alcohol-free moisturizer immediately after shaving.

▶ Shave at the beginning of your bath, not at the end. Soaking in the tub causes the skin to swell so your razor cannot reach the base of the hair on the skin.

▶ Don't shave first thing in the morning; wait at least half an hour after you get up. The reason? After lying prone all night, the body accumulates fluids and you can't get a really close shave.

▶ Shave the night before you plan to go to the beach. Just-shaved skin is very sensitive. Suntan lotion or bronzing gels can irritate it, causing tiny bumps.

Hair

▶ Always use alcohol-free styling gels. Products that contain alcohol can cause hair to get sunburned.

▶ Protect color-treated or permed hair from salt or chlorinated water by massaging in a few drops of baby oil from the roots to the ends. Shampoo as soon as you get home.

▶ Before you sun, use a hot-oil treatment or apply olive or safflower oil. Be sure to rinse it out thoroughly.

▶ Always wear a bathing cap when swimming and rinse your hair after you come out of the water to remove chlorine or salt. If you're not near a shower, pour on some salt-free club soda and comb through; it has the same effect as water.

▶ Protect your hair from overdrying at the beach by combing on conditioner before you go out. Leave it on until you return home, then wash your hair thoroughly.

▶ To de-snarl wet hair, pack a spray bottle filled with conditioner and water. After your swim, spritz on the mixture and comb it through.

▶ For a special summer evening out, dress up your hair with your favorite fragrance. Add a few drops to a pitcherful of water and use it as the final rinse after you shampoo.

On-The-Go Beauty

From quick touch-ups to emergency fixes, here are beauty tricks to take you from morning until evening just the way you want to go—looking your best.

Fresh feeling

For instant freshening, splash your face with warm water and spritz with seltzer. Pat it dry gently.

Buff up

When you can't take time out for a manicure, buff your nails to a soft pink finish. Buff in one direction only and stop when the nails feel hot.

Quick remover

You're not stuck when you discover that you're all out of nail polish remover. Paint a generous amount of base coat over your nail, wait 20 seconds and wipe the nail with a tissue or cotton ball, pressing firmly. Repeat until the polish is removed.

No shine

Can't get to a sink to wash your face? Try using oil-blotting tissues. They get rid of shine but leave makeup intact.

Bath bonus

Taking a bath after a long, hard day is wonderful; there's nothing like it to unwind. You can use this bathtime for a beauty treatment, too. Add 2 cups instant non-fat dried milk to the water to soften skin, or massage your body with vegetable or baby oil before stepping in the tub. After soaking for a few minutes, rub your body down with a loofah. This not only gets rid of dead, flaky skin but wakes you up so you'll be ready for a night out.

Faded to fresh

▶ When you're too rushed to take time out for a recharge, you can give your face a healthy glow with this mix-in-a-minute combo. Combine a bit of cream blush with your moisturizer (a one to four ratio) and apply it over your entire face. Smooth with a facial sponge and finish with translucent powder.

► All you need is your blush for this transformation! Put more blush high on the cheekbones into the temples. Brush a bit along the eyebone under the brow, at the tip of the nose and at the bottom of the chin.

► Try heading for the kitchen when you want to add a rosy glow to your face. Mix 1 teaspoon thyme into 1 cup boiling water, let it steep for 10 minutes and apply the solution to your face with cotton balls. Let it dry, rinse with cold water and you're ready to go.

Fix-up for the frizzies

Give your hairbrush a dusting of antistatic fabric spray and run it through your hair. Instant manageability! You can smooth a sheet of anticling fabric softener— the kind you put in the dryer—over your hair for the same effect.

Long-lasting makeup

► Pat an ice cube gently over your face after applying makeup. It "seals" color in and gives you a fresh, dewy look.

► For lips that won't need retouching for hours, use a lip-coloring pencil on the entire surface of the lips and slick gloss over it.

Rx for puffy eyes

A fast cure for puffy eyelids is to lie down and place steeped chamomile tea bags on closed lids for 10 minutes. The tannic acid reduces the swelling like magic.

Smear tactic

You're all made up and ready to go— and your mascara smears. Don't start over. Dip a cotton swab in eye makeup remover and whisk off the smudges.

Putting on the glitz

► Don't have time for a day-into-evening makeover? Add a metallic or glitter eye shadow shade right over your matte color.

► A few strokes of a highlighter in a pale silver shade will light up your eyes and your whole face. Stroke it on the browbone, sweeping to the outer corner of the eye.

Perm pick-up

If your perm has pooped out, leaving you with a droopy crown and straight-ish sides, try this: Spray the crown with water. Using your fingers, squeeze small handfuls of hair as it dries. You'll have curls galore! For the sides, spray and fluff the hair with your fingers. Pull one side back and secure it with a decorative comb.

Under cover

To hide a blemish, paint it out. Dab on an astringent and apply a heavy coating of undereye cover-up. Dip a small makeup brush into liquid foundation and stroke it over the blemish, feathering at the edges.

Look Great In Glasses

Selecting flattering glasses shouldn't be a hit-or-miss proposition. Here's how to choose the best frame shapes and lenses for your face, plus smart makeup strategies.

Round face

Squared-off frames de-emphasize roundness. Select styles that are slightly wider than the widest point of your face for a slimming effect. The bridge of the frames should be wide as well and somewhat arched.

Triangular face

To give better "balance" to your face, the top half of the frames should not extend past your temples. A bridge that's softly curved and the lower half of the frame in a down-sweep are most flattering for you.

Oval face

Because the oval face is ideal, you can experiment with many different types of frames to find the best one for you. However, it's important not to detract from the natural symmetry of your face, so don't go for a shape that's *too* way out.

Rectangular face

To create the illusion of a broader face, keep the overall width of the frames within the border of the widest point of your cheekbones. The bridge of the frames should be slightly curved.

Square face

Gracefully curved frames relieve the angular shape of a square face. The frames should be slightly wider than the widest point of your jawline, with the bridge arched. The lower part should sweep up toward the brows.

Lenses: hints on tints

Tinted lenses in glasses can complement your frames, your eyes and your complexion.

▶ Select lenses that are in the same color family as your frames. For example, if your frames are warm-toned—brown, coral, bronze, cinnamon, gold—the lenses should have gold or yellow undertones. For cool-toned frames—blue, plum, rose, gray, taupe—lenses with blue or pink undertones work best.

▶ Another choice is gradient lenses. This type of lens has graduated levels of color: The most intense tones are on top and the color fades toward the bottom. Gradient lenses can be especially flattering for shades such as blue, which is lovely at lid level but can make you look just plain tired when the deep color extends below the eye.

Brow-beautiful advice

Select frames that cover your browline or you'll get a "double-brow" look. If your browline is below your frames, dust a bit of blush above your brows to lessen the double-brow effect. Be sure to keep your eyebrows neatly plucked underneath the natural line.

Framing blush

If blush looks unnatural under your glasses, try wearing your glasses when you apply it. Stroke it on, following the line of the frame from the center of your cheeks up toward your temples in a gentle curve. Blend well. This will accent your cheeks in line with your frames so that the blush doesn't "change color" when seen through tinted lenses.

Eye-catching makeup

▶ The rule to remember when applying eye makeup under tinted lenses is to choose colors that are close to each other in the color spectrum. For example, rose-tinted lenses won't be attractive over green eye shadow. The combination creates a muddy effect. However, rose lenses with blue eye makeup gives you a soft mauve—very pretty.

▶ If you're farsighted, your type of lenses magnify the eyes. To counteract this effect, choose eye makeup in neutral tones—browns, grays, soft plums. With eye shadow brush or eye pencil, draw a line close to the lashes on the upper lids and brush or finger-smudge the line up toward the brow and out (away from the nose). The idea is to have deep color close to the lashes, very subtle color on the lids and below the brows. If you wish, lightly apply a coat of mascara and brush the lashes with a clean mascara brush. Any clumping of mascara will be magnified under these lenses; take care to keep the lashes separated. Choose vibrant-toned lipsticks. Since the lenses magnify your eyes, your lips should be just as outstanding. Try ruby red, deep plum, hot raspberry.

▶ If you're nearsighted, your lenses make your eyes look smaller, so your eyes need more definition. Use a soft pencil and rim your lower lids, keeping the color close to your lashes. Good color choices are turquoise or light gray, which make the whites of your eyes appear brighter. Then use a dark-colored shadow (navy, brown, teal, plum) and line the outer halves of both the upper and lower lids. Lightly extend the color of the upper lid to just under the brows. Highlight under the arch of the eyebrows with a pale eye shadow or blush. Apply two coats of mascara, allowing ample time in between to let the first coat dry. Stick to pinks, corals and peaches for your lips. Since your eyes are already diminished by your lenses, you don't want an overpowering mouth.

Jewelry

If you wear glasses frequently but not all the time, select your earrings with your glasses on. A couple of hints to keep in mind:

▶ Oversized earrings may look "clunky" with oversized frames. Think of your face as a unit, not separate parts, and keep proportion in mind.

▶ If your glasses are silver- or gold-toned, you may want to choose earrings in the same color to keep your face "color-coordinated."

Balancing act

Lipstick can be your number one beauty essential. The reason is that glasses draw attention to the upper part of your face. A bit of color on your lips (subtle or vibrant, depending on your frame color) will give your face a more "balanced" appearance.

11.
Here's To Your Health!

How To Cut Calories—And
Enjoy Eating

Eat, Drink and Be Merry . . .
Without Gaining Weight

Dieting Success Strategies

Healthful Habits

Common Exercise Mistakes And
How To Correct Them

Medicines That Don't Mix

How To Cut Calories And Enjoy Eating

Worried about extra pounds, but tired of fad diets that never seem to work for you? These tips will help you trim calories every day from breakfast through dinner—without actually dieting. What could be easier!

Breakfast

▶ Start the day with fresh fruit rather than fruit juice. Half a grapefruit, for example, has 60 fewer calories than eight oz of unsweetened grapefruit juice and you get important fiber as a bonus.

▶ Prepare French toast in a non-stick frying pan and serve with unsweetened applesauce, stewed fruit or unsweetened fruit butter instead of maple syrup.

▶ Make a 2-egg omelet, using 1 whole egg with just the white of the other egg. By eliminating the second egg yolk, you'll save more than 250 mg of cholesterol and over 65 calories.

▶ Switch from whole milk to skim. If you've never been able to get used to the taste of skim milk, mix half whole with half skim. You'll cut 36 calories from each 8-ounce glass. For even easier calorie cutting, switch to 2% or 1% milk, which has fewer calories but retains more body than skim.

▶ Instead of American cheese as an omelet filling, substitute leftover steamed vegetables and herbs. You'll save about 210 calories and 16 grams of fat per two oz of cheese.

▶ For a delicious spread you can use on toast or pancakes, purée fresh fruit, such as blueberries or strawberries, in a blender to keep handy in the refrigerator.

▶ For an even faster low-calorie fruit spread, open a small jar of puréed baby food.

▶ After toasting your bread, let it cool. It will absorb less butter.

Lunch

▶ When you order a hamburger, instead of eating only half of the bun to save calories (the usual dieter's ploy), eat the whole bun but only half to two-thirds of the meat. Each ounce of meat you forego saves you about 80 calories, 52 of them from fat.

▶ Pass up catsup (each tablespoon has 16 calories). Instead, have a slice of tomato on your hamburger; only four calories and no sugar added.

▶ The calories in a restaurant diet platter (usually hamburger, fruit and cottage cheese) are no bargain. Opt for a bowl of soup and a small salad instead.

▶ In place of mayonnaise-loaded tuna salad, have a small individual-size can of water-packed tuna with a squeeze of lemon. You could save over 200 calories.

▶ For a low-fat, low-cal sandwich, have a slice of cheese, lettuce and tomato on whole-wheat toast. A real bargain at under 250 calories.

▶ Create a healthful, low-calorie thirst-quencher by mixing ½ cup mineral water with ⅓ cup of your favorite juice.

▶ Another low-cal, healthful drink is two oz of orange juice mixed with a squeeze of lime and enough cold water to make 1 cup. It has only about 30 calories.

▶ Try two shredded wheat biscuits with four oz of skim milk for a filling, low-fat, high-fiber, 225-calorie lunchtime meal.

▶ Have a low-cal California-style salad. Slices of oranges and fresh spinach leaves make a salad with lots of eye appeal that is also high in iron and vitamin C. Sprinkle it with lemon, vinegar or a low-cal dressing.

▶ To get a taste of salad dressing without calorie-laden oil, dilute the dressing with water. Then spray it on the salad with a plant mister.

Main meal tactics

▶ Turn the salad course into the appetizer. This will quell your hunger and contribute important vitamins, minerals and fiber.

▶ A half-dozen raw clams or oysters makes a nutritious appetizer with fewer than 60 calories.

▶ To keep chicken moist, cook it with the skin on. Trim calories and fat by removing the skin before serving.

▶ Opt for white meat over dark. It has fewer calories and about one-third less fat.

▶ Make soups a day ahead and refrigerate them. Before reheating, skim the congealed fat off the top.

▶ Don't fry chicken in oil. Instead, try oven-baked "fried" chicken. Coat chicken pieces as you normally do and bake them for about an hour. Periodically baste them with a few tablespoons of orange juice to enhance the flavor and prevent drying out.

▶ To reduce the fat content in ground beef recipes, sauté lean beef in a nonstick pan. After the meat browns, place it in a colander so the excess fat can drain off. Then press the beef against the sides of the colander with a large spoon to remove more fat. Continue preparing the recipe as usual.

▶ When making chili, cut the amount of ground beef in half. For each ½ pound of raw meat you omit, substitute ½ cup cooked bulgur wheat or ½ cup cooked brown rice. You'll reduce the fat, save up to 500 calories (depending on the percentage of fat in the meat) and increase the fiber content.

► When preparing stuffed cabbage or stuffed peppers, substitute ½ cup cooked lentils for ½ pound raw ground beef. You can save as much as 500 calories.

► Tomato juice makes a flavorful, fat-free liquid for pot roast.

► For stews, switch occasionally from beef to leaner chunks of veal. Stew them with vegetables, such as carrots, squash and potatoes, in an electric slow cooker. Limit your portion to about two oz veal.

► Instead of high-fat veal parmigiana, try veal sautéed with mushrooms in a few tablespoons of dry Marsala wine.

► Fish or shellfish appetizers can substitute as a filling, low-calorie main course. A double-size shrimp cocktail, a large portion of ceviche or a dozen clams or oysters are excellent (although pricey) choices.

► Use swordfish or salmon in place of beef when making shish kabob. Alternate with decorative chunks of fresh or unsweetened pineapple and lime for an attractive and healthful meal.

► Instead of meatloaf, try fish loaves or fish burgers. Mix flaked fish with eggs and bread crumbs, shape the mixture into loaves or patties and bake. For every 2 eggs you use, remove 1 yolk and save it for another recipe.

► Save calories when preparing eggplant parmigiana by steaming thin slices of eggplant instead of sautéing them in oil. With a tasty sauce blanketing the dish, you won't notice a difference.

► Use low-fat cottage cheese and low-fat ricotta for stuffed shells and manicotti. Save up to 80 calories per eight oz of low-fat cheese without sacrificing a bit of flavor.

► Make lasagna with cheese and spinach filling instead of beef. Mix equal parts of low-fat cottage cheese and cooked, drained spinach. Spread the mixture over lasagna noodles and cover with tomato sauce.

► "Sauté" onions and other vegetables in broth instead of oil.

► Sprinkle ½ teaspoon Parmesan cheese on half a baked potato with a dash of pepper. Cut the potato into thirds and toast it until crispy. Each third has about 80 calories.

Desserts

► Whenever possible, choose fresh fruit to top off a meal.

► When an apple or a piece of melon won't satisfy your sweet tooth, have fruit ice rather than ice cream or milk sherbet.

► If you must have cake, opt for those that are lowest in calories— sponge cake or angel food cake.

► Have a frozen banana. Slice a very ripe banana, seal it in foil and keep it in the freezer. It's a palate-pleaser for only about 100 calories.

► A dozen frozen grapes (40 calories) makes another tasty treat.

Snacks

► A cup of air-popped popcorn (no butter) makes a low-fat snack for only about 25 calories. Try seasoning it with herbs.

► To save calories, spray popcorn with vegetable cooking spray before adding the salt. It helps the salt stick and only a trace of calories is added.

► For a nutritious high-energy snack, have half a raisin bagel or whole-wheat bagel.

► A glass of skim milk blended with some ripe fruit and crushed ice makes a frothy low-calorie shake.

▶ Instead of reaching for a candy bar when your energy level dips, try eating some dried fruit. Limit yourself to two pieces. Two large apricot halves have about 25 calories.

▶ Make custards and puddings with skim milk and reduce the sugar by half.

▶ Mix ½ cup tangy buttermilk with ½ cup tomato juice. It has just 67 calories.

▶ Mix ½ cup buttermilk with ½ cup of low-calorie borscht. It has only about 60 calories and is a refreshing summer soup.

▶ Boost your calcium intake by adding a tablespoon of dry skim milk powder to a glass of skim milk for only 23 extra calories.

Until dinner is ready

▶ Have ready some low-calorie snacks that are easy to grab: unsalted oyster crackers, tiny cheese tidbits, raw vegetables such as mushrooms, cherry tomatoes, carrots, cucumbers and celery.

▶ Before preparing dinner, sit down and have a glass of vegetable juice or two breadsticks to take the edge off your hunger and prevent excessive "sampling."

▶ Keep your freezer stocked with single-portion containers of low-calorie vegetable soups that you can heat up in minutes. This "first course" will prevent you from overeating at dinner.

While watching TV

▶ If you're used to snacking while watching TV, wear a leotard or gym shorts and do some stretching and toning exercises instead of nibbling.

▶ Keep your hands busy by giving yourself a manicure. By the time your nails dry, your need to nosh may have disappeared.

▶ Keep a pitcher of tomato juice, club soda or ice water at hand. Sip slowly.

▶ Never have dinner in front of the TV; concentrate on one or the other. It's much more satisfying to savor your meal at an attractively set table.

▶ Use the time during commercials for activities other than snacking. Keep your hands occupied with crossword puzzles, a stamp collection, sewing, knitting or balancing the checkbook.

Handling the food-craving crazies

▶ Instead of a chocolate bar, treat yourself to one or two chocolate-covered cherries, about 67 calories each, or 10 to 15 chocolate-covered raisins, about four calories each.

▶ Try one of the reduced-calorie hot chocolate drink mixes. For as few as 40 calories, you can get a satisfying chocolate "fix."

▶ Choose vanilla thins, tea biscuits, graham crackers or arrowroot cookies, which are lower in calories than most other varieties.

▶ Low-priced ice creams are also lower in fat and calories—a smart choice when the craving for something cold and creamy hits you.

Fat-free cubes

Busy and weight-conscious families often broil meats but don't make gravy with the pan juices. Don't waste the juices; let them cool and pour them into an icecube tray that has individual lift-out sections. When the fat has risen, skim it off and put the tray in the freezer. Later you can use the cubes to flavor soups, sauces, casseroles.

Eat, Drink And Be Merry. . . Without Gaining Weight

Holiday dinners, drinks and parties don't have to mean extra pounds. These fool-your-appetite tricks and morale-boosters will help keep your weight steady no matter what time of year it is.

Party-goer's do's and don'ts

▶ Don't skip meals the day of a party; going hungry will only make you more susceptible to temptation. Instead, eat a healthy lunch, one that contains a lean source of protein such as poultry or fish plus some complex carbohydrates and have a small bowl of soup with a salad before going out.

▶ Make your first drink a glass of club soda or mineral water. Sip this while you scout around and see the kinds of food available. Then ration your nibbling to the foods on the left column of our "Party Switch Chart." *(See page 248.)*

▶ Find someone interesting to talk to and stay far from the food buffet.

▶ Don't give in to sabotage. Have some ready excuses on hand for the hosts who push drinks or press you to "try this." Some good ones are: "Sorry, doctor's orders," "Thanks, but everything was so delicious I'm stuffed already," "I'm driving."

▶ Don't eat salty foods; they'll only make you thirsty and encourage more drinking.

▶ Leave early. If you thank your hosts profusely and tell them you have an early morning appointment, they'll understand, and you'll remove yourself from the site of temptation. Another option is to arrive fashionably late.

▶ Fill up on crudités first, then head for the more fattening foods—but go easy on these.

Cocktail hour

▶ Steer away from drinks made with fruit juices and milk bases. These increase the calorie count considerably.

▶ Rule of thumb for alcoholic beverages: The "proof" determines the calories; 80 proof vodka instead of 100 proof, for example, saves you about 25 calories per 1½ oz.

▶ Sip your cocktail from a large glass filled with ice. There will be less room for liquid.

▶ Opt for lower calorie dry wines over sweet ones. Champagne is a good choice.

Dinner out

▶ Ask the waiter not to put butter on the table.

▶ In place of dinner rolls, request crackers or breadsticks.

▶ Start the meal with a salad, clear soup or tomato juice. Avoid creamed soups or heavily sauced pasta appetizers.

▶ Order salads without the dressing or with the dressing on the side.

▶ Substitute a squeeze of fresh lemon or vinegar and fresh pepper for the usual dressing.

▶ Ask for steamed vegetables and a baked potato with no butter.

▶ Order broiled meat and fish. Ask how gravies and sauces are prepared. If they're made with butter or cream, request that they be served separately.

How to cope with holiday dinners

▶ Decide in advance to be satisfied with small portions. Have your favorites—you'll feel deprived if you don't—but remember that the fifth bite of pumpkin pie (or the second helping of stuffing, or the fourth glass of wine) doesn't taste any different from the first.

▶ Eat an apple 10 minutes before dining. This way your brain will get a head start on registering satisfaction—it takes 20 minutes for your stomach to signal your brain that you're full—and you won't be as likely to overeat.

▶ Cut food into small pieces and chew each mouthful five times.

▶ Always put down your knife and fork between bites.

▶ Talk up a storm. This will slow down your eating and give you time to feel full.

▶ Don't save the best for last; that always leads to overdoing it.

▶ Eat a *big* salad; the fiber will fill you up quickly.

▶ Tighten your belt before you dig in. The discomfort is a great "stop" signal.

Party Switch Chart

Try This . . .	Instead Of . . .
Wine spritzers; light beer; mineral water or club soda with lime; alcohol mixed with water or club soda	Sweet wines; liqueurs; punch; eggnog; alcohol with sugary mixes
Lean, sliced poultry or roast beef; shrimp	High-fat cold cuts; pâté; sausages; Swedish meatballs
Lower-calorie cheeses like Gouda, Camembert, Provolone, Neufchâtel	High-calorie cheeses like creamed cottage cheese, Brie, Roquefort
Flatbreads; pretzels; popcorn; breadsticks; whole grain crackers	Potato, corn or taco chips; salted nuts
Plain crudités	Crudités with dips
Oil and vinegar or plain lemon juice	Blue cheese, Roquefort and Russian dressings
Raisins; dried fruits; fresh apples and pears; hard candy	Fruitcake; gingerbread; Christmas cookies; pie; fudge

Dieting Success Strategies

Slim-down tactics that really work.

Smart ways to meet your dieting goals

▶ Build confidence in your ability to succeed by setting reasonable goals for yourself. It's better to commit to just 15 minutes of exercise three times a week, for example, than an unrealistic goal of 30 minutes every day.

▶ Be specific. "I'm going to lose weight this year" is too vague. Instead, decide to join a weight-loss group and/or to cut out 150 calories a day and/or to substitute fruit for dessert three times a week. Select whatever strategies work for you.

▶ Make a written contract with yourself. If you want to lose more after your first goal is met, renew the contract.

▶ Make sure you really *want* to lose. Otherwise, you're doomed from the start. Key words that may indicate you're not quite ready: "I wish, I hope, I'll try."

▶ Share your plans with those you can count on for support. But keep your goals to yourself if you suspect someone is going to be watching for your first slip-up.

▶ Be prepared for setbacks, and when they occur (as they inevitably will), don't berate yourself. Making changes often involves two steps forward and one step backward. Losing weight is no exception.

▶ Decide to lose weight out of self-love, not out of self-hate. Perhaps your body type or bone structure is such that you can be content to wear a size 10 rather than a size 8. If you can get yourself into reasonable physical shape and feel good about yourself, a few pounds more or less really don't matter.

▶ Learn to reprogram your mental dialogue. When your mind tells you, "I can't pass up that incredible dessert," realize that you *don't* have to listen.

▶ Enjoy a treat occasionally. Sometimes you may choose to tell yourself, "Yes, tonight I'll treat myself to a slice of cake." That's fine, provided you are in charge of that decision.

▶ Make use of mental pictures. Every day, sit quietly for a few minutes and visualize yourself walking or jogging briskly, weighing five pounds less, feeling good about yourself.

▶ Eat regular meals and have your biggest meal when you are most active. This allows your body to burn calories more efficiently.

▶ Drink at least six 8-ounce glasses of water a day. Try mixing a little fruit juice with the water. Drink half an hour before meals. Juice will cut your appetite by raising your blood-sugar level.

▶ When marketing, concentrate on the outer aisles, where fresh vegetables and dairy products are. Inner aisles usually carry processed, calorie-dense foods.

▶ Use nonstick pots and pans whenever possible to cut down on fats.

Fun reminders

When your children outgrow playing with magnetic plastic alphabet letters, "write" messages on the refrigerator to remind yourself to stick to your diet—"eat a carrot," "think thin" and so on. The letters are bright and eye-catching, and you can easily change the messages so that you won't get used to seeing them too often and ignore them. If that doesn't work, hang a favorite piece of clothing that you can't fit into— slacks or a skirt, for example— beside the refrigerator.

Ride and run

If you have a very busy schedule, make your time with your spouse meaningful. Try sharing a form of exercise—running. If your spouse can run faster and farther than you, ride a bike while he or she runs. Then switch off and let him or her ride while you run. This provides a warmup or cool-down period for the person pedaling and at the same time allows both of you to run the distance most comfortable for each.

The heart of the matter

You may be trying to stay fit but don't have time to take a class or join a club, so you exercise at home. If you know the importance of keeping track of your heart rate, but find it impossible to count heart-beats and seconds at the same time, here's a solution: Set the timer on your microwave oven on defrost for six seconds while you take your pulse and multiply by 10. Now you have an accurate reading of your heart rate during exercise.

Shape-up pen pals

Do you have an out-of-town friend you can share information about diet and exercise endeavors with? Try collecting articles and ideas from magazines and other people to send along with your letters. Sharing health- and diet-related information will not only keep you well informed, but can help you stick to your diet and exercise routines. And it gives you an added reason to write regularly.

Run, Walk, Bike or Swim Off
Your Favorite Foods

Sample Food	Calories	How to Burn Them Off (for the avg. 150-lb. indiv.)
3 oz beefsteak	330	Run 25 minutes
5.2 oz broiled chicken	250	Walk 68 minutes
1 slice pizza	145	Swim 18 minutes
1 cup macaroni & cheese	430	Bike 68 minutes
4 oz hamburger w/roll	418	Run 32 minutes
3 oz bluefish	135	Walk 36 minutes
1 med. baked potato	145	Swim 18 minutes
1 ham & cheese sandwich	458	Bike 72 minutes
1 fried egg	115	Run 9 minutes
2 strips bacon	85	Walk 22 minutes
1 oz pretzels	110	Swim 14 minutes
1 oz Cheddar cheese	113	Bike 17 minutes
1 cup roasted peanuts	842	Run 64 minutes
1 oz potato chips	150	Walk 39 minutes
1 Tbs. peanut butter	95	Swim 12 minutes
1 oz jelly beans	28	Bike 4 minutes
1 apple	80	Run 6 minutes
4 cookies	200	Walk 53 minutes
1 Danish pastry	275	Swim 34 minutes
1 slice chocolate cake w/chocolate icing	365	Bike 60 minutes
1 banana split	540	Run 41 minutes
1 cup ice cream	270	Walk 71 minutes
1 cup pea soup	164	Swim 21 minutes
¾ cup chili w/beans	250	Bike 39 minutes
Beverages		
1 cup orange juice	120	Run 9 minutes
1 cup apple juice	117	Walk 30 minutes
1 cup whole milk	150	Bike 24 minutes
12 oz cola	144	Swim 18 minutes
3½ oz white wine or Champagne	85	Bike 13 minutes
12 oz beer	150	Run 11 minutes
2½ oz martini, dry	140	Walk 37 minutes

Calorie Burn-Off Chart

Activities	Calories Burned Per Hour	Activities	Calories Burned Per Hour
Aerobics	396	Running (9-minute mile)	786
Archery	264	Shoveling snow	600
Badminton	396	Singing	add 50 cal. per hour to whatever activity you're doing while singing
Basketball	564		
Bicycling (9.4 mph)	381		
Card playing	102	Skiing—cross-country	582
Cleaning windows	240-300	Skiing—downhill	402
Climbing stairs	150	Snowshoeing	678
Cooking	75-80	Squash	864
Dancing—ballroom	210	Swimming	486
Dancing—rock	420	Stocking wood	294-312
Driving a car	70	Table tennis	276
Gardening—digging	516	Tennis	444
Gardening—mowing	456	Vacuum cleaning	100
Gardening—raking	222	Volleyball	204
Golf	348	Walking (3 mph)	228
Ironing	110-200	Walking while pushing a baby carriage	100-250
Mopping floors	240-300	Washing dishes	59

Healthful Habits

Here's how to help your whole family—even your kids—love nutritious food and get into the wholesome eating habit.

Introduce new foods and dishes gradually

Developing new eating habits doesn't happen overnight. You're making changes not only in what your family eats, but in their attitudes toward food. Some suggestions: When serving brown rice for the first time, use it in a favorite family casserole instead of as a plain side dish. Include a new vegetable as one of several in a stir-fry dish or in a salad.

Stop buying sweet and salty snacks

Instead stock up on fresh and dried fruits, unsalted nuts, trail mix and popcorn. When you're thirsty, try just water or fruit juice.

Try a variety of flours

Make whole-wheat bread as well as quick breads from rye, soy bean and rice flours or cornmeal.

De-emphasize meat

Serve smaller portions of meat; you get all the protein you need for one day in only six ounces of beef. Rely more on vegetables and interesting side dishes. Or include meat as one ingredient in a dish such as a vegetable and flank steak stir-fry served with brown rice.

Serve more vegetables

These help fill you up and add variety to meals. To get even more vegetables into your family's fare, chop them raw into salads.

Take the saltshaker off the table

Flavor food with herbs and spices.

Use more low-fat dairy products

Substitute low-fat milk and yogurt for the whole-milk variety. Use regular cheese only twice a week.

Include more legumes and grains

Add beans to soups and throw some barley into stews. Get in the habit of making them part of a dish.

Be certain everyone gets a good breakfast

Try serving oatmeal with honey, raisins and 2%-fat milk, or make whole-wheat pancakes or rice pudding.

Don't deny a sweet tooth!

Most of us have one and a little honey added to breads, rice pudding or granola will satisfy the craving.

Add nutritious touches

▶ Make a more nutritious applesauce by cooking washed and cored apples with their skins until tender. Then blend them at purée speed until smooth. Sprinkle with a little wheat germ and cinnamon to serve.

▶ If you sprinkle the pastry board with 3 to 4 tablespoons of quick rolled oats before rolling out dough, you can give pie crusts, fruit pies especially, a "nutty" flavor and an extra boost of nutrition.

▶ When a recipe calls for the cake pan to be dusted with flour after greasing, use wheat germ instead. It keeps your cake from sticking and adds flavor and nutrition.

▶ If you're preparing French toast, pour some wheat germ in a separate dish. After dipping the bread in the egg, also dip it in the wheat germ.

Don't ban foods

This only makes them more enticing to the kids. Let them eat cake at a friend's birthday party or have what's on the school lunch menu, even if you don't serve some of those foods at home.

Get the whole family involved in being nutrition-conscious

Take your kids along to the supermarket because shared motivation increases cooperation. Explain to them why you buy certain foods and not others. Assign the older children the important task of reading labels.

Read all food labels carefully

Check for hidden salt, sugar, fats. Remember, the term "natural" doesn't mean salt- or sugar-free.

Discourage snacks an hour before meals

This is especially important when you are introducing a new way of eating. Hungry kids tend to eat what's in front of them!

Plan menus a week in advance

This avoids having to go out for "fast food" because there's nothing in the cupboard.

Keep up with diet and health news

Read magazine and newspaper articles on health and nutrition, and watch reports on TV.

Common Exercise Mistakes And How To Correct Them

Your calisthenics routine may be doing you more harm than good. Look over these most common exercise blunders and be sure that you're not making the same mistakes.

Spine strainers

Blunder: shoulder stand leg bicycling
Cycling the legs in the air while propping the entire torso up with the arms.

▶ This position can hurt the neck muscles and their connective tissues if you lack the strength, flexibility and balance needed to hold your body up this way. Shoulder stands also create a forward slouching of the head, which strains the muscles behind the neck and promotes a rounding of the shoulders.

▶ Remedy: Do leg cycling with the shoulders and back *flat* on the floor and prop up the buttocks only.

Blunder: prone chest lift
Lying on the stomach, arms at the sides and arching the spine as you raise the upper body.

▶ This exercise exaggerates any curvature of the spine while shortening and tightening the lower back muscles. It can cause pain and strain if you have a weak lower back or any other back problems.

▶ Remedy: Do your chest lift push-up style. Lie on your stomach, bend the knees and place the hands at shoulder level. Using the arms, lift the upper body off the floor, but remember to hold the neck and back straight and keep the stomach muscles tightened.

Blunder: back bends and waist circles

Any standing position where you bend backward as a stretch or twist.

▶ If you have a lower spine problem or previous injury to the joints of the spinal column, bending backward can cause pain and injury.

▶ Remedy: Bend the body forward or to the sides only.

Blunder: pelvic tilt

Lying on the back with bent knees and pushing the buttocks high up off the floor as you tighten them and the stomach muscles.

▶ Pushing the buttocks so high up will cause your back to arch and puts a strain on the neck and shoulders. It also makes it harder to tighten the buttocks muscles, and that's the movement you need to raise and shape your fanny.

▶ Remedy: Move your feet closer to your body and, keeping the small of the back on the floor, tip the buttocks up to no more than five inches. From there, squeeze them and tighten the abdominals.

Abdominal bloopers

Blunder: straight leg sit-ups

Doing sit-ups from a totally prone position, legs and heels flat on the floor.

▶ These put pressure on the hip flexors (the muscles that bend the hip joints), which in turn put excessive pressure on the lower spine. When the legs are straight, you also use the hip flexors more than the abdominals to sit up, defeating the purpose of the exercise. Exercising the hip flexors can increase a curvature of the lower spine.

▶ Remedy: Do bent-knee sit-ups, which fully exercise the abdominals while protecting the lower back.

Blunder: full sit-ups

Bringing the body up to a total sitting posture from a straight-leg or bent-knee position.

▶ These are also counter-productive to the abdominals. Once you raise your shoulders higher than a 45° angle to the body, the hip flexor muscles do the primary work so your stomach muscles don't get the full benefits of the exercise. As mentioned previously, overuse of the hip flexor muscles can increase a curvature of the spine. Full sit-ups are stressful if you have any type of lower back problem as well.

▶ Remedy: Do abdominal curls by raising your body only halfway up from a bent-knee position (go to no higher than a 45° angle) and slowly lowering.

Blunder: double or high leg lifts

Raising or lowering both legs simultaneously or raising the legs 12 inches above the floor or higher.

▶ Both of these exercises cause the hip flexors to do more work than the abdominals, contributing to a curvature of the spine and putting stress on the lower back.

▶ Remedy: Lift one leg at a time, raising it just a few inches off the floor, so the abdominal muscles do most of the work. *Note:* You can keep both legs in a raised position, just don't *lift* them together.

Lower body stressers

Blunders: full squats, squat thrusts, Russian bounces and deep knee bends
Kicking the legs forward or to the sides from a squat position or lowering the body to a squat position.

▶ All of these offer absolutely no fitness benefit. They stretch and weaken tendons and supporting ligaments that hold the knee in place, leading to knee pain and injury.

▶ Remedy: Avoid these exercises entirely.

Blunder: straight-leg toe-touches
Reaching for your toes with locked knees.

▶ In this position, you stretch the supporting ligaments on each side of the knee and strain lower back muscles, connective tissues and nerves.

▶ Remedy: Keep the knees slightly bent while doing toe-touches and any other standing exercise.

Jogging your memory

▶ Can't remember the right moves to your exercise routine? Read the exercises into a tape recorder, with appropriate pauses between each. It's like having a private instructor put you through your paces.

▶ Another idea: Buy different-colored sheets of poster board. On each one, post the sequence of steps in a particular workout, from stretching and warming up to cooling down.

Medicines That Don't Mix

All drugs—even the nonprescription, over-the-counter variety—can have unpleasant side effects. And many interact in potentially dangerous ways. Following are some of the more common troublemakers.

Analgesics

To fight pain and fever.

Acetaminophen

(e.g. Tylenol) Can be toxic to the liver, especially if taken with barbiturates or alcohol. May boost the effects of anticoagulants and the tranquilizer *diazepam (Valium)*.

Aspirin

Can block the action of the anti-hypertensive medications bumetanide *(Bumex)*, captopril *(Capoten)* and furosemide *(Lasix)*.

Antacids and corticosteroids can block its action. The antiulcer drug cimetidine *(Tagamet)* may boost its effects. Can hinder blood clotting, especially with alcohol, anticoagulants or the antibiotic moxalactam *(Moxam)*. May harm the liver and irritate the digestive system.

Ibuprofen

(Motrin by prescription, *Nuprin* and *Advil* over-the-counter) Can block the action of some diuretics. Anyone with impaired kidney function who is taking a potassium-sparing diuretic may be in danger of retaining too much potassium. Can cause gastrointestinal bleeding (less often

than aspirin, which has a similar side effect). Can hinder blood clotting (especially with alcohol or anticoagulants).

Indomethacin

(Indocin) May block the action of antihypertensive medications, including beta-blockers *(Inderal)*, captopril *(Capoten)*, furosemide *(Lasix)*, prozosin *(Minipress)*, thiazide diuretics and the diuretic bumetanide *(Bumex)*. Antacids can block its action. Indomethacin can cause severe drowsiness with the antipsychotic haloperidol *(Haldol)*. It can hinder blood clotting (especially with alcohol or anticoagulants).

Antiasthma Drugs

To relieve wheezing.

Inhaled corticosteroids

(e.g. Vanceril, Beclovent, AeroBid) Occasionally can cause fatal adrenal suppression. Therefore, these drugs should be reserved for persons whose asthma can't be adequately controlled with nonsteroid drugs. Antacids, barbiturates, the bronchodilator ephedrine *(Vatronol)*, the anticonvulsant phenytoin *(Dilantin)* and the antibiotic rifampin *(Rifadin)* may block their action.

Sympathomimetic bronchodilators

(e.g. Aerolone, Brethine) Beta-blockers can interfere with their action. They may disturb heart rhythm with theophylline.

Theophylline

(e.g. Aerolate, Slo-Phyllin, Theo-Dur) Flu vaccine can temporarily boost its effects, increasing the potential for toxicity. So can the antiulcer drug cimetidine *(Tagamet)*, the beta-blocker propranolol *(Inderal)*, the antigout drug allopurinol *(Zyloprim)* and antibiotics such as erythromycin *(Erythrocin)*. Smoking, the anticonvulsant phenytoin *(Dilantin)* and barbiturates may block its action.

Antibiotics

To fight selected infections.

Aminoglycosides

(e.g. Garamycin, Myciguent, Nebcin) The antibiotic carbenicillin *(Geocillin)* and the heart drug digoxin *(Lanoxin)* may block the action of aminoglycosides. The diuretics bumetanide *(Bumex)* and ethacrynic acid *(Edecrin)* increase the risk of ear damage. There is increased risk of ear and kidney damage with the anti-hypertensive furosemide *(Lasix)*. Aminoglycosides may cause paralysis in people with abnormal kidney function or low calcium levels. The topical antibiotic neomycin can cause skin rashes and conjunctivitis when applied to eyes, mucuous membranes or the skin.

Cephalosporins

(e.g. Mandol, Moxam) Can hinder blood clotting with aspirin or anticoagulants. They can increase the risk of kidney damage in combination with aminoglycoside antibiotics and the diuretics ethacrynic acid *(Edecrin)* and furosemide *(Lasix)*. Avoid alcohol.

Chloramphenicol

(e.g. Chloromycetin, Ophthochlor, Ophthocort) Can cause aplastic anemia, particularly with the anti-ulcer drug cimetidine *(Tagamet)*. It may boost the effects of barbiturates, the anticonvulsant phenytoin *(Dilantin)* and the antiasthma drug theophylline. Barbiturates and phenytoin can block its action. Acetaminophen may boost its effects. Avoid alcohol.

Erythromycin

(e.g. Erythrocin, E-Mycin) Probably is the safest of the antibiotics, especially if taken with meals to avoid gastrointestinal side effects. However, it can boost the effects of anticoagulants, caffeine, the anticonvulsant carbamazepine *(Tegretol)*, the heart drug digoxin *(Lanoxin)* and the antiasthma drug theophylline. One type, erythromycin estolate *(Ilosone)*, may cause hepatitis in adults.

Penicillins

(e.g. Amcill, Bicillin) Can block the action of aminoglycoside antibiotics. Ampicillin *(Amcill)* may decrease the effectiveness of oral contraceptives.

Rifampin

(e.g. Rifadin, Rifamate, Rimactane) May block the action of oral contraceptives, anticoagulants, barbiturates, beta-blockers, corticosteroids, diazepam *(Valium)* and the heart drugs digoxin *(Lanoxin)* and disopyramide *(Norpace)*.

Sulfonamides

(e.g. Gantanol, Gantrisin) May boost the effects of anticoagulants and the anticonvulsant phenytoin *(Dilantin)*. They can block the action of the heart drug digoxin *(Lanoxin)*.

Tetracyclines

(e.g. Vibramycin, Achromycin, Minocin) Their action can be blocked if taken with milk, iron supplements, antacids, barbiturates or bismuth subsalicylate *(Pepto-Bismol)*. The exceptions are doxycycline and minocycline, which can be taken with milk. Tetracyclines may boost the effects of anticoagulants, the heart drug digoxin *(Lanoxin)* and lithium. They can decrease the effectiveness of oral contraceptives. They can permanently stain teeth if taken by children under 8 years of age or by pregnant women.

Antihypertensives

To treat high blood pressure.

Central-blockers

(e.g. Catapres) Tricyclic antidepressants, such as amitriptyline *(Elavil)*, can block their action. Central-blockers may block the action of the anti-Parkinson's drug levodopa *(Larodopa)*. They can *raise* blood pressure with beta-blockers.

Beta-blockers

(e.g. Lopressor, Inderal) Alcohol, barbiturates, calcium-containing antacids, the analgesic indomethacin *(Indocin)*, the antibiotic rifampin *(Rifadin)* and smoking can interfere with their action. The tranquilizer chlorpromazine *(Thorazine)*, the antihypertensive furosemide *(Lasix)*, oral contraceptives and the antiulcer drugs cimetidine *(Tagamet)* and ranitidine *(Zantac)* may boost their effects. Beta-blockers can heighten the effects of the tranquilizer chlorpromazine and the antiasthma drug theophylline. Paradoxically, they can raise blood pressure with the central-blocker clonidine *(Catapres)*. With calcium-channel blockers or the heart drug disopyramide *(Norpace)*, they may cause heart failure.

Calcium-channel blockers

(e.g. Cardizem, Procardia) The antiulcer drugs cimetidine *(Tagamet)* and ranitidine *(Zantac)* may boost the effects of Procardia. Calcium-channel blockers can boost the effects of the heart drug digoxin *(Lanoxin)*.

With beta-blockers, they may cause heart failure.

Captopril

(Capoten) Aspirin and indomethacin *(Indocin)* can block its action.

Guanethidine

(e.g. Esimil, Ismelin) Tricyclic antidepressants, oral contraceptives, the bronchodilator ephedrine *(Vatronol)* and the tranquilizer chlorpromazine *(Thorazine)* may block its action.

Thiazide diuretics

(e.g. Aquatensen, Diuril) With corticosteroids, can deplete blood potassium levels. They may boost the effects of the antigout drug allopurinol *(Zyloprim)*, the heart drug digitalis and the tranquilizer lithium. They can boost the effects of the antihypertensive diazoxide *(Proglycem)*. Their action may be blocked by the analgesic indomethacin *(Indocin)*.

Antidepressants

To alleviate depression.

Monoamine oxidase inhibitors

(e.g. Marplan, Nardil, Parnate) Don't take them with decongestants, the anti-Parkinson's drug levodopa *(Larodopa)* or tricyclic antidepressants. They can elevate blood pressure if taken with any tyramine-rich food (e.g. aged cheese, red wine, pickled herring).

Tricyclic antidepressants

(e.g. Elavil, Tofranil) Don't take them with decongestants, disulfiram *(Antabuse)* or monoamine oxidase inhibitors. They can block the action of the antihypertensives clonidine *(Catapres)*, guanethidine *(Esimil, Ismelin)* and the anti-Parkinson's drug levodopa *(Larodopa)*. They may boost the effects of the anticonvulsant phenytoin *(Dilantin)*. Barbiturates can block their action. The antiulcer drug cimetidine *(Tagamet)* and phenothiazine tranquilizers may boost their effects.

Cold and Cough Remedies

To relieve symptoms of coughs and colds.

Antihistamines

(e.g. Chlor-Trimeton, Benadryl) Avoid taking them with alcohol and the antiulcer drug cimetidine *(Tagamet)*.

Decongestants

(e.g. Vatronol, Sudafed) Can cause severe headaches, elevated blood pressure and, occasionally, a disturbance in heart rhythm in combination with monoamine oxidase inhibitors. Many decongestants aggravate high blood pressure, especially when taken orally. Oxymetazoline *(Afrin)* may cause low blood pressure.

Gastrointestinal Drugs

To treat a variety of digestive problems.

Antacids

(e.g. Di-Gel, Gelusil, Tums) Can block the action of aspirin, corticosteroids, the analgesic indomethacin, the antibiotic tetracycline, the heart drug digoxin *(Lanoxin)*, the antifungal agent ketoconazole *(Nizoral)*, the tranquilizer diazepam *(Valium)* and the antiulcer medications cimetidine *(Tagamet)* and ranitidine *(Zantac)*. May increase the effects of pseudoephedrine *(Sudafed)* and the long-acting preparations of the antiasthma drug theophylline. Aluminum-containing antacids *(e.g. Mylanta)* can block the action of fluoride. Magnesium-containing antacids *(e.g. Maalox)* can be harmful to patients on dialysis. Calcium-containing antacids *(e.g. Tums)* can block the action of the beta-blocker atenolol *(Tenormin)*.

Bismuth subsalicylate

(e.g. Pepto-Bismol) Can block the action of tetracycline. Not for aspirin-caused digestive upsets.

Cimetidine *(Tagamet)* and ranitidine *(Zantac)*

Can boost the effects of beta-blockers and the calcium-channel blocker nifedipine *(Procardia)*. Antacids may block their action. Cimetidine may boost the effects of alcohol, anticoagulants, benzodiazepine tranquilizers, beta-blockers, the heart drug digitoxin, the anticonvulsant phenytoin (*Dilantin*) and the antiasthma drug theophylline. Cimetidine can block the action of iron and the antifungal agent ketoconazole (*Nizoral*).

Metoclopramide

(*e.g. Reglan*) Can block the action of cimetidine (*Tagamet*).

Mineral oil

May decrease the absorption of fat-soluble vitamins (A, D, E and K). To avoid this effect, take at bedtime.

Diet Aids

To help lose weight.

Phenylpropanolamine (PPA)

(*e.g. Acutrim, Dexatrim*) Can raise blood pressure, derange heart rhythm and cause seizures, stroke, heart attack and kidney failure, especially in combination with caffeine. *Caution:* PPA is often an ingredient in combination decongestants and cold remedies.

Mineral Supplements

To prevent deficiencies.

Caution: Only three mineral supplements—calcium, iron and zinc—have been approved as safe and effective by the FDA.

Calcium

Can block tetracycline's action, cause kidney damage or stones.

Iron

Can block tetracycline's action. Cimetidine (*Tagamet*) and caffeine can block the action of iron. Keep iron tablets away from children; poisoning is a potential danger.

Zinc

Zinc sulfate is the only approved form. May block tetracycline's action. Oral contraceptives can lower zinc levels in the blood.

Sleeping Pills

For short-term treatment of insomnia.

Barbiturates

(*e.g. Amytal, Nembutal, Seconal*) Can block the actions of anti-coagulants, beta-blockers, the antibiotic chloramphenical, corticosteroids, the heart drug digitoxin, the antibiotic doxycycline, the antipsychotic haloperidol, phenothiazine tranquilizers, the antiasthma drug theophylline and oral contraceptives. May decrease the effects of tricyclic anti-depressants. One antibiotic, rifampin (*Rifadin*), can block their action, but another, chloramphenicol, may boost their effects. May cause vitamin D deficiency. Don't drink alcohol with these drugs.

Topical Medications

To treat a variety of "skin-deep problems."

Acne drugs

(*e.g. Clearasil, Fostex*) Mixing two or more topical acne drug products can increase skin dryness or irritation.

Lindane

(*e.g. Kwell, Scabene*) Can cause seizures when not used strictly according to package instructions.

Topical anesthetics

(*e.g. Nupercainal, Xylocaine*) Benzocaine may sensitize skin, leading to an allergic reaction upon subsequent application of other drugs in the -caine family. In large amounts, lidocaine can disturb heart rhythm.

Miscellaneous topical medications

Topical antibiotics, antihistamines and PABA-containing sunscreens and cosmetics may cause allergic skin rashes.

Tranquilizers

To allay anxiety.

Benzodiazepines

(*e.g. Valium, Librium, Serax*) Can boost the effects of the heart drug digoxin. May block the action of the anti-Parkinson's drug levodopa (*Larodopa*). Antacids and caffeine can block their action. Acetaminophen (*Tylenol*) may boost their effects. Avoid alchohol.

Oral Contraceptives

To prevent pregnancy.

Oral contraceptives

(*e.g. Brevicon, Enovid, Norinyl, Ortho-Novum, Tri-Norinyl*) May lower zinc levels in the blood. Can boost the effects of beta-blockers and the anticonvulsant phenytoin (*Dilantin*). May block the action of acetaminophen (*e.g. Tylenol*), anticoagulants, the antihypertensives guanethidine (*Esimil, Ismelin*) and methyldopa (*Aldomet*) and the tranquilizer oxazepam (*Serax*). High doses of vitamin C (1,000 mg a day) can boost the side effects of estrogens in oral contraceptives. Barbiturates, anticonvulsants and many antibiotics may block their effectiveness. Use a condom or diaphragm as back-up protection while you are taking any of these drugs.

More Medicine

Further thoughts on keeping healthy.

Swallowing capsules

For an easy way to swallow capsules, put the medication in your mouth with a small amount of water and tilt your head or upper body forward. The capsule will float backward where it is more easily swallowed.

Careful prescriptions

Certain drugs commonly prescribed to treat the elderly for insomnia, anxiety or depression can also make them drowsy, dizzy and disoriented. Even when taken in prescribed doses, tranquilizers such as Librium and Valium and antidepressants such as Elavil and Dalmane, (frequently prescribed for insomnia,) can have lingering sedative effects. The occurrence of hip fractures resulting from a fall (a major cause of disability and death) increases with the corresponding number of recently filled prescriptions for tranquilizers and antidepressants. If drugs are discontinued, the likelihood of falls will decrease. Always consult your doctor about *any* effect a prescription or non-prescription drug may have on your body.

Stop the itching

The worst part of wearing a cast is the itching underneath. Take an ordinary hair dryer, turn it on the high/cool setting and blow air into the area between the skin and cast. What a relief!

When to call the doctor

▶ Chest pains even if caused by a strained muscle.

▶ A rash that does not look like an allergy, especially if it is accompanied by an elevation in temperature. This could mean a strep infection or other problems that need immediate treatment.

▶ An earache, or a sore throat without a fever, that persists for more than 48 hours (again the possibility of a strep infection).

▶ A yellowish color in the eyes or the skin (possible hepatitis or other liver problem).

▶ Urine that looks the color of tea.

▶ Diarrhea for more than three or four days.

▶ Can't keep liquids down for more than 24 hours.

▶ A stiff neck for more than a day.

▶ A severe stomach ache that lasts for more than 24 hours.

Penny wise . . .

Though generic drugs are widely believed to be medicine's cost-cutting equivalent to buying "house" brands of groceries, they are not always such a bargain. On average, the retail price of generic prescription drugs is lower than that of name brand prescription drugs but, when filling any individual prescription, you may be charged more for the generic version. Although it costs pharmacists less to buy generic drugs, they frequently mark up the price sharply. Therefore, a smart consumer should not assume that a generic drug is always cheaper. Shop around.

12.
Decorating
Know-How

Dollarwise Decorating
Easy Ways To Pretty Up A Room
Super Storage Solutions

Dollarwise Decorating

No need to strain your decorating budget—with these clever techniques, you can spruce up your home for far less than you thought. You'll find something for every room in the house, from bedroom to kitchen.

Kitchen makeovers

▶ One of the easiest—and cheapest—ways to "redo" your kitchen is to give cabinets a new look. Use panels of wallpaper or caning on drawers and door fronts, and trim them with molding.

▶ Use a fool-the-eye technique in a windowless kitchen. Paint a scene you'd like to see on the wall, complete with a window frame and curtains.

▶ Another neat idea: Tack part of a colorful print bed sheet onto a wooden canvas stretcher to make a quick and inexpensive "window" over the sink.

Dining room disguise

Don't get rid of ugly, old dining-room fixtures. Hide them under a 4 x 8-foot lattice panel suspended from the ceiling. You'll find you get a softer light, too.

Living room "facelifts"

▶ This won't cost you a penny. Turn your coffee table at a 45° angle to the sofa rather than placing it square. You'll be amazed at the change in the room.

▶ Classy columns bring drama to a humdrum living room entry. You'll need porch posts from an old house, which you strip and paint in pastel hues. Place them at either side of the entry and watch guests take a second look!

▶ Even if your front door opens directly into the living room, you can have a foyer. Hang a single curtain panel about three or four feet into the room, tying it back with a thick, tassled cord. Less work than that: Put up a decorative folding floor screen and form a foyer area instantly.

▶ For a dollar-smart version of a

fireplace mantel, try a wall-hung shelf with kitchen utensil hooks to hold all your fireplace tools.

▶ Why buy a new coffee table for your living room when you can put one together yourself? Place a poster (options are limitless) inside a large plastic picture frame and rest it on a smaller plastic cube.

▶ Draw attention to your favorite print by "hanging" it from a bow. Tack ribbon to the wall at the center of the picture frame. Hand-stitch the center of the bow and tack it to the ribbon.

▶ Can't decide where to hang your new print? Don't! Lean it on the mantel or on the floor, gallery-style.

Hallway helpers

▶ Bring a long, drab hallway to life with color. Get a multicolored rag rug runner for the floor and paint each door a different pastel found in the rug.

▶ For a front hall that gives a personal welcome, hang a collection of family photos, old prints or other personal treasures. Frame the area with a stenciled border.

▶ Instead of sticking your child's artwork on the refrigerator, use it as a decorative border in a hall. Mount all drawings on the same-size mats and hang them in a row at eye level.

Kids' rooms revitalizers

▶ Kids will love this one-of-a-kind art in their room: a kite! Hang it on the wall or suspend it from the ceiling with fishing line.

▶ Clever seating-storage for the kids' room: Arrange three 36-inch-high bookshelves in a U shape. Inside that space, put down lots of comfy floor pillows for "seats" and pillows all around the sides for "backs."

Bathroom brighteners

▶ When you must replace the bathroom sink, try this moneysaver: Buy a two-legged model from a salvage shop and enclose it in a new laminate countertop and vanity.

▶ Replace chrome faucets with a colorful pair, put out towels to match and you'll have an almost-new bathroom.

▶ Love the look of lace-edged bath towels? Buy regular coordinated towels. Then purchase a yard of lace for a reasonable price at a sewing center and hem it onto the bottom of the towels.

▶ An inexpensive straw beach mat makes an interesting "natural" floor covering in the bathroom. Pair it with bamboo shades and green plants.

Bedroom perk-ups

▶ To soften the stark look of platform beds, attach a fabric ruffle around the platform with Velcro.

▶ Living room or bedroom platforms become magical at night when lit up with white mini-Christmas lights. If you have a platform with a slight extension or lip, string lights from cup hooks on the underside of the lip.

▶ When the bed must go under an eave, hang prints in a straight row above the top of the bed to give the effect of a headboard.

▶ Swivel-based artist's lamps are convenient and inexpensive bedside reading lamps. Attach them to wall brackets or stand them on a night table.

Dress it up

▶ Pillows are one of the easiest and cheapest ways to accessorize a room. Make an armful from scraps of floral prints, one print per pillow, and scatter them throughout the room.

▶ Stripes give a room real pizzazz. Pinch pennies by using seersucker or striped dress fabric instead of costlier wallcoverings and decorating fabrics. Other options are to paint stripes on walls and trim or create stripes with colored tape.

▶ Pretty up a window by putting shirred fabric panels on the top half, shutters with matching fabric inserts on the bottom half. Change the fabric whenever you want a new look.

▶ Customize a ceiling fan by hand-painting or stenciling a simple motif on the paddles. Tie a ribbon to the pull chain, if it's right for your decor.

▶ Give solid-colored rag rugs a new look by sewing strips of pastel fabric around the edges. Little work but big results.

▶ Why spend a lot of money reupholstering a worn sofa in the family room? Instead, wrap cushions in blankets and throw a folded blanket across the sofa back. Use bright buffalo plaids or "trapper" stripes for a warm, rustic look.

▶ Rev up painted white floors with stenciled-on splashy floral patterns or tropical ferns. This works well on plain window shades too.

▶ For an inexpensive room divider that also shows off your prettiest hanging plants, use a portable aluminum clothes rack. Try to arrange such hanging plants as ivy, philodendron and Boston fern at different heights to fill the space.

▶ For prints to hang on your wall, try your local library instead of an expensive art gallery. Most libraries have an extensive choice of good reproductions of famous artists' works that you can borrow for a month for a minimal fee.

▶ When does a beach towel become a work of art? When it's put into a frame. With the many designs to choose from, there is sure to be one to suit the kitchen, bath, den or baby's room. It's a great "conversation piece," too.

▶ Bare walls and nothing to put on them? Take your camera to parks and other garden areas to photograph flowers. Focus on a small cluster and move in close enough to fill the entire viewing lens with blooms. Have your photographs enlarged in various sizes, and mat and frame them.

▶ One of the quickest ways to brighten up a room and create the illusion of space is by the use of mirrors. Place them to catch sunlight or lamplight, or to reflect your favorite item.

▶ For a lovely "antique" picture, buy an inexpensive frame (garage sales and thrift stores are terrific for these). Gently glue pressed flowers, dried autumn leaves and greenery to parchment-like paper and frame.

Paint it

▶ Don't stop once you've put up painted wood shutters on the inside of your windows. Paint the window molding a matching color.

▶ Painted borders—around windows, doors, ceilings and floors— add flair to any room. Choose a motif that echoes one in your fabric, such as a leafy border with a floral sofa.

▶ Bold, dark colors can really make a room come alive. Use deep green, navy or black for the ceiling and wainscoting area, a lighter shade for the walls in between.

▶ It's not always necessary to repaint the walls to wake up a room. A bold spot of color, such as yellow or turquoise, may be all it takes. Try it on a plant stand, mirror frame or chair that's seen better days.

▶ Tired of your drab rattan or bamboo accessories? Give them a makeover. Spray-paint them white or a bright color and use a brush to paint on little flowers or vines. On baskets, weave colored ribbons through the handles for an extra romantic touch.

▶ All those unmatched chairs you don't know what to do with can be transformed into a new "set" for your dining nook. Paint them all the same color. Or, for real pizzazz, do each a different high-gloss shade.

▶ Forget about *one* strip of molding—grouping them in rows of two or three is much more interesting. Paint unfinished molding strips, which don't cost much, different colors to coordinate with your room. Put them up on walls, ceilings, etc.

▶ Revitalize battered, hand-me-down furniture by painting it in bold, high gloss colors: fire-engine red, cobalt blue, jet black, lemon yellow. Add new knobs in contrasting colors and coordinate with colorful fabrics.

▶ If you have some artistic talent, you can dramatically decorate your child's or any other room by painting your own mural. Find a design you like and enlarge it for the wall. Take up your paints and away you go. Instant forests, gardens, castles; your imagination is the only limit.

No fire, but . . .

Make the most of a nonworking fireplace. Use these ideas to perk it up.

▶ Place a pretty vase with a floral arrangement inside the fireplace.

▶ Creat mini-bookshelves.

▶ Store a sewing machine.

▶ Create an arrangement of tall candles.

▶ Place small houseplants that don't require a lot of light inside it.

▶ Use it to hold an aquarium (check with your pet store to see if you need to add artificial light).

Easy Ways To Pretty Up A Room

You don't need a total redo for a new look. You'll find little touches like these can make a big difference.

Give your home country charm

▶ Change the look of a room with the season. Cozy up a living room in winter by draping blankets over the sofa and chairs. Give a bedroom a new "face" for spring by replacing dark-colored bedding with white.

▶ The key to making different patterns work together, such as patchwork and florals, is to keep them in the same color family and tones. For example, royal purple, blue and deep red is a successful combo, but pastels with deep, dark hues is not.

▶ Store china and glassware in open cupboards.

▶ Benches are always handy. Turn them into extra tables and chairs. They're also great coffee tables.

Change the rug

Layer an area rug over your wall-to-wall carpeting or tiles. Dhurries, kilims and rag rugs can be inexpensive ways to help set a warmer mood.

Personalize bath towels

Embroider family members' names with large chain stitches on their towels for a personal touch.

Frame-up

An unused picture frame can become an elegant vanity tray for combs, brushes and the like. Replace the picture with giftwrap or wallpaper.

Picture windows

Need privacy yet don't want to shut out the sun with curtains or shades? "See-through pictures" let the sun shine in. Dry and press ferns and flowers (primroses, Johnny jump-ups or almost any garden flower) and mount them on clear adhesive-backed plastic. To create a pleasing design, trace a pattern of the leaves and flowers on paper, set the nonadhesive side of the clear plastic over the paper and follow the pattern as you position each plant on the adhesive side. Carefully set the adhesive side of the plastic on the window pane.

Sentimental keepsake

▶ If you have a beautiful antique pin, such as a cameo, don't hide it in your jewelry drawer. Mount it by buying a small, inexpensive 3½ x 4½-inch gold frame, removing the glass and gluing black velvet to the back where the picture mounting would be. Pin your keepsake on the velvet and hang the frame. You can easily unpin the brooch to wear on special occasions.

▶ To display a collection of award pins acquired over the years—from Brownie scouts to retirement—pin them to a piece of brown felt, frame the "picture" and hang it on the wall.

Brighten up your closet

An excellent way to brighten up a dark closet and create the illusion of more space is to cover the floor with light-colored carpeting. In place of carpeting, white paint or light-colored tiles work well.

Shelf improvement

To protect and enhance the wooden shelves in your kitchen cabinets, center lace paper doilies on the adhesive-backed side of clear vinyl before affixing it to the shelves.

Wonderful windows

▶ Store-bought lace curtains attached to inexpensive brass clips and hung from a brass rod have a delightful, old-time effect.

▶ If one of your heirlooms is an old table scarf and you haven't a place to show it off—use a window. Sew a thin strip of fabric across the top for a rod pocket and hang on a bedroom or den window.

▶ Create a colorful carefree window garden in your kitchen or dining room by placing bright blooms in pretty water-filled bottles.

▶ Gather homespun checked fabric on a dowel and suspend it from brackets. Then stencil around the window frame with a pretty pattern to match your trim color.

▶ If you have a window that doesn't get much sunlight, you can still have a lovely "garden view". Install shelves, and place flourescent bulbs on each shelf. Then, select plants that require medium amounts of light. *(See Plants For Every Window, page 284.)* You'll have a lovely window in a jiffy!

▶ Do you have a wall that is broken up by a small, awkward window? Pretend it's not there. Tack a large basket over it and put up the rest of your collection. Or make it the "centerpiece" by placing a stained glass ornament in it.

Country in the kitchen

▶ For a homey look, hang baskets, colanders, ladles, egg beaters, molds and the like on walls, from beams or racks. Do this with those things you use every day as well as with collectibles you want to show off.

▶ Kitchen windows are perfect places for your bottle collection. Put it on glass shelves to reflect even more light and leave the window curtainless.

▶ Hang pots and pans from an overhead rack or put pegboard on a wall with hooks for pot handles.

▶ For the look of a farmhouse window, put cafe curtains on wood rods with matching wood rings. (Find them ready-to-finish at lumber yards.) Paint, stain and varnish them to fit your color scheme. Make curtains from classic checks, calico, homespun, stripes or gingham.

▶ A rocking chair in the kitchen invites cozy visiting.

▶ Install real brick or stone flooring, or brick-patterned vinyl.

▶ For old-fashioned storage, use a country cupboard (corner ones are great space-savers), pie safes, dry sinks or simple wall-to-wall shelving with wooden shutters for doors.

▶ Paint a wooden floor an earth color, such as rust, and add several coats of varnish. Or decorate your floor with stencils around the edge or across the entire surface.

Get your home summer-ready

▶ Replace an overhead light fixture with a ceiling fan with white, pastel or wicker paddles.

▶ Use fresh flowers and fruit as centerpieces.

▶ Set out open jars of floral-scented potpourri.

▶ Replace heavy, dark-colored pillows with chintz prints or pastels.

▶ Introduce a fresh white wicker, rattan or bamboo accessory—a chair, plant stand or roll-up shades.

▶ Replace wool area rugs with inexpensive sisal ones.

▶ Take down draperies and hang breezy pastel sheers in their place.

▶ Use white lampshades only and tone down the wattage of your bulbs.

Super Storage Solutions

Uncover hidden storage areas in your home and find a place for everything you own.

Sports basket

A wire bicycle basket hung on the wall just inside your back entryway provides a neat storage place for athletic gear—tennis balls, baseballs and bats, footballs and helmets.

A place for your tapes

Plastic shoe boxes, purchased in dime stores, make excellent and inexpensive cassette tape holders. It's easy to see the titles, the lid keeps out dust and the tapes stay organized in one spot.

Handy rack

A large rattan wine rack is an attractive and easy way to store slippers and shoes (especially damp jogging ones) inside the back door.

A place for "little" accessories

Use a 15-drawer storage chest (the kind used for storing nails, screws, nuts and bolts) in your daughter's room to hold her hair ribbons, barrettes, pins and necklaces.

Tray smart

Keep your set of folding TV trays in a large-size plastic garbage bag. It not only keeps them dust-free and together, but makes it easier to carry them to an eating spot or on a picnic.

Shoe storage

An old curtain rod makes a handy shoe rack. Tack it to the inside of a closet door and hang shoes on it by their heels.

Catchall

For instant organizing, make a "find and return rack," a small wine rack filled with empty wallpaper-covered cans. When a friend leaves something behind, place it in one of the cans to be returned on his or her next visit. Gloves, scarves, toys, even recipes or clippings are returned much sooner.

Double-duty storage

Short of closet space? Consider making infrequently used items do double duty. "Store" extra blankets by putting them on the guest bed. If the blankets aren't needed when guests arrive (say, in summer), they are easily removed. Fill rarely used suitcases with off-season clothing. Other tips: Turn a roasting pan into a catchall for awkward-to-store kitchen gadgets, temporarily putting them in a plastic bag when the roaster is in use. Arrange small gardening tools in an unused flowerpot.

Storing Fido's food

Use a 15-gallon plastic garbage container to hold the contents of an entire 40-pound bag of dog food. It's convenient, easy to store and keeps the food fresh.

Crafts closet

To keep crafts projects organized, place the supplies for each in a white plastic kitchen garbage bag. Label the bag with a felt-tip marker, tie it with a simple knot and hang the bag in a closet.

Kitchen space savers

▶ To make the best use of limited space in the kitchen, hang a macramé plant hanger with a deep ceramic or plastic pot over the kitchen sink and fill it with wooden mixing spoons, wire whisks, spatulas and so on.

▶ If your small kitchen doesn't have space for storing often-used place mats, place them in an artist's paper portfolio. It fits perfectly in the narrow space between the refrigerator and cupboard. Or neatly attach the mats to a clipboard and hang the board on the inside of a cabinet door.

▶ Kitchen too small for a china cabinet? Not if you remove the back of an old cabinet with glass doors and place it in *front* of the window.

▶ Another sparkly solution: Install glass shelves on clips in the recess of a no-view window and line up glassware or show off collectibles.

▶ To keep bottle brushes and pot scrubbers organized and handy, place an inexpensive plastic flowerpot with a drip tray on the counter next to the sink. It is attractive and the utensils are always within reach.

▶ To prevent refrigerator chaos, use a single-tier lazy Susan-type turntable on the top shelf. Instead of moving cartons or pitchers to get the beverage you want, just spin the turntable to the desired container.

No-slip quilts

Store slippery satin quilts or polyester bedspreads in old cotton pillowcases. They will be easier to stack.

Banish bathroom clutter

▶ To keep the bathtub uncluttered and children's bath toys drained, take a rubber-covered wire undershelf basket (meant to give you extra storage space in the closet) and bend the hooks in the opposite direction so they hang over the side of the tub. Stow the toys in the basket and they're out of the way.

▶ To keep shampoo and lotions handy in the bathroom, place a decorative ceramic pot in a macramé plant holder and hang it close to the sink. No more clutter on the counter, and hairspray and other necessities are within easy reach. You can also hang a pot next to a narrow shower stall and shower items will be easily accessible.

▶ If you like to use the mirror over the sink when you put on makeup or fix your hair but your bathroom has no counter space, make some. Place a large wooden cutting board on top of the sink and you have a place for makeup, comb, curling iron and so on that is easy to remove and store when you are done.

Keeping track of accessories

▶ Electric curler clips or hooks entangle very easily. To avoid this, attach a toothbrush holder to the inside of the bathroom cabinet. It is out of sight and each hole on the holder can be used for a color-coded clip.

▶ Attach a few good-size magnets to the inside of your metal bathroom cabinet. Safety pins, hair pins, tweezers, nail files and other small metal objects can be found at a glance.

▶ To avoid frantic rummaging around in the morning, put a small piece of fastening tape on each of your small, easily lost cosmetic brushes. Put another piece of tape inside a drawer and attach the brushes to it.

Hidden storage

▶ Finding spare closet and drawer space for guests is always a problem. A simple solution: Buy an old steamer trunk with drawers and a rod for hanging clothes. When not in use, the trunk can serve as a coffee table in a recreation room or a storage cupboard for guest sheets and towels.

▶ Where can you store spare blankets and extra pillows? Right on your beds. Make extra pillow shams to coordinate with your bedrooms. When folded to the correct size, blankets fit in these decorative cases just as well as pillows. You can even roll a blanket into a long bolster shape and cover it with the bedspread before adding the decorative pillows.

▶ Here's an ingenious idea for a little extra storage space in your home. Fill a metal garbage can with all your Christmas ornaments and finish it off with a round tabletop made from scrap Formica (available at building supply stores). Over that, place a pretty floral tablecloth. It makes a nice addition to the family room and the decorations stay clean and undamaged until needed each year.

13.
Green
Thumb
Gardening

Indoors: Wonderful Window Gardens
Outdoors: Frontyard/Backyard
Flowers And Herbs: Not Just
For The Garden!

Indoors: Wonderful Window Gardens

Your houseplants can be healthy and beautiful with these handy facts at your fingertips.

Seasonal care for houseplants

Spring care includes repotting plants that have outgrown their containers (roots may be wound around the soil ball, new growth may be minimal and small) and top dressing large plants.

▶ Plants are beginning to put out new growth, so they may need more frequent watering and feeding.

▶ Cut back rampant growers to keep them shapely and compact, and use the cuttings to increase your collection.

Summer care for houseplants involves taking many of them outside to a patio or deck, or to hang from the branch of a shade tree.

▶ Don't take plants out too soon. Wait till nights are warm and don't place them in a spot that gets direct midday sun.

▶ Plants in containers outdoors can dry out very quickly. Check them daily. In very hot weather you may have to water every day and mist twice a day.

▶ Indoors, make sure plants don't bake or sunburn by being too close to a window that receives direct sun.

▶ Move plants away from drafts caused by air-conditioners.

Autumn care begins with bringing indoors the houseplants you put outside for the summer. Time the relocation so that outdoor temperatures equal those indoors— early September or, in the south/southwest, October.

▶ Don't bring bugs inside: Wash off foliage with spray from the hose. Unpot plants and check the soil for slugs or insects; repot in fresh soil if any are present. If a plant has grown a lot, repot it into a larger container.

▶ Plant growth slows in autumn, so plants require less light, water and fertilizer. Nature takes care of the light, since the sun isn't as bright. Water only to keep plants from wilting and don't feed them. Exceptions: African violets, gardenias, holiday cactus, wax begonias, kalanchoes, geraniums for winter bloom.

Winter care is minimal for most houseplants. They grow little if at all. Many go completely dormant (caladium, achimenes, Amorphophallus). But they still require your attention. The hot, dry atmosphere of heated homes causes browned leaf tips and promotes attacks by red spider mites.

▶ Use a humidifier, especially if you have hot air heat.

▶ Mist around plants often.

▶ Group plants together. Transpiration of moisture from their leaves raises the humidity near them.

▶ Guard plants against sudden drops in temperature, drafts and the cold air near a windowpane. Leaves that touch cold glass can freeze, turning brown and mushy. If that happens, remove the affected leaves and stems, and move the plants away from the windowpane.

Three ways to water houseplants

From the top:

▶ Pour water around the inside rim of the pot, not near the center of the plant. (That can cause rot.)

▶ Don't get water on the leaves, which on some plants (African violets, teddy bear vine) will spot if you do. Water until it seeps out the drainage hole(s) into the saucer and empty the saucer.

From the bottom:

▶ This takes a bit more time, but it's most effective for plants susceptible to crown rot or leaf spot. Fill the kitchen sink, bathtub or dishpan with one to three inches of

water (depending on pot sizes), set the pots (without saucers) in and leave them until moisture beads up on the soil surface. Thoroughly drain them. *Never* bottom water succulents or cacti.

With a wick:

▶ An easy method, especially for plants that prefer evenly moist soil— and for people away from home on business or vacation.

▶ Before potting a plant, insert a wick (a piece of nylon clothesline, strips cut from nylon stockings, acrylic yarn) into the drainage hole. Hold it upright while filling the pot partway with soil. Put more soil on top, then the plant. Place the end of the wick from the drainage hole in a container of water. Keep the container filled.

▶ Wick watering works best if you pot the plant with vermiculite only (wash old soil from the plant's roots) or a soilless medium.

How to groom houseplants

▶ Groom houseplants regularly by wiping large-leaved plants with a cloth dampened in water or a mild soap/water solution. Spritz small-leaved plants with the kitchen sink sprayer or a mister. Spray the underside of leaves as well as the top.

▶ Remove flowers from plants as they fade so that the plants' energy doesn't go into producing seeds. Clean hairy-leaved plants (African violets) and cacti with a *soft* brush. Pinch off (with your fingers) the growing tips of stems of young plants to promote bushy, not lanky, growth; removing the tip causes dormant buds below to begin growing.

Potting pointers

▶ Upright plants do well in pots ⅓ to ½ their height, while plants that grow horizontally (African violets) like pots ⅓ to ½ their width. A 12-inch-tall plant needs a 4- to 6-inch diameter pot; a violet nine inches across, a 3- to 5-inch pot.

▶ Sterilize used pots by soaking them for 20 to 30 minutes in a solution of ¾ cup bleach to 1 gallon water. This method also cleans tools.

▶ To plug up a too-large opening at the bottom of a flower pot, fit a 4-hole button into the space. It slows down drainage and prevents loss of soil.

▶ Have you ever wondered what to do with your children's Frisbees when they no longer play with them? Place upside down Frisbees under pots as saucers. They come in various sizes and will fit almost any pot.

▶ To keep toddlers from scooping out handfuls of potting soil from floor plants, place a snug-fitting "collar" of plastic needlepoint canvas over the surface of the soil, with a keyhole opening cut in the canvas for the stem. The canvas is available in crafts stores and comes in both black and brown, so it blends nicely with the soil. The plant still gets the necessary air and water.

Pest prevention

▶ Rubbing alcohol can't be beat for getting rid of mealy bugs. Dip a cotton swab in alcohol and touch each bug. Repeat as needed till the infestation is gone.

▶ If powdery mildew attacks begonias or African violets, brush Rootone (a rooting hormone powder) on the affected area.

Everblooming African violets

To have African violets bloom all year round, keep the plants in a north/northwest window. Water them lightly from the bottom every other day and feed them every four weeks with 5-10-3 food. Repot them once a year.

Encouraging poinsettias to bloom

Getting this festive plant to bloom isn't simple but it is a lot easier with this holiday schedule.

▶ Cut back the bracts (the large, brightly colored modified leaves that are often mistakenly called flowers) on *St. Patrick's Day.*

▶ Repot the plant in a larger container on *Memorial Day* and put the plant outdoors for the summer.

▶ Cut all stems back by six inches on *Independence Day.*

▶ Move the plant indoors to a sunny window on *Labor Day.*

▶ On *Columbus Day*, start giving the plant 14 hours of darkness daily. The poinsettia is a photoperiodic plant, setting colorful bracts and blooms in response to shorter daylight periods. Cover it with a large cardboard box if you don't have a light-tight closet—it must have *absolute* darkness. Continue the darkness treatment for 8 to 10 weeks, putting the plant in a window during the day where it will receive four to six hours of direct sun. Water and feed it as usual. As soon as the poinsettia comes into bloom, discontinue the closet procedure.

To dry flowers

Pick flowers before they are fully open. Use a drying mix of 3 parts borax to 10 parts cornmeal in a box with a lid. Thoroughly cover the flower heads, which dry in 3 to 10 days. Carefully remove the dried flowers from the borax mix, dust off the excess mix and store the flowers in covered containers until you're ready to use them.

Natural pesticides

Aphids, mites and other harmful bugs can often be controlled with sprays you can make yourself.

▶ Garlic spray controls aphids, caterpillars and onionflies. Grind 3 oz garlic and add 2 teaspoons mineral oil. Stir well and let the mixture soak for 24 hours. In 1 pint warm water, dissolve ¼ oz pure soap shavings. Mix the garlic/oil mixture with soapy water. Let it stand for several hours and strain it through cheesecloth. Store it in a glass or plastic container. To use, mix 1 part mixture with 10 parts water. Spray plants once a week, making sure the underside of the leaves are well covered. Apply more often for heavy infestations.

▶ Buttermilk spray controls spider and other mites. Mix ½ cup buttermilk and 4 cups wheat flour in 5 gallons water. Use the spray as often as necessary.

▶ Hot pepper spray controls ants, spiders, cabbageworms, caterpillars and tomato hornworms. Purée 2 to 3 hot peppers, 1 clove garlic, ½ mild green pepper and ½ onion in a blender. Let the mixture stand for a day or two, then strain it. Adding a little soap (see Garlic spray) will improve its effectiveness. This spray can be frozen and used over a period of several months. Use it as often as necessary.

Special plants for special rooms

▶ Kitchen plants like humidity and can stand grease and smoke.

Grape ivy	Pothos
Kangaroo vine	Schefflera
Peperomia	Bromeliad
Orchids, such as	Episcia
Phalaenopsis	Streptocarpus
Dendrobium	African violet
Cattleya	

Note: While hairy leaves (episcia, streptocarpus, African violet) and grease don't mix well, individual leaves don't live for more than a few months. They are constantly replaced by new, clean ones.

▶ Bathroom plants like warmth and humidity and will thrive in almost any light. Keep their leaves clean and their soil nicely moist.

Rosary vine	Aglaonema
Snake plant	Sweet flag
Piggyback plant	Maidenhair fern
Cyperus	Peperomia
Creeping fig	Episcia
Spathiphyllum	Mini sinningia

▶ Office plants are tough, adaptable to less than ideal conditions and vary from tree forms to trailers.

Dracaena	Sansevieria
Chamaedorea	Avocado
German ivy	Kentia palm
African violet	Rhapis (palm
Amaryllis	for low light)
Chinese evergreen	Spathiphyllum

Plants for every window

North

North-facing windows receive the least amount of sun, almost all of it indirect; northeast and northwest windows receive more light than those facing due north. For these low-light places try the following:

☐ Dieffenbachia
☐ Peace Lily
☐ Aglaonema
☐ Bird's Nest Fern
☐ Sago Palm
☐ Creeping Fig
☐ Prayer Plant
☐ Wandering Jew
☐ Aspidistra
☐ Squirrel's Foot Fern
☐ Philodendron 'Majesty'
☐ Earth Star
☐ Haemaria
☐ Holly Fern

East

Windows facing East receive the morning sun, which means bright light for at least four hours a day. Plants that thrive here include:

☐ Cape Primrose
☐ Ficus benjamina
☐ Walking Iris
☐ Rex Begonia
☐ Fittonia
☐ Oxalis
☐ Lady Palm
☐ Nematanthus
☐ Boston Fern
☐ Firecracker Vine
☐ Norfolk Island Pine
☐ Staghorn Fern
☐ Crossandra

South

A window looking South receives the most sun of all. Those facing southeast and southwest get less light but more than one facing east or west. These plants love the strong rays of the sun:

☐ Passion Flower
☐ Jade Plant
☐ Mexican Gem
☐ Strawberry Geranium
☐ Ponytail Palm
☐ Hawaiian Schefflera
☐ Geranium
☐ Aloe Vera
☐ German Ivy
☐ Ixora
☐ English Ivy

West

A West window receives afternoon sun, which is hotter than morning sun. Some plants that thrive in a West window:

☐ Monstera deliciosa variegata
☐ Natal plum
☐ Syngonium
☐ Begonia
☐ Bear's Paw Fern
☐ Bromeliad
☐ Snake Plant
☐ Episcia
☐ Rosary Vine
☐ Parlor Palm
☐ Rubber Tree
☐ Columnia
☐ African Violet 'Happy'
☐ Miniature African violets: 'Doodle Pink,' 'Tanager' and 'Pixie Blue.'

For all window plants

▶ Don't overestimate the amount of light you have. For best results, always grow plants in more than the minimum light required.

▶ Proper watering, soil conditions, fertilizing and humidity are also important for healthy plants; be sure to check these conditions before choosing a plant.

▶ Dust on leaves cuts down on the light a plant receives. To clean large leaves quickly, shower your plants. Tie a large plastic bag around the pot to cover the soil and set the plant in the shower under a gentle stream of tepid water. Shower smaller plants in the kitchen sink.

▶ Your plant is getting too much light if its leaves turn down (trying to escape the light) and get a bleached-out look. It's suffering from too little light (which it needs to produce its food) if it slowly loses old leaves, produces even smaller new ones and becomes tall and spindly.

How much light does your window get?

Always choose a plant for the kind of light that enters your window, not just the direction the window faces. Remember that glass cuts down on light transmitted, despite clean windows. Curtains, even sheer ones, can turn a west window into a north one. Shade from trees, awnings or buildings can turn a south window into one suitable only for north window plants.

How far can they go?

The amount of light available to a plant decreases rapidly as you move it away from a window. Place your plants as close as possible to the window without letting them touch the glass. To grow a plant more than two feet from an east or west window, choose one recommended for a northern exposure. Plants can be grown farther from a south window than any other: Northern exposure plants thrive six to eight feet from a bright south window; plants for east or west windows do well three to four feet from one. In winter, when light levels are lower, move plants closer to, but not touching, the window.

How light can be increased

White walls or strategically placed mirrors reflect light onto plants. Or use a fluorescent fixture with one "cool-white" and one "warm-white" tube. Most plants in a very dark window need 12 to 14 hours of supplemental light a day. During the winter months, all plants may benefit from a few hours of artificial light.

Planting a dark spot?

If you have a dark corner or window that's crying out for a cheerful plant, try twins! Buy two identical plants and rotate them between the dark space and a bright window. Both will thrive as long as each gets its place in the sun every other week. For best results, select one of the plants that are listed for a north window.

Succulents

Because these plants store water in their leaves or stems, they like warm, sunny days. They also aren't particular about humidity in the air, which makes them adapt easily to most home environments.

▶ **Light:** Cactuses and most succulents will survive without much light, but during their prime growth period—spring to fall—they prefer the strong, natural light of an east or south window where they'll receive at least four hours of direct sun daily. Most young succulents grow well in fluorescent-light gardens, although they will bloom only occasionally without some natural light.

▶ **Water:** Consistently wet or even damp soil is the one thing that will do in a succulent, especially cactuses. Although they store moisture, they need a thorough drenching periodically. Water plants when the soil is dry to a depth of an inch or so: once a month in winter, every week to ten days in summer. Water with lukewarm water until the excess spills out of the drainage holes. Keep water away from the crowns of the plants and off of stems and foliage.

▶ **Fertilizer:** Succulents need a little fertilizer during their heavy growth period, from spring to summer, and none for the rest of the year. Use a water-soluble type that's high in phosphorus (indicated on the label by the second number—5-10-5, 5-15-10, etc.) and feed once a month beginning in late April. Make sure you wet the soil thoroughly before feeding.

▶ **Temperature:** Most succulents adapt to our indoor living conditions, but *cactuses* do best in a warm summer/cool winter (50°) environment while *other succulents* prefer up to 90° in summer and no more than 65° in winter.

▶ **Pots and soil:** Use clay pots—they're porous and allow excess water to evaporate—and a coarse, fast-draining soil mix.

30 exotic no-fuss houseplants

- ☐ African mild tree *Euphorbia trigona*
- ☐ Baby toes *Fenestraria rhopalophylla*
- ☐ Ball cactus *Notocactus claviceps*
- ☐ Barrel cactus *Ferocactus*
- ☐ Bunny ears *Opuntia microdasys*
- ☐ *Cereus tetragonus*
- ☐ Chin cactus *Gymnocalycium delaetii*
- ☐ Christmas cactus *Zygocatus*
- ☐ Cob cactus *Lobivia*
- ☐ *Cotyledon wallichii*
- ☐ Crown-of-thorns *Euphorbia splendens*
- ☐ Curiosity plant *Cereus peruvianus monstrosus*
- ☐ Black Prince *Echeveria*
- ☐ *Echinopsis turbinata*
- ☐ Felt plant *Kalanchoe beharensis*
- ☐ Golden barrel cactus *Echinocactus grusonii*
- ☐ "Golden stars" pincushion cactus *Mammillaria elongata*
- ☐ Jade plant *Crassula argentea*
- ☐ King agave *Agave ferdinandi-regis*
- ☐ Medicine plant *Aloe vera*
- ☐ *Neochilenia occulta*
- ☐ Old man cactus *Cephalocereus senilis*
- ☐ Peanut cactus *Chamaecereus sylvestri*
- ☐ Pearly dots *Haworthia papillosa*
- ☐ Ponytail palm *Beaucarnea recurvata*
- ☐ Rainbow bush *Portulacaria afra variegata*
- ☐ 'Candy' *Sedum sieboldii*
- ☐ *Sempervivum globosianum*
- ☐ *Senecio trapaeolifolius*
- ☐ Snake plant *Sansevieria trifasciata*

Outdoors: Frontyard/ Backyard

Yes, your yard can be a showplace!

Lawn care

▶ Leave grass clippings on your lawn. They are full of valuable nutrients and recycle rapidly in a healthy lawn.

▶ Remove grass clippings from your lawn only while treating it for a severe thatch problem.

▶ Cut your lawn often enough to keep clippings below 1½ inches in length.

▶ Allow your grass to grow longer in the spring for better development and in the fall for better root development.

▶ An extra feeding in the fall will help your lawn handle winter better.

▶ In hot, dry weather, don't cut grass shorter than two inches.

Planting chart

Plot your vegetable garden with chalk! Draw the outline on a chalkboard. Then draw in crop locations and revise them easily with an eraser. When you at last find the perfect arrangement, copy the chalk diagram on paper.

Planning a small-space vegetable garden

▶ Put fall-bearing plants, like kale and Brussels sprouts, at the garden edge so that you can turn under the rest of the garden in the fall.

▶ Keep tall plants, like tomatoes, on the *north* side of the plot so they don't shade other crops.

▶ If your garden is on a slope, run rows parallel to it, not straight up and down, to prevent soil runoff.

▶ Stagger your rows so that the rows are closer together but the plants keep the same distance.

▶ Choose continuous-bearing vegetables. Some crops—peas and spinach, for instance—have a very short harvest of two weeks or so. Other vegetables produce until frost: tomatoes, broccoli, kale, squash, eggplant and peppers.

▶ Put ramblers, like squash, at the edge of the garden or on trellises.

▶ Make frequent small plantings of radishes and lettuce instead of planting once in one long row.

▶ Succession planting can double your garden's yield. Replace a row of vegetables that have finished bearing with a new planting of another vegetable. For example, follow leaf lettuce with carrots or snap beans, carrots with fall spinach or kale, beets with escarole and cabbage with beans. To figure out other practical combinations, substitute crops with maturity dates similar to these.

▶ Your average fall frost date will determine what you can plant and how late. (Consult your local county agricultural agent for frost dates in your area.) In warm regions, three and even four succession crops may be grown on the same piece of ground.

▶ Rotate different kinds of plants, root vegetables with leafy vegetables for instance, because each uses different combinations of soil nutrients.

▶ For the second crop, choose vegetables that grow best when they mature in cool weather.

▶ Interplanting—in the same row or area—combines different kinds of plants that grow well together. They may even complement each other because one is ready for the harvest early in the season, leaving room for the other to spread. Good interplanting combinations include radishes/squash, lettuce/tomatoes, lettuce/radishes and early peas/squash (the vines take over when the peas are finished).

Seedling "tents"

In case of late frosts when growing seedlings, make protective "tents" for the seedlings by cutting the bottoms off 2-liter plastic soda and large bleach bottles.

Easy tie-ups

The very best thing for tying up plants is old nylon hose. It is flexible enough not to chafe the stems and is exceedingly strong. If you want the ties to be almost invisible, cut them into narrow strips.

Pest prevention

For easy-to-make scarecrows that keep birds away, spray-paint foil pie pans yellow. Hang them in the garden. You can also coat your foil pan scarecrows with cooking or motor oil—the yellow-sticky surface attracts and traps many damaging insects.

Saving seeds

Store leftover vegetable seeds to use next year in airtight plastic bags in a cool, dark place. Seeds to save: beans, peas, tomatoes, beets, carrots and spinach.

Transplanting

▶ When transplanting bare-root nursery stock, soak the roots in water for 24 to 48 hours before planting.

▶ Keep container-grown plants shaded, sheltered and watered for a few days. Then plant and water them, and mulch the roots.

Weed woes

▶ If dandelions set seed before you can root the plants out, use the hose attachment of the vacuum cleaner to collect the seeds before they scatter.

▶ Fight weeds and cut down on watering chores by using mulches, one to two inches deep, around plants from spring to fall.

▶ Instead of digging by hand, get rid of weeds and unwanted grass in walks and the driveway by pouring boiling-hot salt water on invasive growths. (Keep the solution away from desirable plants and the lawn.)

▶ Cut down on spade work and weeding in new garden beds by covering the area for three weeks with black plastic. It kills growth underneath and softens the soil.

Fast, frugal yard makeovers

▶ For older shrubs that have become leggy and brown at the base, trim dead branches and build up the soil at the base of the shrubs. Then bring attention to ground level with plantings of ground covers and/or colorful flowering plants and bulbs.

▶ "Hiding" eyesores such as air-conditioning units or trash cans with shrubbery only draws the eye to the objects you want hidden. Instead, draw the eye *away* with plantings 2 to 15 feet from the eyesore: Mass brilliant flowers, such as pansies, zinnias and petunias, or invest in a flowering shrub.

Make-it-yourself birdfeeder

Cut or drill four equidistant holes around the rim of a Frisbee. Knot four lengths of twine, pull them through the holes and tie them to a tree limb. Fill the Frisbee with feed.

Pretty camouflage

To camouflage an unsightly tree stump, build a loose, 1-foot-high stone wall around it and fill it in with soil. Then plant colorful geraniums and petunias in the circular flower bed, turning an eyesore into a lovely addition to your yard.

Easy care ideas

▶ Plant groundcover under trees and shrubs that have a tendency to litter to eliminate cleanup of leaves, pods, etc.

▶ Save fallen leaves. Shred and distribute them around the garden. They'll decompose over the winter and enrich the soil.

▶ Spread grass clippings, 1-inch-thick, to retain moisture in the soil around vegetables and flowers.

▶ If you plan to install trellises along the sides of the house, hinge them so that they can be pulled away slightly to make house painting and maintenance easier.

▶ When digging post holes in dry, compacted soil, make a starter hole, fill it with water and wait for it to soak in before you proceed. This technique saves time and potential blisters.

Plastic pots

Patio plants potted in plastic containers usually need water only half as often as those in clay.

Planning your garden

When planning free-form garden beds, pools and other outdoor features, use a garden hose to lay out the design on the ground. Once you're satisfied with the design you've made, use the hose "template" as a digging guide.

Save your back

Move shrubs, heavy bags of fertilizer, etc. by using a shovel as a sled. This is a time and back saver when you are transplanting lots of stock.

Bulb marker

In the spring, when tulips and crocuses bloom, you may find empty spots in the garden where bulbs have died during the previous winter or been dug up and eaten by squirrels. Use a brightly colored nail polish to paint the tops of wooden clothespins and stick the prongs into the soil wherever you see a bare spot. The clothespins will clearly show you where to plant bulbs come fall.

Storing bulbs

Store bulbs throughout the winter in old nylons. Knot the stockings to separate kinds and colors of bulbs. The bulbs will be well aired and also be easy to hang out of the way.

Garden gloves

Lined latex gloves work just as well in the garden as they do in the kitchen. You don't have any messy fabric gloves to clean—the dirt washes right off the rubber gloves. If you put on a little hand lotion before using them, your hands will get a moisturizing treatment while they're pulling weeds and digging in soil.

Taking care of tools

▶ Paint the handles of garden tools a bright color so you can spot them easily among the plants and grass. Also, if friends borrow your tools, they will always know who to return them to.

▶ Save time next spring: Clean, sharpen and oil all your gardening tools before putting them away for the winter.

A portable greenhouse

A child's small plastic wagon makes a moveable greenhouse. Filled with dirt, planted with seeds and covered with a piece of glass from a window or building supply store, it makes a convenient indoor garden to start seeds for transplanting later in the garden. The wagon is watertight, so dripping won't be a problem. It can be moved with ease to sunny or shady, warmer or cooler spots—wherever necessary. Best of all, once the weather is warmer, it can easily be moved throughout the garden as you transplant seedlings.

Make a garden trellis

▶ A garden trellis for roses or climbing vines can be easily made from a youngster's old safety gate. Give it a coat of white paint and attach it vertically with hooks to two upright posts.

▶ A section of vinyl-coated wire fencing hung vertically or horizontally on the side of the house makes a good trellis for climbing plants—and it never needs painting.

A spritz will do it!

Vegetable cooking spray, which keeps food from sticking to pans and skillets, has wonderful additional uses—it prevents dirt from clinging to small gardening tools and keeps snow from sticking to shovels.

Bulb Planting Chart

Key: Planting depth is measured from the base of the bulb.
*North, Northeast and Canada: areas where winter temperatures
are consistently below freezing.
**South & Southwest: areas where winter temperatures are mild.

VL = Very Low (up to 6″) **L** = Low (6″ to 12″) **MH** = Medium High (12″ to 20″)
H = High (20″ to 28″)   **VH** = Very High (over 28″)

Flowering Schedule	Planting Depth (in inches) In The North*	Planting Depth (in inches) In The South**	Spacing (in inches)	Flowering Height
Very Early (to mid-March)				
Galanthus (Snowdrops)	4 for all	2 for all	3	VL
Eranthis (Winter Aconite)			3	VL
Iris reticulata			3	VL
Crocus			3	VL
Chionodoxa (Glory of the Snow)			3	VL
Puschkinia libanotioa			4	VL
Fritillaria meleagris			4	L
Early (late March)				
Anemone blanda	4	2	3	VL
Kaufmanniana Tulips	8	4	6	VL
Muscari (Grape Hyacinth)	4	2	3	VL
Fosteriana Tulips	8	4	6	L
Single Early, Double Early Tulips	8	4	6	L
Miniature Daffodils	6	4	4	L
Hyacinths	8	4	6	L
Trumpet Daffodils	8	4	6	MH
Mid Season (April)				
Triteleia uniflora	4	2	3	VL
Mendel & Triumph Tulips	8	4	5	MH
Daffodils	8	4	6	MH
Darwin Hybrid Tulips	8	4	6	H
Greigii Tulips	8	4	6	L/MH
Fritillaria imperialis	8	4	12	H
Leucojum aestivum	4	2	4	L
Late (May)				
Scilla campanulata (Spanish Squill)	4	2	5	L
Parrot Tulips	8	4	6	MH
Double Late Tulips	8	4	6	MH
Lily-flowered Tulips	8	4	6	H
Darwin Tulips	8	4	6	H/VH
Cottage Tulips	8	4	6	H/VH
Rembrandt Tulips	8	4	6	H
Allium aflatunense	8	4	4	H
Allium karataviense	8	4	6	L
Ornithogalum	4	2	3	VL
Very Late (to mid-June)				
Dutch Iris	6	4	4	MH
Allium albopilosum	4	2	6	H
Allium moly	4	2	3	L
Alium giganteum and Drumstick Allium	8	4	6	VH

For beautiful flowers

Turn your dreams of glorious flowers into reality by following these growing hints.

Annuals:

▶ If you have a fluorescent light setup, you can start coleus, cosmos, marigolds and zinnias indoors from seed. When these seedlings are transplanted outdoors, they will bloom faster than those sown directly in the ground.

▶ To spur growth, water indoor seedlings of impatiens, petunias and snapdragons with an application of water-soluble fertilizer at one-fourth the strength recommended on the package label.

▶ If the weather has settled and the ground is dried out and workable, seed these easy-to-grow annuals directly outdoors: aster, bachelor button, celosia, cleome, cosmos, marigold, nasturtium, poppy, salvia, sweet alyssum and zinnia.

▶ Because the following plants need a long growing season—and if you haven't started them indoors— plan to buy seedlings from garden centers: ageratum, fibrous-rooted begonia, gerbera, impatiens, petunia and snapdragon.

▶ Snap off the faded flowers of pansies promptly so that additional flowering will continue into the early summer months.

▶ To break up large expanses of flower color and rest the viewer's eye, incorporate a few gray-leaved dusty miller plants in your border.

▶ Geraniums are especially regal when planted in window boxes, patio tubs and deck planters. Trim the planters with trailers such as ivy or vinca, which will drape gracefully over the sides.

▶ Other showy flowers to brighten patios, decks and terraces are begonias, cleome, gerberas and petunias. Plant them in redwood tubs or clay pots. Add cascading plants such as lobelia or sweet alyssum.

▶ Plant sweet peas along a fence or on a trellis because these climbing vines need a sturdy support.

▶ Nip out the growing tips of tall and floppy cosmos and snapdragons to force them to branch.

▶ If annuals sown directly in the garden come up too thickly, thin them to four inches apart by transplanting some of the strongest young plants to fill in blank spaces in other parts of your flower borders.

▶ Where the soil gets a lot of sun and is well drained, set out tubers of the large "dinner-plate size" dahlias, or buy started seedlings of the dwarf, low-growing dahlias to show off in garden borders.

▶ Where there is little sunlight, impatiens seedlings will thrive and flower to make bright color accents all season long.

▶ Plant verbena for brilliant touches of color along the patio or by the edges of a swimming pool.

▶ After using hand tools, remove the soil and wipe them with an oiled cloth to prevent rust.

Perennials:

▶ Cut to the ground any stalks left over from last year's bloom.

▶ As soon as oak leaves are the size of a mouse's ears, remove leafy winter mulches from perennial beds.

▶ When new leaves of perennials poke aboveground, make a circle of general garden fertilizer around each cluster; work it into the soil lightly to strengthen growth and summer flowers.

▶ When working around perennials, be careful not to trample late risers such as hostas and balloon flowers.

▶ If you are gardening for the first time, try one or all of these easy-to-grow perennials: astilbe, rudbeckia, daylily, columbine, phlox, peony, Oriental poppy, veronica, Shasta daisy and bleeding heart.

▶ For shady yards, choose from these perennials: Jacob's ladder, hosta, astilbe, hardy geraniums (*Geranium*, not *Pelargonium)* and liriope.

▶ Stake delphiniums, foxgloves and weak-stemmed peonies with bamboo; tie them securely with pieces cut from old nylon stockings.

▶ Use prunings from a privet hedge to stake floppy, wide-spreading perennials such as coreopsis and gaillardia. Simply stick them in the ground; the plants will grow up around them.

▶ Use a half-moon edging tool to define the outlines of the flower border along the lawn.

▶ Keep a rubber kneeling pad in the toolshed and use it when you have to reach far into borders to pull weeks or cultivate soil; this way, you don't step directly on the soil.

▶ Dig, divide and replant the young outer shoots of chrysanthemums and asters and discard the old centers.

▶ Cut off faded blooms of columbines and forget-me-nots so they do not reseed and become weeds.

▶ To keep down weed growth after planting, mulch the soil with a thick (3- to 4-inch) layer of chopped compost, pine needles or bark nuggets.

▶ Use labels to identify unusual cultivars or special plants given to you by neighbors and friends.

Roses:

▶ When new red/green growth buds begin to swell on stems, prune out winterkill (dead wood) and cut tall canes (stems) down to size.

▶ Remove mounds of winter protective mulch from the crowns.

▶ Trace one-quarter cup of rose food in a circle around the base of each plant.

▶ Start protective spraying to prevent rose disease. The spray should include the fungicide Funginex, which protects the plants against mildew and black spot, two harmful fungus diseases.

▶ When planting new rosebushes, make sure you keep the grafted knob no less than two inches below the soil line.

▶ Replace any winter-killed rosebushes some of the newer All-American Rose Selections: 'Bonica,' 'New Year' or 'Sheer Bliss.'

▶ Choose miniature roses as edging plants for your rose garden.

▶ After lightly cultivating and feeding roses, mulch the soil with buckwheat hulls to conserve soil moisture and control weed growth.

▶ If spring rains are infrequent, water the rose garden weekly with a *soaker hose*; never use an overhead hose, which encourages disease.

Flowers And Herbs: Not Just For The Garden!

Try these unusual ways to use your garden's bounty.

Surprising sweets

▶ Add a pleasant scent to white or yellow cake by placing a rose geranium leaf in the bottom of the pan before pouring in the batter.

▶ Fresh fruit compote becomes a surprising dessert when made with sweet cicely, mint or basil.

▶ Make an old-fashioned "Grandma's Seed Cake" in a jiffy by adding 1 tablespoon anise, fennel or caraway seeds to a yellow pound cake mix.

▶ Herb sugars are an easy way to brighten the taste of simple foods. Add them to tea or coffee, or sprinkle on sugar cookies. To make them, layer brown or white sugar with dried herbs. Close the container tightly. After several weeks, combine the mixture thoroughly in a blender. Try lemon verbena, mint or marjoram. *Note:* In selecting flowers and herbs for use in kitchen recipes, never use any that have been sprayed with pesticides or insecticides. Always rinse off blossoms, leaves and/or stems before using them.

Wet potpourri

▶ In a large jar, combine 2 cups each of rose petals, rosemary and mint with ½ cup whole allspice, 4 cinnamon sticks and 2 garlic cloves. Fill the jar with hot white distilled vinegar to cover. Cover the jar and let it set for one week. The longer the herbs soak, the stronger the scent. Experiment with your own favorite fragrant blossoms and herbs such as lavender, lemon verbena or sage.

▶ Soak cotton balls in the wet potpourri. When dry, they make simple sachets for lingerie or linens.

▶ Sprinkle wet potpourri in musty places—on the floor under beds and in closets, for example. Use it in an atomizer to spray as a room deodorizer or leave the jar uncapped briefly for an old-fashioned room scent.

▶ To clean no-wax floors, mix ½ cup wet potpourri with 1 quart water. This no-rinse solution leaves floors with a spicy mint scent.

▶ Use wet potpourri undiluted in a spray bottle to clean mirrors and counter tops.

Beverages

▶ Add zest to everyday beverages by garnishing them with herbs: lemonade with lemon balm, tomato juice with oregano or basil, mineral water with rose geranium, white wine with borage blossoms or iced tea with mint.

▶ Say goodnight with a cup of milk sweetened with honey and heated with 2 to 3 teaspoons fresh fennel, anise, mint or dried sweet woodruff.

▶ Make herbal "tisanes" (teas). Steep 2 to 3 teaspoons fresh, or 1 to 2 teaspoons dried, leafy herbs such as chamomile, mint, marjoram, borage or scented geranium for each cup of hot water. Tisanes are refreshing drinks whether they're served hot or cold.

▶ To perk up ice, freeze a sprig of mint or a borage flower in each cube.

Lettuce, plus . . .

▶ Instead of lettuce, use herbs on your sandwiches. Try basil with tuna salad, savory with sliced chicken, dill with egg salad and oregano with grilled cheese.

▶ Fresh herbs also make snappy salads. Tear nasturtium, sorrel, cress and basil leaves into pieces and mix with tossed greens. Mince strong herbs such as savory, dill and thyme.

▶ Green fennel seeds tossed in salads add pockets of spice.

▶ Fruit salad is cool and refreshing when served on a bed of mint.

▶ Garnish tacos with a sprig of cilantro or serve with a bit of minced oregano added to the shredded lettuce.

At the barbecue

▶ Throw herbs on the coals when grilling. Cover the grill if possible or make a foil tent to allow the spicy smoke to penetrate the meat. Try stalks of savory, sage or rosemary, or whole star-anise, fennel or dried basil seed pods.

▶ Skewer herbs, à la shish kabob, between pieces of fish or meat. Alternate bay leaves with swordfish, fresh dill with lamb or basil with beef.

▶ Slip in a sprig of marjoram when you wrap corn in aluminum foil and roast it on the barbecue.

▶ Use sprigs of herbs tied together as a spicy brush when basting meat.

▶ Grill fish wrapped in a foil package with a slice of lemon and a sprig of dill.

Miscellaneous

For laundry with an outdoor scent, use herbal packets when you do the wash. Tie ½ cup of your favorite dried herbs in the foot cut from an old pair of pantyhose. Add the packet to the wash during the rinse cycle and include it with the laundry in the dryer. The herbs dry with the clothes and can be tucked away as a sachet when the folded clothes are returned to the drawer. Lavender and lemon verbena add delicate fragrance to lingerie. Sweet woodruff scents linen with a hint of new-mown hay.

14.
Great Ideas For Friends, Family – Even Pets!

Smart Ideas
Thoughtful Ideas
Fun Ideas
Pets

Smart Ideas

This everyday wisdom will really go far!

Key exchange

It's not a good idea to have your name and address attached to your car and house keys because anyone who finds them has access to your property. So arrange with a friend to put her name and address on your key rings and yours on hers. Your lost keys will then be useless to the finder—and might even be returned to your friend.

House-sitters

Here's a marvelous way to find reliable house-sitters. When you go away on vacation, ask neighborhood friends if they are planning, or would like to plan, to entertain out-of-towners during the time you will be away. If so, offer them the perfect place for their guests to stay—your house, right in the neighborhood. Your neighbors have a chance to entertain without overcrowding at home, their guests have proximity and independence without hotel bills and you have peace of mind.

A rewarding solution

Whenever your home or appliances need repairing, one member of a working couple must usually take the day off to wait for the repair person. Instead introduce yourself to some senior citizens at a local home for the elderly and work out a "barter system." If a repair person is coming, ask one of the residents to spend the day at your house. In exchange, you might take your valuable neighbor grocery shopping, to the theater or to a variety of places. This is also a great way to find loving, reliable babysitters.

Sure return

There is more to "pot-luck" parties than the food; it's also "pot-luck" whether or not you get your own bowl or platter back! A quick way to make sure you do is to stick a self-adhesive name and address label on the bottom of each dish. For extra insurance, add your phone number.

Neighborhood clothing exchange

Instead of discarding good-as-new clothing, try setting up a "laundry store." Hang freshly laundered and neatly pressed clothing in the laundry room of your apartment building. Trips to the laundry room can become exciting, free "shopping" ventures that reap considerable savings for you and your neighbors.

Tried and true

Before buying an expensive appliance, such as a microwave oven or a food processor, borrow a friend's or rent one from a rental agency. This way you can test it out and determine whether you can or cannot live without it *before* buying it.

Memory machine

▶ Use your telephone answering machine as your memory. If you're at work or out shopping and there's something you want to do when you get home, call and leave yourself a reminder. No more lost notes.

▶ If your children are home alone after school, you can leave them messages about chores to do, instructions for starting supper or just "I love you—see you soon."

Inexpensive and versatile paper

Purchase inexpensive "roll-ends" of newsprint paper at your local newspaper office. They are available in several sizes; the 36-inch-wide roll is the most versatile and easy to handle. The paper is clean and is especially good for wrapping glassware or other breakables when moving, drawing patterns or encouraging children's artistic talents.

Simple wrap-around

Whenever you have to wrap a large or bulky gift, wind a string around it to measure the amount of wrapping paper you need to cut.

Finding your way

Put even dabs of fluorescent paint around keyholes and the edges of driveways, stairs and house numbers, and you'll be able to see them more easily in the dark. Fluorescent tape will do the same thing, but it's not as long lasting.

The family dot

When a number of families get together to hold a garage sale, assign a different colored stick-on dot to each family. Put one of these dots on each item to prevent mix-ups later.

Polish it up

Red nail polish has many uses besides its cosmetic one. To quickly spot the arrow on childproof medicine-bottle caps, paint the arrow red. Dab some polish on the "OFF" button on your calculator—it saves time and batteries. Paint the "OFF" button on your camera flash attachment so you can tell at once whether or not it's turned off.

Dial "memory"

Here is a foolproof way to keep track of outgoing calls each month, especially long-distance ones. Keep a calendar near the telephone and record each call as you make it by jotting down the party's name and number. Next time the bill arrives, simply compare the charges with your calendar record.

Rise and shine

If you always sleep through the alarm in the morning, put the alarm clock in a metal wastebasket or large tin pot. When it rings, you'll wake up!

Adding on

Use a roll of adding machine tape as a paperweight on your desk. Whenever you need a piece of scratch paper to jot down a shopping list or other note, rip off a piece of your ever-handy paperweight.

A pick-up basket

An excellent method for avoiding excess stress on the family when your home is for sale is to use a "pick-up" basket. Items of clothing, books, letters, school papers and such can be removed quickly following a call from the realtor. Stash the basket out of sight in a closet before the prospective buyer arrives.

The right touch

Shampoo and conditioner often come in very similar containers. If you have difficulty telling them apart in the shower, put a strip of masking tape around the shampoo bottle.

Perfect match

When you put winter coats and jackets away for the summer, include the matching scarf, hat and gloves in a self-sealing plastic bag that you attach to the coat's hanger. In the fall, when you want to wear a particular coat, the matching accessories are right there.

The cold freeze

Anyone who has ever come home from a vacation or arrived at a summer place to discover that the freezer has defrosted because of mechanical or power failure knows the headache that can ensue. Has the food spoiled by being refrozen? You'll be able to check on this if you keep a few ice cubes in a sealed glass container in the freezer. If the cubes are intact, so is the food. If they appear to have melted, you can be sure the food has defrosted and refrozen while you were away.

Easy I.D.

When there is more than one child using the same clothes closet, assign a different color to each child and paint each child's hangers his or her particular color. Kids won't have any trouble finding their outfits.

Tie a red ribbon . . .

When storing Christmas decorations each year, tie each box, bag, etc. with a red ribbon. You will be able to tell at a glance which boxes in the attic hold holiday decorations.

Cedar scents

Here is how to create the expensive smell of cedar-lined closets without the expense. Purchase a bag of cedar shavings from your local pet store. Cut a 12-inch square of thin cotton material and put a large handful of the shavings into the center of it. Tie up the corners with a colorful ribbon and hang it in your closet.

Visitor comfort

If you have frequent guests, here's a way to make sure towels don't get mixed up. Hang a small chalkboard trimmed in paint to match your bathroom along the wall above each towel rack. On each board write the guests' names so that everyone has his or her own towels. This saves a lot of confusion.

Table linens

A permanent-press flat sheet makes an ideal tablecloth. It washes like a dream, needs no ironing, comes in a variety of colors and, best of all, is easy on the budget.

Pouring solution

To identify which glass decanter holds the scotch, bourbon, gin or vodka, remove the label from each bottle, cut out the name and tape it to the bottom of the corresponding decanter. You can easily identify the contents of each by checking the bottom.

Cover-up

Before hanging pictures on papered walls, take a razor blade, cut a small V in the wallpaper, carefully peel it back and hammer in the nail. When you want to rearrange your pictures, you can repaste the small flap of paper back into place and no ugly nail holes show.

Staying put

Attach a piece of double-faced tape to the bottom of bookends to keep them from sliding out of place.

Waterproofing the wall

When adding a shower attachment to a bathtub, it is a good idea to waterproof the wall beside the tub. Cover the wall with clear adhesive-backed vinyl. To further protect it, run a bead of silicone sealant between the bottom edge of the vinyl and the tile border around the tub. This works even over wallcovering.

Clever protection

To prevent bar soap from dissolving on the shower caddy shelf, cover it with an upside-down soap dish. Soap is protected from the spray, yet can dry out between showers.

Soap sense

To make bar soap last longer and to add a decorator's touch in the bathroom, place a giant brandy snifter (a wide-mouth vase would do as well) on the bathroom vanity and put unwrapped bars of your favorite bath soap in it. It also adds a nice, mild fragrance to the bathroom.

Caring for outdoor furniture

Large plastic garbage bags make handy and inexpensive protective covers for aluminum lawn chairs and chaises. When folded, the chairs slide into the bags easily and can be stored outside without being damaged by rain.

Quick I.D.

A good way to identify your folding lawn chairs when taking them to summertime outings is to use inexpensive luggage tags and attach them through the webbing of the chairs. One quick glance will tell you which chairs are yours.

Sinking lawn chairs

Lawn furniture has small legs that easily sink into the ground when people sit down on them. Solve this problem by slipping a jar lid under each leg before sitting down.

Protective tie-up

To protect a patio umbrella from blowing open and getting wind- or storm-damaged, buckle a man's stretch belt around the middle of the umbrella when it's closed and not in use.

No more mix-up

Do your tennis balls get mixed up with those from the next court? Use felt pens to draw funny faces on them. Not only are they easy to spot, they are usually returned with a smile.

An efficient checkout system

Establish a "checkout system" so favorite books that are borrowed will never be lost again. Whenever you lend a book, keep the jacket and write the name and telephone number of the borrower inside. This lets you know where the book is, and also preserves the jacket.

For bookworms

If you often lend books to friends but cringe when they're returned with dog-eared pages, start attaching colorful paper clips to the books. Mention to your friends that they should use the clips as bookmarks.

No more dirty books

To keep paperback books in good condition, give each one a thin coat of kitchen floor wax as soon as you buy it. Allowed to dry and buffed, the wax protects the books from dirt and stains and makes them easier to slide on and off the shelf.

Easy book I.D.

After purchasing a book, paste your address label on the inside cover. If it is ever lent out, friends will remember where to return it.

Photo finish

Has a film-processing company ever lost rolls of film that you sent away to be developed? Whenever you load your camera, take the first shot of a piece of paper with the sentence, "These pictures belong to (your name and address)" written on it. The developed roll will always be sure to find its way back to you.

Instant raincoats

When you go on a family outing, always bring along a few plastic trash bags—lawn and garden size for you and your spouse, the tall kitchen size for children. You'll have instant raincoats and windbreakers; just cut holes for the head and arms.

Learning aid

Do you have a personal computer at home that you still don't know how to use? Does the manual seem to be written in Greek? Check out a computer "how-to" book from the children's section of the public library. They are a cinch to follow and can give you a good basic understanding of computers so that you can go on to the more complicated manuals.

A "gentle" reminder

It isn't easy to ask friends to remember not to smoke in your car. As a solution, "plant" a small artificial violet in the car ashtray. They'll get the hint!

Welcome relief

For family outings at the ice rink in winter, bring along small, hot, damp towels in a thermos bottle to warm cold faces and hands on the trip back home. During summer trips to the beach, substitute cool towels.

Indelible ink

After addressing packages with a felt-tip marker, rub a white candle over the writing. The wax seals it and rain, sleet or snow won't smudge it.

Perking up roses

When cut roses begin to droop or wilt, submerge the entire flower flat in a pan of warm water. Gently straighten the heads and cut off the stems—under water—two inches from the ends. Allow the roses to stay two hours in the water to revive.

To hold flowers

If your clear glass flower vase is a bit too large, crumble a piece of plastic wrap and put it in the bottom. It will hold the flowers and hide the stems.

Table service

Want an eat-in kitchen but don't have the room? Make an "instant table" by nailing cleats to the bottom of a thin piece of wood to make a large tray that fits securely over a drawer. There's enough room for two to dine.

Tile a table top

Give new life to an old table. Use bathroom tiles and cover the top in a colorful design. Paint the table legs to match the tiled top.

Clear directions

When you are driving to an unfamiliar place, simplify following the directions by writing them in large print on a 3 x 5-inch index card. Attach this to the dashboard right next to the steering wheel so that the directions are easily in sight. Later save the card for a "directions file."

On-the-road reading

Make sure to keep a small, pocket-size magnifying glass in the glove compartment of your car. When you need to consult a map under less than perfect illumination, you'll find small letters and fine lines easier to read.

Frost-free mirror

If your car isn't garaged overnight during cold weather, cover the side-view mirror with a plastic bag held in place with a clothespin. The mirror will be clear in the morning.

Thoughtful Ideas

Show your family and friends that you care!

Leaving your mark

The next time you borrow a book from a friend, return it with this thoughtful thank you: an inexpensive bookmark along with a short comment about your enjoyment of the book. Date and sign your thank-you bookmark so your friend knows you returned it without delay and with appreciation.

For a friend in the hospital

There isn't a finer gift for a hospitalized friend than a box of stationery with stamps already on the envelopes, a clipboard for writing and a pen.

Make returns easy

When buying gifts for family or friends, ask the salesperson to give you two receipts. The one that you keep has the price on it and the other has all the important information except the price. Enclose this receipt with the gift in case it has to be exchanged or returned.

Keep a coloring book

The cleverest household gift for a friend can backfire if it's the wrong color. After visiting your friends, write down the color schemes of their kitchen, bath and bedroom in your address book and you'll be prepared when gift time comes around.

Cheery pass-along

When friends need their spirits lifted, present them with "sunshine bouquets"—garage-sale vases filled with flowers from your garden. Ask that each recipient refill the vase and pass it along to someone else whose day needs brightening.

Happy birthday to you!

Many restaurants have "birthday discount specials." As you discover them, make a note on your calendar and when a family member's big day arrives, take advantage of these offers. You save money and the birthday person feels extra important.

Welcome home

Next time you watch your neighbors' house while they vacation, why not give them a special "welcome." Prepare a meal and leave it in the refrigerator for them. They will love having their dinner waiting for them on their return.

A gallery of dreams

If you have close friends building a long-awaited dream house, here's an idea they'll appreciate: Photograph the house in various stages of construction (the foundation being poured, frame being raised, roofing nailed in place and the final coat of paint). At their housewarming party, present them with the four framed pictures.

Little surprise

Don't confine your gift-giving just to the "traditional" times—Christmas, birthdays or Valentine's Day. An unexpected bouquet of seasonal flowers, a pretty or funny mug with some special tea alongside can be a sign of love all year long.

Don't throw out old magazines

When magazines pile up around the house, take them to a local nursing home where they will be greatly enjoyed by the residents.

Thinking of you!

Make pretty, one-of-a-kind picture postcards by cutting the front from glossy greeting cards that are too pretty to throw away. Use a ruler to draw a straight line, sectioning the back side into halves. This defines the area for postage and the address, and leaves the other half for a quick "thinking of you" message for a special friend.

Fun Ideas

Just for the fun of it!

"Smart" meals

Here's an enjoyable way to spark up your family's dinnertime conversations and enrich your vocabulary as well. Ask each member to look up the definition of at least one word they may have discovered while reading a newspaper or magazine or have seen or heard during the day. At dinner, exchange "words." Often your discoveries will lead to very funny conversations and become the starting point for many interesting—and educational—discussions.

Bud vases

Can't think of what to use as vases for short-stemmed flowers such as miniature roses, violets and pansies? Try clear cologne and perfume bottles. With pliers, remove the metal cap holding the atomizer. Since these bottles come in various sizes and shapes, you can use them grouped as a centerpiece, individually at each place setting or as accents on an end table. This is a great way to make a few flowers go a long way.

Family news chain

Do you find you have little time and money to call or write family members who live far away? Start a "family news chain." To begin, contact family members to see who wants to participate and list them in alphabetical order. Write a page of interesting anecdotes about your immediate family and pass it on to the next person on the list. He or she will write their letter, include it with yours and send it on to the *next* in line. Each participating family receives a packet of "news" letters once every four to eight weeks. The last receiving family then discards its old letter, writes a page of current happenings and sends the packet on its way to start the next round of news.

Two jobs in one

To make better use of exercising time while riding a stationary bicycle, attach a basket to the handle bars to hold nonurgent mail, catalogs, magazines, a radio headset and the like.

Our feathered friends

Does your dishwashing rinse agent come in little plastic baskets? Don't throw them out when they're empty. Wash and rinse them thoroughly, and fill them with raisins, sunflower seeds, popcorn or birdseed from your local pet store. Then hang them outside for wild birds. This is especially nice to do in the winter when food is scarce.

Speaking of feathers...

If you have found lovely feathers on your walks through parks or the woods and haven't known what to do with them, here's a solution: Wash a feather thoroughly, dry it and gently brush it out. When it is completely dry, carefully push an ordinary ball point pen refill into the hollow end at the base of the feather. Secure the refill with a few drops of quick-bonding glue and you have a beautiful and unique quill pen.

Cool balloons

Going on a picnic and don't have an ice chest? The day before, fill several small balloons with cold water, knot the openings carefully and put them in the freezer; don't fill them too full or they might break. When you're packing the picnic basket in the morning, place the balloons gently into the basket and pack the food around them. The food will stay cool without getting wet.

A puzzlement!

▶ If you like jigsaw puzzles but don't like the mess they can make or the space they can take up, here's an idea: Buy a large desk blotter and lay out your puzzle on it. It can easily be moved from room to room without disturbing the puzzle.

▶ Another solution to the puzzle dilemma is a portable puzzle board. Sand a piece of plywood and edge it with molding to keep the pieces from sliding off.

Pets

*From Fido to felines, this advice
really works.*

Sure sign

If your dog gets fed only once a day, you need a way for all family members to know when Fido has already eaten. Buy an inexpensive plastic place mat and, using colored tape, put "FED" on one side and "NOT FED" on the other side. Each time you feed the dog, turn up the "FED" side.

Bowl anchor

To keep your dog from overturning his bowl outdoors, use a tube baking pan to hold his drinking water. Drive a wooden stake into the ground and place the tube pan over the stake. No more spills.

Manageable hair

To cut down on the hair your pet sheds in the house, staple Velcro® around his flexible pet door. When he brushes against the strips, the loose hair will stay behind.

Off the furniture

To keep your dog from sleeping on your sofas and chairs, put a piece of aluminum foil on top of each cushion. The rustle of the foil frightens the dog and he will soon get out of the habit.

"Sibling rivalry"

Quite often a pet is acquired before starting a family, and when you do have a child, sibling rivalry ensues between the pet who is used to considering itself your baby and the new baby in the house. A pet's reactions may range from avoidance to hostility toward the infant, but you *can* help your pet to accept and love your new baby.

Before the baby is born:

▶ Be sure your pet is healthy and has up-to-date immunizations. Poor health can cause crankiness. For the baby's health, the animal should be clean, free of parasites and have its nails trimmed.

▶ If your pet has never been around babies, try to accustom it to your infant's smells and sounds. For example, have someone bring a blanket or piece of your baby's clothing from the hospital before you return so that your pet can become familiar with the baby's smell.

▶ Make arrangements for your pet's care during and right after your child's birth. A pet that is suddenly ignored may connect the lack of attention with the baby's arrival.

After the baby is born:

▶ When you and your baby come home, take time to greet your pet and make a fuss over it.

▶ Make sure your pet receives as much love and attention as before. Don't shoo it away, no matter how busy or tired you may be. Try to have your pet's feeding, play and other routines remain as unchanged as possible.

▶ Be especially aware of changes in your pet's behavior. Sudden possessiveness of food or toys, hostile or fearful behavior—growling, barking or hissing excessively—are all signs of jealousy and aggression.

▶ Most important, *never* leave a dog or cat alone with an infant. *Do* encourage a pet to interact with a baby *but only under supervision.* Snatching the pet away can provoke jealousy and will make a pet overly curious. Take time to introduce your pet to your baby and your baby to your pet—and you could have the beginning of a beautiful relationship.

Dog trot

Don't assume that because your dog looks healthy, he or she is fit to run long distances. If you want to run regularly with your dog, take the dog to a vet for a complete physical examination and explain that you'd like to include your dog in your exercise program. Particular attention should be paid to the animal's heart to rule out any defects which may previously have been overlooked. Heartworm must also be ruled out and preventive medication given, if indicated. The joints and spine should be checked; many dogs suffer from skeletal problems which don't show up with normal activity, but might cause trouble under continuous stress. Have the dog's feet examined and its nails clipped. Remember, running on a track, dirt path or grass is fine, but hard surfaces, such as cement or asphalt, can make a dog's footpads very sore.

Flea, flee!

▶ The most reliable way to kill fleas on an animal is with an insecticidal dip. However, dips have little residual action, so dusts and/or sprays should be used between dips for more control. Flea collars and medallions are helpful, but not if the infestation is severe. Your veterinarian will know which of the many types and brands of commercial flea-control products are the most effective in your geographical area.

▶ Environmental control should include daily vacuuming of carpets and the use of sprays and home foggers to kill both fleas and larvae. If the infestation is severe, a professional exterminator may be needed. Outdoor runs and pet houses also must be treated regularly to prevent re-infestation.

Chow time

Feeding your cat or dog can be a confusing process with all the new types of food on the market. Here's an explanation of what your pet needs to be both happy and healthy.

▶ Read the labels. Dogs and cats require balanced diets containing an optimum amount of required nutrients and sufficient calories for your particular pet (this varies depending on your animal's individual metabolism, activity level and age). The labels on your pet's food will provide you with information on each ingredient in the food, shown in decreasing order of weight or proportion. Meat, meat by-products and dairy products generally provide higher-quality protein than vegetables.

▶ Test it out. Whether or not a particular food is suitable for a pet also depends on its taste and digestibility. After you have read the label and have determined as much as you can about the nutritional value of the food, try feeding it to your pet. Sometimes several types of food must be tested before finding one that suits your particular animal.

▶ Always consult with your veterinarian if special conditions arise which might alter an animal's nutritional needs: unusual stress, pregnancy, lactation or illness.

▶ Home cooking can be all right in supplying a dog's or cat's nutritional needs, but home-prepared pet food requires a good deal of effort by you to ensure a well-balanced diet for your pet.

Happy cat

Here's some advice to help you give your cat a longer, healthier life.

▶ Preventive care: Just like other animals, cats should have regular veterinary checkups and immunizations throughout their lives. Very young and very old cats are more susceptible to illness, so it's important to begin your kitten's immunizations immediately. Keep in mind that immunity to disease wears off and your pet will need annual booster shots throughout its lifetime. Vaccinations can protect your cat against serious infectious diseases (such as feline panleukopenia). All cats should be immunized against feline distemper. There is also a preventive vaccine against the feline leukemia virus (FeLV).

▶ Neutering: This can also be an important preventive health care procedure. A neutered male cat will no longer fight and roam; this can cut down on the chances of injury and contact with possibly diseased cats. A spayed female cat will be spared heat periods and pregnancies, which cuts down on unwanted kittens, and will no longer be susceptible to reproductive tract disorders.

▶ Routine care: This must include fresh food and water every day. Some dry food in your cat's diet will help keep its teeth clean too. You should brush and comb your cat as often as necessary to keep it clean and free of loose hair; otherwise it will swallow the hair while cleaning itself and hair balls will form. While you are grooming your cat, check carefully for ticks and fleas. If you notice any sudden change in your cat's behavior or normal habits, check immediately with your veterinarian for a cause.

▶ Safety first: Because cats are very curious—about everything— they are often accidentally injured. Be sure to put screens in windows and to protect your cat from running motors or fans. Even an old cat may chew and swallow small objects or needles and threads. If you suspect that your cat has eaten something dangerous, check with your vet immediately.

▶ Cats are not human—no matter how much they may seem to be at times. *Never* give a cat medicine intended for a person. It is generally well known that aspirin is toxic to cats but aspirin substitutes are even more dangerous and *can be fatal*. Do not give a cat any medication without a veterinarian's advice.

What To Consider When Choosing A Dog

Breed	Human-Attention Needs 10 = a lot	Good With Children 10 = ex.	Good in City 10 = ex.	Activity Level 10 = high
Airedale*	8	10	0	7
Beagle	6	10	0	5
Boxer	8	10	0	2
Irish Wolfhound	5	10	0	0
New-foundland	5	10	0	0
Retrievers:				
• Flat-Coated	7	10	9	3
• Golden	8	10	0	3
• Labrador	7	10	0	3
Standard Poodle*	10	9	4	7-8
Spaniels:				
• Cocker	10	10	10	10
• Springer	8	10	8	9
Yorkshire Terrier*	10	10**	9	10
Whippet	10	10**	10	10

* = Coat needs regular professional grooming.
** = Fragile — can't stand roughhousing. Good with one child, or older child.
Ex. — Excellent